D1564942

Debating Darwin

Other Books by the Author

The Death of Adam: Evolution and Its Impact on Western Thought (1959/Mentor Books, 1961)

Darwin and the Modern World View (1963)

The Science of Minerals in the Age of Jefferson (1978)
with John G. Burke

Science, Ideology and World View: Essays in the History of Evolutionary Ideas (1981)

American Science in the Age of Jefferson (1984)

DEBATING DARWIN

Adventures of a Scholar

John C. Greene

Regina Books
Claremont, California

Library of Congress Cataloging-in-Publication Data
Greene, John C.
      Debating Darwin : adventures of a scholar / John C. Greene.
          p. cm.
      Includes bibliographical references and index.
      ISBN 0-941690-85-7 (cloth)
      1. Evolution (Biology)   I. Title.
QH366.2.G74   1999   98-54671
576.8—dc21   CIP

Regina Books
Post Office Box 280
Claremont, California 91711
Tel: (909) 624-8466 Fax: (909) 626-1345

Manufactured in the United States of America.

CONTENTS

For Ernst Mayr,
in Friendship

INTRODUCTION

1

I DISCOVER DARWIN & THE DARWINIANS

I first encountered a dedicated Darwinian, although without quite realizing it, when, as a senior at the University of South Dakota in 1938, I signed up for a course in ancient history taught by a brand new Ph.D. from Harvard named Bert Loewenberg. A native of Brookline, Massachusetts, Loewenberg had recently completed a dissertation on the reception of Charles Darwin's ideas in the United States in the late nineteenth century and had found a job in far away South Dakota at a time when teaching jobs were hard to find. The transition from Brookline to Vermillion, a university and market town of about 3500 inhabitants (800 of whom were college students) cannot have been easy. Loewenberg had had a course in ancient history at Harvard, but his real love was American intellectual history, especially Darwin's influence. Like John Dewey, whose writings he admired greatly, he looked to Darwin as the prophet of twentieth-century revolutions in science, philosophy, and world view. I knew little or nothing about Darwin at that time, being immersed in writers like Henri Bergson and Alfred North Whitehead in my extracurricular reading, but I found Loewenberg's conversation and teaching intensely stimulating, and I sought him out at every opportunity. He eventually went on to a long and successful career as a teacher and Darwin scholar at Sarah Lawrence College.[1] Meanwhile, thanks to his recommendation, I was launched on a career of graduate study in American intellectual history under his old mentor, Professor Arthur Meier Schlesinger.

Darwin was the last thing on my mind during my pre-war years at Harvard. It was sociological, not biological theory that provided

intellectual excitement for me in these years. Through Crane
Brinton's course in European intellectual history I got interested in
Vilfredo Pareto's ideas and began to audit Talcott Parsons' seminar
in sociological theory and to read Parsons, Durkheim, and Max
Weber, none of whom had much to say about Darwin. The door that
eventually led to Darwin was opened inadvertently when I walked
into Professor Schlesinger's office toward the close of my second
year of graduate study to discuss possible topics for a doctoral
dissertation. He offered quite a list of possibilities, ranging from the
study of immigrant groups to the history of state lotteries, but the
topic that struck my fancy was "Geology and Religion in the United
States 1820-1860." I suppose that my longstanding interest in the
relations between science and religion, and possibly my discussions
with Bert Loewenberg, influenced my choice. In any case, the
choice proved to be a fateful one.

As I dug deeper and deeper into the subject I had chosen, I
discovered two things. First, it became clear that geology was but
one of the sciences that were raising problems for traditional
religious beliefs. The nebular hypothesis in astronomy, the so-called
development [evolutionary] hypothesis in natural history, the
investigation of racial differences, the progress of Egyptology and
Biblical criticism—all these were posing difficulties for traditional
interpretations of the Bible. Second, it seemed clear that the crucial
Christian doctrine in relation to these sciences was the doctrine of
the plenary inspiration of the Bible—not the *literal* truth (although
many Christians asserted this) but rather the idea held by leading
scientists like Benjamin Silliman, James Dwight Dana, Joseph
Henry, and others that everything in the Bible, properly interpreted,
was substantially true whether it concerned moral and spiritual or
historical and scientific matters. The result was that when I was
interviewed as a candidate for membership in the Society of Fellows
at Harvard, an appointment that would give me three years of
independent study, I built my research proposal around the historical
fortunes of the doctrine of plenary inspiration in the period 1820-
1860.

After a year and a half of research I went to Professor
Schlesinger and said that I thought I was ready to begin writing my

dissertation, except that I had as yet done no research for the introductory chapter setting the stage for developments after 1820. I was eager to start writing as soon as possible, but he instructed me to do the research for the introductory chapter before beginning to write. That, too, was a fateful decision.

As I delved into the controversies between Christians like Timothy Dwight, president of Yale College, and deists like Thomas Jefferson, Thomas Paine, and Ethan Allen, I was immediately struck by the fact that, whereas the two contending parties were at absolute loggerheads with respect to the inspiration of the Bible, they were in perfect agreement in their view of nature as a wisely designed set of stable structures subservient to the needs—physical, moral, and intellectual—of intelligent moral beings. The deists had retained Christian natural theology lock, stock, and barrel. No less astonishing to me was the great difference between this view of nature and the one I had grown up with in the post-Darwinian era. As time went on, I became less interested in the fortunes of the doctrine of Biblical inspiration and more and more interested in the structure of the static view of nature and natural science and in the causes of its gradual decline and its replacement by evolutionary views.

Up to this time I had been working only on American writers, but since these writers referred frequently to the works of Isaac Newton, Robert Boyle, Carl Linnaeus, the Count de Buffon and other European scientists, I began to read those works too. As I read I began to discern the outlines not only of a dominant static view of nature and natural science but also of an earlier subdominant view of the world in terms of decline from original perfection and an incipient new view of nature as a lawbound system of matter in motion. Moreover, these three different ways of looking at nature were not the disparate views of particular individuals or groups of individuals but rather could be detected interacting side by side with each other in the writings of a single author. Thus, in Newton's works the majestic conception of nature as a lawbound system of matter in motion was conjoined with a static creationism in which the Creator was thought to have so ordered the properties and motions of the atoms of matter that they should produce from the

beginning the harmonious universe we now behold. The problem
for me, then, was to discover the process by which the dynamic and
causal view of nature as a system of matter in motion undermined
and gradually replaced the dominant static view of nature.

I decided to trace this process not only in geology and
paleontology but also in astronomy, in botany and zoology, and in
anthropology. Unfortunately, however, my three year term in the
Society of Fellows expired, and I was thrown out on the academic
world without a Ph.D. (Junior Fellows were not supposed to need a
Ph.D.) And this with a wife and child, presently two children, to
provide for, at first as an instructor in Robert Hutchins' general
education college at the University of Chicago and subsequently as
an assistant professor at the University of Wisconsin. Reading and
discussing the "great books" from Hobbes and Locke to Durkheim
and Max Weber at the college was highly stimulating intellectually,
but I soon realized that I would need a Ph.D. Such chapters of my
grand project as were in reasonable shape were submitted as a
dissertation in 1952, and I received the sacred union ticket just
before I went to the University of Wisconsin.

Teaching American history while working on a book which now
had little to do with American history was not easy. Finishing THE
BOOK (as it came to be known in our family) became a continuing
obsession. I well remember taking the entire family to the library of
the university to view my first article, pilfered from THE BOOK, in
the pages of the *American Anthropologist*, only to hear my eight-
year-old daughter exclaim: "Oh, Daddy, The Book!" I devoutly
wished it had been, for I was then thirty-seven years old.

By this time, however, I had managed to pull together my ideas
about changing presuppositions of thought in successive historical
periods and express them in a paper which I read at a meeting of the
Mississippi Valley Historical Association and published in its
Review in 1957.[2] In that article, entitled "Objectives and Methods in
Intellectual History," I sketched the results of my researches to that
date and charted my course for the future. Intellectual history, for
me, was to consist in delineating the basic presuppositions of
thought (dominant, subdominant, and incipient) in given periods

and in explaining as far as possible the transitions from the dominance of one set of presuppositions to the next. So far as I know, the article did not attract much immediate attention, but I was comforted by a letter from a former graduate student at Wisconsin assuring me: "Immortality is surely thine!"

Meanwhile a basic change had taken place in my academic career. By what I can only regard as a merciful dispensation of Providence, at the very moment when my professional prospects at Wisconsin looked dim indeed an opportunity presented itself to go to Iowa State University to introduce a course in the history of science. I had no training in that field except my work on THE BOOK, but I decided that my research had pointed me toward the history of science and that I might as well make a virtue of necessity.

There followed six busy and successful years at Iowa State University, during which I learned a lot about the history of science and continued working on THE BOOK. The manuscript thereof, in various stages of completion, had been submitted to several presses, academic and commercial, without success but with substantial improvements resulting from criticisms by various readers. Then, in 1958, the Iowa State University Press offered a prize for the best manuscript submitted, with a guarantee of publication, and my manuscript won the prize. Hallelujah! Since the Press was now branching out from books on practical subjects such as poultry husbandry, engineering, statistics, and the like, they decided to publish my manuscript handsomely with many illustrations. But the title I had chosen, "The Genesis of the Evolutionary Idea," did not seem sufficiently dramatic, and I was asked to suggest other titles. The choice fell on *The Death of Adam: Evolution and Its Impact on Western Thought*, a title that was to provoke criticism in conservative religious circles.

But there was another difficulty to be overcome. My manuscript carried the story only through the careers of Georges Cuvier and Jean Baptiste de Lamarck, i.e. to about 1830. My plan had been to produce eventually a second volume which would begin about 1830 and move forward on the same broad basis to the climax in Charles

Darwin's *Origin of Species* and *Descent of Man*. But it was now 1958, and the Darwin centennial year loomed straight ahead. Somehow or other Darwin had to be brought into the picture.

Thus, despite the title of this book, it was not until my forty-first year that I met Charles Darwin as I worked feverishly through the published Darwin materials then available, the *Journal of Researches*, the transmutation notebooks recently published by Sir Gavin de Beer, the sketches Darwin wrote of his theory in 1842 and 1844, and the correspondence published by his son Francis—less than half of what is now available in print. The result, at the end of six months, was the last two chapters of *The Death of Adam*, appropriately titled "The Triumph of Chance and Change" and "Darwin and Adam". The book appeared in the nick of time, one month before the end of the Darwin centennial year. Fortunately it was picked up by the New American Library for their Mentor Books series and thus made available for classroom use at seventy-five cents a copy.

Meanwhile I had already begun reaping the fruits of my suddenly acquired interest in Charles Darwin. When the American Philosophical Society was making plans for its commemoration of the centennial of Darwin's *Origin of Species* early in 1959, a speaker was needed to discuss the topic "Darwin and Religion". The Society's librarian, Richard H. Shryock, had seen and liked my article "Objectives and Methods in Intellectual History" and now suggested that I be asked to deliver the needed lecture on Darwin. Only too glad to oblige, I showed up at the centennial observance of the Society in April of 1959, manuscript in hand, and there found myself surrounded by distinguished neo-Darwinian scientists, founders of what Sir Julian Huxley had called the "modern synthesis." At the reception before the papers were read I found myself standing next to one of these resurrectors of Darwin's theory of natural selection, the famous geneticist Theodosius Dobzhansky. By way of making conversation I told him that I was planning to say a few words in criticism of the similes and metaphors that he and Julian Huxley used in describing evolutionary processes. "Pray, sir," he admonished me, "do not bracket me with Julian Huxley. He is an atheist. I am a Christian." We discussed the matter further, and

I promised not to mention him in this connection in my paper. Apparently he liked the paper, for he praised it warmly and urged me to call him and come for dinner at the Dobzhansky apartment in New York when next I visited that city.

Precisely what Dobzhansky admired in my paper I am not sure—perhaps the fact that I took religion seriously. But he cannot have accepted fully my conclusion that Darwin, like Herbert Spencer, became involved in hopeless contradictions in his attempt to apply biology to human history.

> Biology [I maintained] afforded no criterion of progress for a creature like man, and Darwin was forced to bring in other criteria, imported surreptitiously from his Christian background. To the very end he failed to appreciate the morally ambiguous character of human progress. He failed because, like many social scientists today, he had no adequate conception of man. Whatever his origin, man is a very peculiar creature, whose inmost being eludes the abstractions of science. For science, since it adopts the point of view of the disinterested observer, has no access to those aspects of reality which can be known only from the point of view of the actor. Yet, ultimately, the scientist himself is an actor in the difficult human situation, and science becomes pointless and even destructive unless it takes on significance and direction from a religious affirmation concerning the meaning and value of human existence.[3]

As we shall see, Dobzhansky was fully prepared to make such an affirmation, but not to concede that science, conceived since the seventeenth century as a search for the laws governing natural processes, excludes value judgments about those processes and hence forswears all attempts to find moral significance in natural events. On this point he and I were to exchange a series of letters in the 1960s, some of which are reproduced in this volume.

My drift toward making Darwin and Darwinism central to my research and writing was accelerated markedly when William V. Houston, president of Rice University, who had heard my lecture on Darwin and religion, wrote asking me to give three Rockwell lectures on that subject in the spring of 1960 at his institution. I now began to delve into Biblical criticism and natural theology, both Protestant and Catholic, and into the writings of social evolutionists like V. Gordon Childe, Leslie White, and Julian Steward as well. My lecture "Darwin and the Bible" drew a packed audience, the ones on natural theology and social evolution a somewhat smaller one. When the lectures were published by the Louisiana State University Press, I had the pleasure of dedicating the book to my former teacher Bert Loewenberg. At the same time I was able to define more clearly my position with respect to the relations between science and religion.

> Every great scientific synthesis stimulates efforts to view the whole of reality in its terms, and Darwin's theory of natural selection was no exception. But the views of reality that originate in this way are not themselves scientific, nor are they subject to scientific verification. They attempt to make sense not only of the facts "out there," held at arm's length by the observer, but also of the facts "in here", facts such as our awareness of our own act of existence, our sense of moral accountability, our communion with the source of being. Facts of the latter kind lie close to the heart of reality, but they do not lend themselves to scientific formulation. Attempts to explain them scientifically end by explaining them away. But science itself then becomes unintelligible.[4]

In the meanwhile I had encountered Theodosius Dobzhansky again at the Darwin centennial celebration at the University of Chicago in the fall of 1959, and Julian Huxley as well. By this time Dobzhansky had read the copy of *The Death of Adam* I had sent him, for he greeted me with: "Professor Greene, why are you so pessimistic?" I presumed he was referring to the last paragraph of the book, in which I expressed my reservations about Julian Huxley's proclamation (quoted by Dobzhansky) that man was on the verge of becoming "business manager for the cosmic process of evolution." Concerning that vision of the human future I had written:

> Is man in truth a kind of Prometheus unbound, ready and able to assume control of his own and cosmic destiny? Or is he, as the Bible represents him, a God-like creature who, having denied his creatureliness and arrogated to himself the role of Creator, contemplates his own handiwork with fear and trembling lest he reap the wages of sin, namely, death? The events of the twentieth century bear tragic witness to the realism of the

Biblical portrait of man.... The historical Adam is dead, a casualty of scientific progress, but the Adam in whom all men die lives on, the creature and creator of history, a moral being whose every intellectual triumph is at once a temptation to evil and a power for good.[5]

I was never introduced to Julian Huxley, but I saw him in action at the session on evolution and religion. Unfortunately, I missed his sermon on evolutionary humanism preached from the pulpit of Rockefeller Chapel, where I had sung in the choir during my teaching years at the University. I did send him a copy of *The Death of Adam*, however, and many years later found it marked with his annotations in the Huxley collections at Rice University. The chapter which seems to have interested him most was "The Perfectible Animal"!

My correspondence with Dobzhansky after the Chicago symposium centered on the concept of biological progress, a concept which I had seen creeping into the literature of natural history in the late eighteenth century and early nineteenth century, partly in connection with the evolutionary speculations of Erasmus Darwin, Lamarck, Lacépède, and others, partly in the anthropological inquiries of Rousseau and Lord Monboddo, and partly in the idea of successive progressive creations advanced to explain the paleontological discoveries of Georges Cuvier and his contemporaries. As I traced this idea up to and on through Darwin's writings I gradually became aware of its ambiguous status in a scientific world increasingly dominated by mechanistic conceptions of nature and science. After trying out my ideas on this subject on various biologists at Iowa State University and on a conference of botanists at Vanderbilt University, but without arousing any great interest in my auditors, I decided to develop my ideas more fully in a lecture to the History of Ideas Club at the Johns Hopkins University. This was a club founded and dominated by Arthur O. Lovejoy, a philosopher whose writings on intellectual history, and especially on the history of evolutionary ideas, had done much to influence my own thinking. Unfortunately Lovejoy, then in his eighties, was not well enough to attend the lecture, but it generated sufficient interest to bring about its publication in *The Johns Hopkins Magazine* under the title "Evolution and Progress".

Biologists, I urged, should either stop using words like "higher" and "lower" and "progress" and the figures of speech accompanying them or they should revise their philosophy of nature and natural science to make room for concepts of this kind. But I thought it unlikely that they would adopt either course of action.

> Belief in progress through the accumulation and dissemination of knowledge is the belief that sustains the whole fabric of modern society, Communist and non-Communist.
>
> Is it surprising, then, that the idea of progress should play an equivocal role in modern biology? As a biologist, the student of evolution can say of the idea of progress what Laplace said of the idea of God: "I have no need of that hypothesis." But as a human being seeking some motive of action beyond the needs of the moment he stands in desperate need of that hypothesis. No one can live without hope, and modern man's hope is in progress.[6]

The response to my lecture from members of the History of Ideas Club came largely from professors of literature and philosophy, but the published article eventually elicited an interesting and well considered comment from Professor Walter Bock, an ornithologist and evolutionary biologist then teaching at the University of Illinois. To my delight he thought that my analysis of the problem of progress in evolutionary theory gave an accurate picture of the psychological factors underlying biologists' frequent resort to the language of progress in formulating evolutionary concepts. For his own part, he added: "I do not see the need for a notion of progress in evolutionary biology and have rejected it from my thinking.... I am currently attempting to formulate statements about evolution without progress and with something else in its place."

Twenty-five years later Professor Bock was still considering the issue (letter of May 3, 1989):

> .... the problem always arises of establishing the standard against which progress is judged. As far as I have been able to judge, the standards used by almost everyone in discussing evolutionary progress can be shot down readily. There is one exception, which was developed by my colleague Gerd von Wahlert.... He argues that progress could be equated with greater use

of the available solar energy. But care should be taken not to equate this "progress" with "better", rather to indicate a directional change.... Humans can be considered to be evolutionarily very progressive as they use huge amounts of available energy. But they may be also causing their own extinction because of this great utilization of available energy.

With the publication of *The Death of Adam* and *Darwin and the Modern World View*, both available in cheap Mentor Books editions, I was now a Darwin expert, or so the unsuspecting public thought. Whether I liked it or not, I had become involved in what soon came to be known as "the Darwin industry", a scholarly enterprise which attracted not only aspiring young historians of culture like James Moore and Dov Ospovat but also distinguished scientists who had played leading roles in founding and extending the neo-Darwinian synthesis of the 1930s and 1940s—men like Julian Huxley, George Gaylord Simpson, Theodosius Dobzhansky, Ernst Mayr, and G. Ledyard Stebbins, all of whom looked to Darwin as their patron saint.

As I read what these scientists had to say about Darwin and Darwinism, I soon realized that their interpretations were different in important respects from my own. I had come to Darwin, not from the perspective of twentieth-century neo-Darwinism, but from my researches on the interaction of science and world view in the development of systematic natural history from the late seventeenth century to the overthrow of the static view of nature and natural history in Darwin's time. To me it seemed obvious that the Darwin of the *Origin of Species* was, like his grandfather Erasmus Darwin, an evolutionary theist who saw in the processes of evolution a set of secondary causes by which the Creator had brought about, and was bringing about, adaptation and improvement in the organic realm, including human history. I viewed Darwin also in the context of British *laissez-faire* political economy, British natural theology, and British overseas exploration and colonization among the "lesser breeds without the law," as Kipling called them. But Julian Huxley, Simpson, Mayr, and others wanted to see Darwin as a pure scientist uncontaminated by what came to be known as "social Darwinism" and completely emancipated from both natural and revealed theology—an atheist or at best an agnostic. Indeed, Julian Huxley

aspired to ground a new ethics and a new secular religion of
evolutionary progress in neo-Darwinian biology, and this aspiration
was echoed in varying degrees in the writings of Mayr, Simpson,
Edward O. Wilson, and others. It manifested itself in the highly
teleological, vitalistic, and anthropocentric figures of speech they
used in describing evolutionary processes. Evolution, they said,
was opportunistic, involving trial and error, success and failure,
progress and retrogression, escape from blind alleys, and overall
advance toward higher forms of organization. Yet at the same time
evolution was said to be mechanistic, blind, and purposeless.

When confronted with the teleological, vitalistic, and
anthropomorphic figures of speech they used, these biologists
mostly excused them as a convenient shorthand for purely scientific
ways of stating facts and theories. As a historian of ideas, however,
I could not take so benign and unproblematic a view of the similes
and metaphors used by twentieth-century biologists. To me they
seemed to reflect underlying tensions in biological thought, tensions
which could be traced back to the writings of Darwin himself and
beyond.

For years I had been impressed with the ambiguous status of the
idea of progress in evolutionary discourse. Biologists, it seemed,
could neither live with it nor without it. They could not live with it
because they could not define it without introducing value judgments
which, according to the conception of science that had prevailed
since the scientific revolution of the seventeenth century, were
supposed to be excluded from science. All attempts to define
biological progress scientifically, and there were a good many,
collapsed into mere survival or likelihood of survival. Yet the
evolutionary literature was full of words like "progress",
"improvement", "advance", "higher", and "lower" and of figures of
speech implying striving, purpose, and achievement. Was it
possible, I asked myself, that these biologists, most of whom had
discarded traditional religious and philosophical ways of giving
meaning to science and to human existence, had adopted the idea of
evolutionary progress as a substitute mode of accomplishing the
same objective and had done so by way of simile and metaphor
because the conception of science and nature they had inherited from

the past proscribed the introduction of teleology and value judgments in scientific writing?

It was not until my sabbatical year in 1974 that I had a chance to do some research in the Darwin materials at Cambridge University, thanks to an appointment as Visiting Scholar at Corpus Christi College. What a pleasure it was to leaf through Darwin's books and reprints, annotated in his own hand! As I examined his annotations, I began to realize how deeply Darwin's thinking on social evolution was embedded in British belief in competition between individuals, tribes, nations and races as an engine of progress in human history. In the resulting essay based on these researches I concluded:

> The idea that Darwin, unlike Herbert Spencer and other contemporaries, was a pure scientist confronting nature unhampered by preconceived ideas about nature, society, man, and God must be abandoned. Like every other scientist, Darwin approached nature, human nature, and society with ideas derived from his culture, however much his scientific researches may have changed those ideas in the long run.[8]

By this time I could see the outlines of a general world view common to the members of the great quadrumvirate of English Darwinists—Darwin, Spencer, Huxley, and Wallace—and I decided to publish an article "Darwinism as a World View" in the hope of clarifying the confused situation produced by conflicting definitions of Darwinism as being, alternatively, the idea of organic evolution, the theory of natural selection, the ideological position known as social Darwinism, etc. etc. Spencero-Darwinism, I argued, was compounded of several historical currents of thought: (1) Cartesian mechanism, (2) evolutionary deism fading into agnosticism, (3) British empiricism verging toward positivism, and (4) belief in progressive development through competitive struggle and the inherited effects of habit and mental and moral training.

> Darwinism as a body of scientific theory [I concluded] is alive and flourishing in a considerably modified form in our own day. Darwinism as a world view.... is also still with us, but in less robust condition. Darwinism as an ideology of social progress through competitive struggle of individuals, tribes, nations, and races is rejected in most quarters but not totally extinct. Like everything else, Darwinism evolves. Only a clear

delineation of the elements that entered into its original constitution will enable us to trace its evolutionary history with any degree of certainty.[9]

As the last sentence indicates, I had begun to envisage the possibility of tracing the fortunes of Darwinism as a world view into the twentieth century and, more generally, of seeking to discover the presuppositions of thought in the scientific literature of that period, beginning with evolutionary biology. It would be a difficult undertaking and one which could scarcely be completed in my remaining years of research, but I decided to give it a try. Accordingly, having moved to the University of Connecticut, I launched a new course, "Darwin and the Modern World", which began rather than ended with Darwin and carried through to the founding of the neo-Darwinian synthesis of the 1930s and 1940s.

The first fruit of these studies was an essay "From Huxley to Huxley: Transformations in the Darwinian Credo", which was published in the *Journal of the History of Biology* and later in a collection of my essays entitled *Science, Ideology, and World View*. In this essay I tried to display the interaction of science, ideology, and world view in the evolutionary writings of Julian Huxley, George Gaylord Simpson, Cyril Darlington, and Edward 0. Wilson and, in particular, to uncover the paradoxes and contradictions arising from their attempt to erect a new vision of human duty and destiny on the basis of a supposedly value-free neo-Darwinian biology. Books like Julian Huxley's *Evolution in Action*, Simpson's *The Meaning of Evolution*, and Edward O. Wilson's *On Human Nature*, I argued, were the twentieth-century equivalents of the famous Bridgewater treatises, in which leading nineteenth century British scientists used astronomy, geology, and biology to prove the existence and wisdom of God.

In both cases [I wrote] the conclusions antedate the investigation and dictate its outcome. Simpson and Huxley did not learn to value the individual, to detest totalitarianism, and to believe in the brotherhood of man from studying biology and paleontology any more than William Buckland and his contemporaries learned to believe in an omnipotent, omniscient, and benevolent Creator from their scientific researches. One group of scientists approached nature as agnostics or atheists, the other as Christians. Each had a moral commitment, the first to vindicate the values they held dear and discredit beliefs they thought would hinder the further progress of science, the second to confound skeptics and corroborate religious doctrines that made human duty and destiny intelligible to them. In both cases science was only a tool, a weapon, in defense of positions that were essentially religious and philosophical.[10]

To my mind, these twentieth-century proponents of science-based conceptions of human duty and destiny were impaled on the scientistic horn of what I called the positivist dilemma.

Whoever regards science as man's sole means of acquiring knowledge of reality [I wrote] must eventually confront that dilemma. If science and the scientific method are defined narrowly so as to exclude value judgments and all nonlogico-experimental statements (to use Vilfredo Pareto's term), it then becomes impossible to say why anything, science included, is important or valuable, why the passion for truth is to be inculcated and respected, and why human beings have any more inherent dignity than starfish or stones. But if, on the contrary, science is declared competent to discover human duty and destiny, as those who choose the other horn of the dilemma assert, one is soon confronted with the conflicting claims of Huxleian science, Freudian science, Marxian science, Comtean science, and a host of other scientisms. In the ensuing struggle the central idea of science as an enterprise in which all qualified observers can agree as to what the evidence proves vanishes from sight. Thus, whichever horn of the dilemma the positivist takes, science is the loser.[11]

As I expected, the essays just described were not greeted with enthusiasm by the surviving founders of neo-Darwinism. By great good fortune, however, they brought me into correspondence with Ernst Mayr, the ornithologist-systematist-evolutionist whose *Systematics and the Origin of Species* (1942) and *Animal Species and Evolution* (1965) had been landmarks in the development of the neo-Darwinian synthesis. Beginning about the time of the Darwinian centennial celebrations in 1958-1959, Mayr had turned his attention increasingly to the history and philosophy of biology. His extensive researches culminated in a series of books and articles defining his position scientifically, philosophically, and historically with respect to the relations among science, philosophy, religion, ideology, and world view and placing Darwin at the center of the intellectual revolution implicit in twentieth-century evolutionary biology. In those same years, as we have seen, I was moving from my earlier studies of the interaction of science and world view in the pre-Darwinian period to an analysis of a similar set of interactions in the writings of twentieth century biologists. Not surprisingly, the trajectory of my research and writing intersected with Mayr's, and a correspondence sprang up between us. Our ideas about history, philosophy, and religion clashed openly, but, thanks to Mayr's willingness to consider my criticisms of his writings, we remained good friends in the midst of our "mutual education correspondence", as Mayr called it.

As the letters reproduced in the present work show, Mayr and I approached the study of Darwin and Darwinism from very different points of view. I came to that subject in the course of my studies of the interaction of science and world view in the pre-Darwinian period, studies motivated to a considerable extent by an interest in the relations of science and religion and undertaken with no formal training in science or theology but with a generally sympathetic attitude toward Christian belief and theistic views of nature. As a youth I had gone with my parents to a liberal, non-doctrinal Congregational church and, unlike Mayr, had found parts of the Bible deeply moving and the Christian conception of human nature highly realistic. As a graduate student at Harvard I sampled religious services in several Protestant denominations and eventually settled on the Episcopal service as most to my liking. In my researches leading to *The Death of Adam* I came to realize that Judaeo-Christian creationism played an important positive (as well as an often negative) role in the birth of modern science. Fused with the Pythagorean-Platonic idea that nature was made according to number and proportion, it helped give rise to a conception of natural philosophy as a quest for the mathematical laws governing the divinely established system of matter in motion. Fused with Aristotle's biological ideas, it spawned a conception of natural history as a search for the natural method of classification of divinely created plants and animals.

Static creationism, I discovered, was a powerful incentive to scientific research, but in its static aspect it was gradually undermined by the drawing out of the speculative implications of the concept of nature as a lawbound system of matter in motion and by successive discoveries in astronomy, geology, paleontology, botany, and zoology which seemed to cast doubt on the absolute stability of the structures of nature. The mechanistic view of nature challenged not only static creationism but also the idea of miracles and prophecies and hence the so-called "external evidences" of the Christian revelation. In the nineteenth century heroic efforts were made to save the static view of nature, natural philosophy, and natural history and traditional ideas about the inspiration of the Bible (by working out a concordance of Genesis and geology), but to no avail. With Spencer and Darwin evolution triumphed. Science, formerly pursued in a largely Christian context, became increasingly specialized, professionalized, and secularized and, at the same time, deified as the one sure way to acquire knowledge of reality.

Pursuing the fortunes of Darwinism into the twentieth century, I encountered the evolutionary humanism of Julian Huxley, George Gaylord Simpson, Ernst Mayr, and other founders of the neo-Darwinian synthesis, a secular faith which regarded Darwin as its prophet and imputed to him the positivistic beliefs and unbeliefs that characterized their own thinking on religious, philosophical, and historical topics. As an amateur philosopher I found their efforts to derive knowledge of human duty and destiny from evolutionary biology unconvincing. As a historian I found their ideas about the role of religion in the rise of evolutionary concepts dubious. In due course my published thoughts on these subjects drew me into the correspondence with Ernst Mayr already mentioned.

In Mayr's case the science-and-religion issue which occupied my attention for many years was settled early in life. Although exposed as a child to traditional Protestant doctrines at school and church, in his mid-teens Mayr decided that the supposed Biblical revelation was totally unbelievable and that theism, "the concept of a just God", could not be reconciled with what he saw going on in the world in the decade of World War I. Some years later he read Julian Huxley's *Religion Without Revelation* and found Huxley's evolutionary humanism congenial to his own way of thinking, although he had none of Huxley's crusading zeal to persuade others to his own beliefs.[12] Natural history, especially ornithology, was his passion, and when his discovery and observations of a pair of migratory Redcrested Pochards in March, 1923 led to an invitation to work with the ornithologist Erwin Stresemann at the Berlin Natural History Museum, he abandoned his medical studies and began a lifelong career as naturalist, systematist, and evolutionary theorist, distinguishing himself successively as a field naturalist in New Guinea and the Solomon Islands, as curator of the magnificent ornithological collections of the American Museum of Natural History, as director of the Museum of Comparative Zoology at Harvard University, and, after his retirement in 1974, as a leading contributor to the history and philosophy of biology.[13] Of special significance in the present context is the fact that when, about the time of the Darwin centennial celebrations in 1958-1959, Mayr first began to look into the history of the rise and development of evolutionary ideas, he was well known as a vigorous defender of the neo-Darwinian synthesis against critics of all kinds—vitalists and finalists, saltationists, molecular geneticists, structuralists, skeptical mathematicians and physicists, logical positivists, and others as well. From that time on Mayr devoted himself to defending the synthesis he had helped to construct and the central role of Darwin in bringing about the revolution in science and world view which, in Mayr's opinion, culminated in that synthesis. If his interpretation of the history of biological thought in the context of Western intellectual history was influenced to a considerable extent by his fierce engagement in the scientific and philosophical battles raging in the twentieth century, no one should be surprised. Nor is it surprising that his historical and philosophical conclusions should have differed from mine.

The Mayr-Greene epistolary dialogue, much of which is reproduced in this volume, began in earnest in the summer and fall of 1979. It displays in bold-relief the extent to which our differences in background, training, and interests and the different routes by which we had come to the study of Darwin and Darwinism influenced the conclusions we drew from the historical record. As a naturalist who early in life had rejected Christianity and theism generally, Mayr found it difficult to believe that anyone who understood the theory of evolution by natural selection, as Darwin certainly did, could be a theist. Darwin, he thought, must have inserted those references to the Creator in the *Origin of Species* out of respect for the deeply felt convictions of his wife and friends. For my part, as a historian who had traced the transition from the static creationism of John Ray and Carl Linnaeus to the static deism of Paine and Jefferson and on to the evolutionary theism of Erasmus Darwin and Lamarck, I thought it natural that Darwin, like his grandfather, should have regarded evolutionary processes as a system of secondary causes designed to bring about adaptation and improvement in organic nature. Had not Darwin, in his unpublished essay of 1844, conjured up the vision of "a Being with penetration sufficient to perceive differences in the outer and innermost organization quite imperceptible to man, and with forethought extending over future centuries to watch with unerring care and select for any object the offspring of an organism produced under the foregoing [environmental] circumstances?"[14]

Again, when it came to defining the nature of "Darwinism", Mayr tended to argue from the understanding of that term current among mid-twentieth century evolutionary biologists, to gloss over those passages in Darwin's writings which fit badly with that understanding, and to impute to Darwin the greater part of the scientific and philosophical ideas and attitudes which characterized his own thinking about evolution. Darwin, he believed, was not only a great scientist but a great philosopher as well, one who singlehandedly had confronted and demolished the false ideologies of creationism, vitalism, Platonic mathematicism and essentialism, cosmic teleology, philosophical idealism, and physicalist reductionism and had replaced them with bold new concepts of nature, science, human nature, and society, including "population thinking", probabilism, teleonomy, and ethical perspectives based on the theory of evolution by natural selection.[15] My own view, emerging from my studies of the interaction of science and world view in the period separating Newton and Darwin, was less apocalyptic. I conceived Darwinism, as expounded in the writings of Darwin, Spencer, Wallace, and Huxley, as a fascinating blend of currents of Western (especially British) thought reaching back at least to the time of René Descartes. I was aware, of course, of the novel elements in Darwin's writings, but I had grave doubts about attributing to Darwin twentieth century neo-Darwinian ideas when the historical record showed that his thinking was deeply colored by the political economy, natural theology, utilitarian social theory, racial and gender prejudices, and empiricist philosophy of his own British culture. It was one thing to say that Darwin's theory implied "population thinking" and a probabilistic conception of order, but quite another to say that Darwin grasped these perspectives philosophically. The idea of an unconscious philosopher seemed to me a contradiction in terms.

The publication of my essay "From Huxley to Huxley: Transformations in the Darwinian Credo" opened up a wide range of philosophical issues between Mayr and me. To Mayr it seemed that my critique of the conclusions drawn by Julian Huxley, George Gaylord Simpson, Cyril Darlington, and Edward 0. Wilson concerning the implications of neo-Darwinian biology for traditional religious beliefs, social ethics, and the like were motivated by religious conservatism. "One continuously reads between the lines let us go back, let us go back to God, then we will be comfortable, and then we can refer all objections to Him."[16] From my point of view, however, my critique was based on certain clearly stated ideas concerning the relations of science, philosophy, and religion, or, more broadly, science and world view. These writers, I argued, were trying to attach the prestige of science to world views which went beyond anything which science as traditionally conceived could verify or falsify—world views, moreover, which were beset with paradoxes and contradictions.

Mayr could not agree. These scientists, he argued, were "valiantly trying to arrive at a non-supernatural basis of human ethics and beliefs." They believed, as George Gaylord Simpson put it, that "as modern scientists we must reject escape into non-material causations, and if we look for the science that can serve as a basis for our interpretations we find that the only one that is suitable for this purpose is evolutionary biology (broadly defined to include psychology and sociology, so far as they are evolutionary)".[17] To me, however, it seemed obvious that science as conceived since the seventeenth century ignored the value aspect of reality in its attempt to discover how nature works and hence was in no position to provide a basis for ethics of any kind. The values espoused by the scientists themselves were derived, not from science, but from the traditional sources of Western values—the literature and philosophy of Greece and Rome, the Judaeo-Christian tradition, and the Enlightenment. They had their roots, not in science, but in philosophical reflection and religious affirmation.

In return, Mayr denied that evolutionary biologists were trying to derive ethics from science. They contended only that ethical principles were indispensable to the functioning of societies and that natural selection had produced in the human animal "open programs" which *permitted* the development of ethical beliefs. In my view, this line of argument conceded what I had been insisting on, namely, that science by its self-definition is confined to the study of what *is* and has no way to ascertain what *ought* to be. As to "non-material causation", the investigator *as a scientist* might choose to reject this idea *a priori*, but that in no way constrained him to do the same in his investigations *as a philosopher*, unless science and philosophy were the same thing (which, I suggested to Mayr, seemed to be the nub of the issue between us). The rules governing science should not be conceived as embracing the entire field of rational inquiry. To do so would make it impossible to say why science itself is valuable or important.

There seems to have been a hiatus in the Mayr-Greene correspondence from May 1980 until October 1985, when it was resumed in somewhat strained circumstances. I had sent Mayr an advance copy of my essay "The History of Ideas Revisited" (reprinted in this volume) which I had written in response to a request from Jacques Roger, one of the editors of the *Revue de Synthèse*. In this essay I summarized my ideas about the interaction of science and world view in the development of natural history from Aristotle to Darwin and thence to the neo-Darwinian synthesis of the mid-twentieth century. Unfortunately, Mayr mistook my line of argument for an all-out attack on Darwinian biology *per se* and, when asked (at my suggestion) to provide a commentary on my essay, mounted a blistering attack on what he thought was my position, alleging that I was a teleologist and a Christian and hence incapable of accepting the theory of natural selection, that I reduced science to ideology, that I was an essentialist, and so forth. Somewhat taken aback, I wrote to Mayr explaining my true views, and he replied in a conciliatory letter which did much to heal the breach that had opened between us.

In the next few years I devoted much of my time to a careful study of the three books—*Evolution and the Diversity of Life*, *The Growth of Biological Thought*, and *Toward a New Philosophy of Biology*—in which Mayr brought together his ideas about the history and philosophy of biology. My reflections on these books were set forth in two articles (reproduced below) in the *Journal of the History of Biology*,[19] both of which were submitted to Mayr in advance of publication and modified somewhat in response to his criticisms. Indeed, he even permitted me to quote from his letters to me with respect to my critique of *The Growth of Biological Thought*, thereby giving the heavily footnoted article the character of a dialogue between us. Our liveliest exchange of views, however, concerned the fourth section, "Science, Value, and the Image of Man", of my critique of his *Toward a New Philosophy of Biology*, in which I raised anew my longstanding objections to his view that the theory of evolution by natural selection had given rise to a new and better image of human nature, duty, and destiny than pre-Darwinian science, philosophy, and religion could provide. Replying in a series of letters, Mayr defended evolutionary naturalism vigorously, denying any intention to discredit religion or to derive ethics from evolutionary biology. He himself, he declared, was a deeply religious person, and so were most of the scientists he knew. Religiosity need not involve theological dogmas based on belief in some supposed revelation from on high. As to ethics, a value system developed from a world view based on scientific investigation could justly be described as derived, if only indirectly, from science. To which I answered that my objections were not to evolution nor to science properly conceived nor to Darwinism as a scientific theory but rather to mechanistic naturalism as a total world view. I admitted that my own Christian belief contained a considerable admixture of agnosticism and that many of my friends who subscribed to some form of naturalism led exemplary lives, much more useful to mankind than mine. But, like Arthur Balfour in the late nineteenth century, I questioned whether agnostic evolutionary naturalism, when shorn of its parasitic borrowings from classical and Judaeo-Christian sources, could long support a high civilization. Time would tell!

Since this exchange of views the Mayr-Greene dialogue has continued in correspondence and in print, with neither of us showing any inclination to adopt the other's point of view nor, on the other hand, to shut off the debate. But I think we have not been without influence on each other. I know that I have been forced to think harder and dig deeper in the sources to defend my positions, and I think I can see some shifts in Mayr's line of argument in response to my criticisms. In any case, I continue to be astonished and grateful that this eminent biologist-historian-philosopher should be sufficiently broad-minded to consider and contend with criticisms grounded in philosophical reflection and sustained analysis of basic texts in the literature of natural history. The better I know the man, the more I like and admire him.

I cannot conclude this narrative of Darwinian encounters, however, without mentioning another and quite different dialogue I have carried on over the past two decades with a fellow historian, James Moore, born and educated in engineering and theology in northern Illinois and transplanted to England on a Marshall Fellowship to study nineteenth-century history. There he developed his own style of Marxist-influenced historical interpretation not long after the publication of his first book, *The Post-Darwinian Controversies*. He then became a major figure in Darwin scholarship and in the work of the Open University at Milton Keynes. Like me, Jim has long been interested in the relations of science and religion, but he has come to view their interaction, not so much as a dialectic of ideas, but rather as the outcome of economic, social, and political institutions and interests prevailing in society at different epochs. During the period of our friendship he has argued the case for this point of view in correspondence and conversation and in several books and articles (most notably in the biography *Darwin* which he wrote in collaboration with Adrian Desmond). "Viewing scientific ideas as embedded in social relationships, in particular economic and political contexts," he contends, "seems to be more faithful to the texture of history as it was actually lived than dealing with the same ideas as freefloating entities that may or may not in some transhistorical sense be 'true'."[20]

On this question I find myself more in accord with Mayr than with Moore. Although Mayr and I disagree widely in our analysis of conceptual developments in Western science, we both stress the central role of ideas in the transition from Aristotle to Darwin, refusing to regard the theoretical constructions of major figures in this transition as completely determined by the social, economic, and political situations in which they worked. General ideas have indeed floated through the centuries, borne along on a sea of written and printed words and combining in fascinating ways to produce new scientific theories and new world views.

> If you want to understand Newton's ideas about mathematics [I told Moore], the answer is not to study the social conditions in England in his time, but to examine Newton's ideas in relation to what Descartes had done, what Apollonius had done, and so on. There is an internal evolution of ideas that both influences and is influenced by other things not so internal. There is a history of thoughts.[21]

Again:

> If ideas are only manifestations of class interests or libidinal drives, then the whole intellectual enterprise is reduced to absurdity. Freud's theory, Marx's theory, Darwin's theory—the notion that any of these could be true goes out the window. All are merely manifestations of something essentially non-ideational, and I certainly do not believe that. There is a life of the mind, and it is very real and very important.[22]

Thus, toward the end of an extended series of Darwinian encounters I find myself more in love with the history of ideas than ever but greatly enriched by the intellectual friendships formed along the way and by the intellectual challenges they have brought. Far from wishing (as Dobzhansky suspected me of doing) that Darwin had never lived, I emerge from four decades of studying his work and influence with the highest admiration for his intellectual integrity, his prowess as a scientist, and the courage and resourcefulness with which he faced the dilemmas created by his determination to view human nature in all its aspects as part and parcel of nature. As the ensuing essays will show, I cannot agree with that view, but I respect Darwin's candor and integrity and acknowledge his far reaching influence in the century now coming to a close. Just as the century beginning about 1740 became Newton's century, so the period beginning about 1930 has become Darwin's century. But Newtonianism as a world view eventually succumbed to changes in science and culture, leaving a solid core of scientific achievement as a permanent monument to Newton's genius, and already there are signs that a similar fate awaits Darwin. My only regret is that I shall not be around to study these changes in science and world view. Whatever happens, it has been a high privilege and an exciting adventure to have known and shared ideas with fellow historians and with two biologists who played leading roles in giving Darwin's vision its twentieth-century form, each in his own way.

NOTES

1.   For a representative listing of Bert Loewenberg's publications on Darwin and Darwinism see the "Bibliography" in James Moore, *The Post-Darwinian Controversies. A Study of the Protestant Struggle to Come to Terms with Darwin in Great Britain and America 1870-1900,* p. 431.

2.   John C. Greene, "Objectives and Methods in Intellectual History," *Mississippi Valley Historical Review* 44 (1957), pp. 58-74.

3.   Greene, "Darwin and Religion," *Proceedings of the American Philosophical Society* 103 (October 1959), p. 725.

4.   Greene, *Darwin and the Modern World View* (Baton Rouge: Louisiana State University Press, 1961), pp. 132-133.

5.   Greene, *The Death of Adam. Evolution and Its Impact on Western Thought* (Ames, Iowa: Iowa State University Press, 1959), pp. 338-339.

6.   Greene, "Evolution and Progress," *The Johns Hopkins Magazine* 14 (October 1962), p. 32.

7.   Gerd von Wahlert, "Evolution als Geschichte des Ökosystems Biosphäre," in U. Kattman, G. v. Wahlert, J. Weninger, *Evolutionsbiologie* (Köln, 1978), pp. 23-68.

8.   Greene, "Darwin as a Social Evolutionist," *Journal of the History of Biology*, 10 (1977), p. 27.

9.   Greene, "Darwinism as a World View," in Greene, *Science, Ideology, and World View. Essays in the History of Evolutionary Ideas* (Berkeley, Los Angeles, London: University of California Press, 1981), p. 151.

10. Ibid. "From Huxley to Huxley: Transformations in the Darwinian Credo," p. 177.

11. Ibid., p. 188.

12. Letter from Mayr to Greene, May 1, 1989.

13. For an overview of Mayr's life and work, see the "Special Issue on Ernst Mayr at Ninety," John Greene and Michael Ruse, ed. *Biology and Philosophy* 9 (July 1994).

14. Charles Darwin, *The Foundations of the Origin of Species; Two Essays Written in 1842 and 1844,* Francis Darwin, ed. (Cambridge, England, 1909), pp. 85-87.

15. For a succinct view of Mayr's ideas concerning Darwin's role in Western thought see his *One Long Argument. Charles Darwin and the Genesis of Modern Evolutionary Thought* (Cambridge, MA: Harvard University Press, 1991), especially Chap. 7. My review of this book appeared in the *Times Higher Education Supplement*, May 29, 1992, p. 25.

16. Mayr to Greene, April 8, 1980.

17. The best introduction to George Gaylord Simpson's views concerning the relations of science, philosophy, and religion is his book *This View of Life. The World of an Evolutionist* (New York: Harcourt, Brace & World, Inc., 1964).

18. My letter to Mayr explaining my views as stated in "The History of Ideas Revisited," *Revue de Synthèse, quatrième série* (juillet-septembre 1986), pp. 201-228, was published in the *Journal of the History of Biology* 22 (Summer 1989), pp. 357-359. Mayr's commentary on my article, "The Death of Darwin?", appeared in the same issue of the *Revue*, pp. 229-235. See Greene to Mayr, June 4, 1986 and Mayr to Greene, June 11, 1986 in the present volume.

19. See Greene, "From Aristotle to Darwin: Reflections on Ernst Mayr's Interpretation in *The Growth of Biological Thought*," *Journal of the History of Biology* 25 (Summer 1992), 257-284, and Greene, "Science, Philosophy, and Metaphor in Ernst Mayr's Writings," in the same journal, 27 (Summer 1994), pp. 311-347.

20. Quoted from the "Introductory Conversation" in James R. Moore, ed., *History, Humanity and Evolution. Essays for John C. Greene* (Cambridge: Cambridge University Press, 1989), p. 11.

21. Ibid.

22. Ibid., p. 10.

I

SCIENCE, RELIGION & PHILOSOPHY IN THE EVOLUTIONARY DEBATE

2

THE RELIGIOUS ROLE OF METAPHOR IN EVOLUTIONARY BIOLOGY

In her challenging book *Evolution as a Religion,* Mary Midgley declares:

> The theory of evolution is not just an inert piece of theoretical science. It is, and cannot help being, also a powerful folktale about human origins....Facts will never appear to us as brute and meaningless; they will always organize themselves into some sort of story, some drama. These dramas can indeed be dangerous. They can distort our theories, and they have distorted the theory of evolution perhaps more than any other. The only way in which we can control this kind of distortion is to bring the dramas themselves out into the open, to give them our full attention, understand them better and see what part, if any, each of them ought to play both in theory and in life.[1]

She dedicates her book "To the Memory of Charles Darwin Who Did Not Say These Things." Alas, Darwin did say some of these things, but he was a very great scientist and an admirable man for all of that.

Our starting point, however, is not Charles Darwin but rather some remarks of Alexandre Koyré about the divorce of science from philosophy and, more generally, from the search for meaning and value that accompanied the seventeenth century revolution in physics and cosmology. The substitution of the mechanical view of nature for Aristotle's world of forms and qualities involved, says Koyré, "the destruction of the Cosmos", the disappearance of "the conception of the world as a finite, closed and hierarchically ordered whole." In its place science erected an indefinite and infinite universe in which all the components of nature were placed on the same level of being, governed by the same laws. This, in turn, involved "the discarding by scientific thought of all considerations based upon value-concepts, such as perfection, harmony, meaning and aim, and finally the utter devalorization of being, the divorce of the world of value from the world of facts."[2]

But although the mechanistic view of nature may seem by hindsight to have implied all that Koyré describes, in practice it was not pushed to any such drastic conclusion. Physical nature may have been stripped of Aristotelean forms and qualities, but they were retained intact in the organic world. Robert Boyle explained the origin of forms and qualities in the physical world in terms of the motions of atoms, but it would be another two centuries before Darwin attempted to explain their origin in the organic world by natural causes. For Newton and most of his contemporaries nature was still a hierarchically ordered whole, a framework of stable structures fitted as a stage for the activities of intelligent beings, whether on this planet or in other regions of space. Matter was regarded as designed to provide a theater for life, and the lower forms of life were viewed as subservient to the needs of the higher.

For this view of nature and natural science the metaphor of nature as a machine seemed entirely appropriate. The word "mechanical" in the phrase "mechanical view of nature" had two different but related meanings, as E. J. Dijksterhuis has noted.[3] On the one hand it meant "reducible to the principles of mechanics", the science of bodies acted on by forces. On the other hand it meant "like a machine", the operation of which could be explained by mechanical principles. The celestial machine, Kepler wrote to von Hohenburg, "is to be likened not to a divine organism but rather to a clockwork...., insofar as nearly all the manifold movements are carried out by means of a single, quite simple magnetic force, as in the case of a clockwork all motions [are caused] by a simple weight. Moreover [Kepler added] I show how this physical conception is to be presented through calculation and geometry."[4]

To say that events in physical nature were reducible to the mathematical rules of the science of mechanics was one thing. It implied nothing concerning the origin of those rules or the significance of the mathematical physicist himself. But to say that nature was a machine was quite something else. A machine is an artifact, designed for some purpose. It presupposes an intelligent designer. And indeed Kepler and Galileo believed that the world machine had such a designer. For them nature was the work of a "divine Artificer", and the science of nature was the divinely appointed task of human artificers whose minds had been created in the image of the Divine Mind. Through mathematical-experimental science, they believed, the natural philosopher would be led up through nature to nature's God and thus to a knowledge of his duty toward God and his fellow human beings. Through science, moreover, mankind would attain to that dominion over nature which their Creator had intended for them. Thus, through the metaphor of the machine, human beings became participators with God in the intellectual pleasures of mathematical physics and in the practical work of subduing nature to divine purposes. The universe might be infinite and the atoms of matter all on the same level, but matter was subservient to life and life to rational existence. As for science, it was increasingly regarded as the supreme human manifestation of divine reason and the surest road to useful knowledge, including knowledge of the Creator's existence and attributes and consequently of human duty and destiny. All this was implicit in the metaphor of the world machine.

All this, too, was called into question when the mechanical view of nature was extended to embrace not only the inorganic but also the organic world, a development that began when Descartes undertook to derive the present state of nature from previous states of the system of matter in motion through the operation of the laws of motion. This Cartesian enterprise was so bold, so appealing to the speculative intellect, that it was soon extended from astronomy and cosmology to geological transformations on the Earth's surface and thence, beginning with Erasmus Darwin and Jean Baptiste de Lamarck, to the origin and development of living forms.

The idea of extending the law-bound system of matter in motion to embrace the organic world seemed perfectly natural to those who proposed it, but the project had unforeseen consequences. It introduced foreign elements into the mechanistic world view—ideas of progress, levels of being, and the like—and thereby undermined the notion of nature as a machine. Animals could be thought of as automata—Descartes had already suggested this—but the idea that machines could evolve from simple to complex forms (including human beings) without the aid of a designing intelligence seemed preposterous. Both Lamarck and Erasmus Darwin felt compelled to postulate a "sublime Author of nature" (Lamarck), a "Cause of causes" (Erasmus Darwin), to explain the ability of animals to respond to the challenge of environmental change by developing new faculties and organs. The function of this supreme being, however, was not to create new organic forms by almighty fiat but rather to design the system of matter in motion in such a way that it would generate the living from the non-living and improve organic forms gradually through the operation of natural causes. Evolutionary theory led, not to atheism or agnosticism, but to evolutionary deism. But there was as yet no appealing metaphor to dramatize the conception of nature as a self-perfecting process of progressive improvement capable of giving rise to the scientist himself, nor was there as yet any scientifically credible "mechanism" (a word derived from the mechanical view of nature) to account for the changes of organic form disclosed in the fossil record.

It was Charles Darwin who coined the master metaphor that eventually dominated evolutionary thinking. Having decided to adopt the transmutation hypothesis shortly after his return from the voyage of the *Beagle*, Darwin began the search for the natural means by which populations of organisms were modified and kept adapted to changing circumstances. Finally, in the fall of 1838, after reading Thomas Malthus' famous *Essay on the Principle of Population*, Darwin hit upon the idea of a general organic struggle for existence in which those members of a species which happened to possess traits favorable to survival in their particular circumstances would be most likely to reach reproductive age and hence would spread those traits through subsequent generations, thereby gradually changing the character of the population. Casting about for a suitable name for this process of variation, population pressure, differential adaptedness, differential survival, and differential reproduction, Darwin chose the term "natural selection", in order, as he said, to "mark its relation to man's power of selection" in producing new breeds of plants and animals.

There was, of course, no selection in nature. Selection implies intelligent choice, of which nature knows nothing. What Darwin called natural selection might better have been called differential reproduction through the luck of the hereditary draw. Why, then, did Darwin choose a metaphor implying intelligent choice to designate a complex set of processes involving random variation, population pressure, and differential survival to reproductive age? He did so, first, because the analogy to the selection practiced by plant and animal breeders served him well, both as a research tool and as a method of making his theory intelligible to fellow scientists and to the general public. But Darwin seems to have had another reason as well, a reason connected with his evolutionary deism. His transmutation notebooks, his essays of 1842 and 1844, and the *Origin* itself all show that Darwin regarded what he called "natural selection" as a set of processes designed by the Creator to produce adaptation and improvement in the organic world. In the essays of 1842 and 1844 Darwin even personified natural selection, asking his readers to imagine "a Being with penetration sufficient to perceive differences in the outer and innermost organization [of plants and animals] quite imperceptible to man, and with forethought extending over future centuries to watch with unerring care and select for any object the offspring of an organism produced under the foregoing [environmental] circumstances." Darwin could see no reason why such a being could not "form a new race (or several were he to separate the stock of the original organism and work on several islands) adapted to new ends." "As we assume his discrimination, and his forethought, and his steadiness of object, to be incomparably greater than those qualities in man," Darwin continued, "so may we suppose the beauty and complication of the adaptations of the new races and their differences from the original stock to be greater than in the domestic races produced by man's agency.... With time enough, such a Being might rationally.... aim at almost any result."[5] Darwin was careful to say that this master Being was not the Creator Himself, but the powers he ascribed to it made it at least the vicegerent of the Creator.

In Darwin's *Origin of Species* there is no explicit mention of the master Being, but he lurks behind the scenes in Darwin's description of natural selection as "daily and hourly scrutinizing, throughout the world, every variation, even the slightest; rejecting that which is bad, preserving and adding up all that is good; silently and insensibly working, whenever and wherever opportunity offers, at the improvement of each organic being in relation to its organic and inorganic conditions of life."[6] The products of this constant, rigorous scrutiny, Darwin observed, "bear the stamp of a far higher workmanship" than those of "feeble man" in his role of plant and animal breeder. Note that, in Darwin's view, the variations "preserved" by natural selection are not merely good in the sense that they promote survival to reproductive age. They are "improvements". Darwin's *Origin* abounds with "improvements" produced by natural selection. "The modified offspring from the later and more highly improved branches in the lines of descent," he wrote, "will.... often take the place of, and so destroy, the earlier and less improved branches. Hence all the intermediate forms between the earlier and later states, that is between the less and more improved state of a species, as well as the original parent-species itself, will generally tend to become extinct."[7]

The influence of the analogy to artificial selection and of Darwin's evolutionary deism is evident in these passages. The variations selected by a plant or animal breeder are improvements from the point of view of the breeder because they move the stock in the direction desired by the breeder. But in nature there is no desired or intended direction of change unless one postulates a master Being who has such a direction in mind. From the point of view of the organism concerned it is doubtless good to survive and reproduce, but to consider the organisms that survive and reproduce as "improvements" on those that do not is to introduce value judgments supposedly outside the domain of science. Is the tapeworm an improvement on its ancestors that had a more complicated structure? Is the modern horse an improvement on Eohippus? A standard of comparison would seem to be required, and, as Darwin himself conceded in his correspondence with Joseph Dalton Hooker, the intuitive standard of comparison is man himself. If human beings are considered higher than amoebas and chimpanzees and if the fossil record seems to indicate an overall succession of forms leading eventually to human beings, organic evolution may be described as a process of progressive improvement, however haphazard and erratic. But without the fossil record and without the assumption that man is the highest organism on earth what reason is there to think that differential reproduction of organisms happening to have traits favorable to survival will produce improvement in the organic world?

To Charles Lyell it seemed evident that the improvement attested by the fossil record must have its source outside of nature, since nothing in Darwin's theory of natural selection seemed to require it. Darwin, however, was convinced that his theory did imply progressive improvement in the long run, although not in every instance of organic change through natural selection. He explained his position as follows in a letter to Lyell:

> .... every step in the natural selection of each species implies improvement in that species in relation to its conditions of life. No modification can be selected without it be an improvement or advantage. Improvement implies, I suppose, each form obtaining many parts or organs, all excellently adapted for their functions. As each species is improved, and as the number of forms will have increased, if we look to the whole course of time, the organic condition of life for other forms will become more complex, and there will be a necessity for other forms to become improved, or they will be exterminated; and I can see no limit to this process of improvement, without the intervention of any other and direct principle of improvement. All this seems to me quite compatible with certain forms fitted for simple conditions, remaining unaltered, or being degraded.
>
> If I have a second edition, I will reiterate 'Natural Selection', and, as a general consequence, Natural Improvement.[8]

Darwin's *Origin* did indeed have a second edition (and a third, fourth, fifth, and sixth), and Darwin continued to the end to insist that the apparent improvement in organic forms disclosed in the fossil record was a necessary long-run consequence of random variation, population pressure, and differential survival to reproductive age. In the sixth edition, as in the first, these processes were represented as constituting "laws impressed on matter by the Creator" and as working "by and for the good of each being", with the result that "all corporeal and mental endowments will tend to progress towards perfection."[9] What better metaphor could Darwin have chosen to designate these agencies of progressive improvement than the term "natural selection," evocative as it was of the benevolent selectivity of the improver of domestic stocks? True, nature's selection was much slower, much more erratic and wasteful than man's, but its superior workmanship was evident in the "endless forms most beautiful and most wonderful" it had produced. The struggle for existence was harsh, but Darwin found consolation in the belief "that the war of nature is not incessant, that no fear is felt, that death is generally prompt, and that the vigorous, the healthy, and the happy survive and multiply."[10] Natural improvement, although costly, slow, and spasmodic, was, happily, inevitable. Having produced the human species, natural selection (aided by the inherited effects of mental and moral training) would, Darwin hoped, eventually evolve creatures who would look back on him and Lyell and Newton as "mere Barbarians".[11] In Darwin's view, natural selection was no mere mechanism of organic modification and co-adaptation. It was also the Great Improver, blind but powerful and inexorable. It had, said Darwin, elevated man to "the very summit of the organic scale" and had thereby given him "hope for a still higher destiny in the distant future."[12]

Darwin's metaphor had taken on a life of its own. Natural selection had become a being with many of the attributes of deity. Its works were manifold, like those of the Biblical Jehovah. Its power was awesome, conferring life and death, creating new and ever more complex organic forms, separating the wheat from the tares, rewarding the efficient and punishing the ineffectual, giving hope of ultimate progress to those who believed in its power and kept its commandments. Nature, said Thomas Henry Huxley, was a great university in which all mankind were enrolled. Those who studied her ways, who learned and obeyed the laws that govern men and things, would be rewarded generously. Nature would be their ever-beneficent Mother, they her ministers, mouthpieces, and interpreters. But those who remained ignorant of her laws would be "plucked", i.e. flunked—"and then you can't come up again. Nature's pluck means extermination."[13]

Huxley eventually parted company with those who looked to nature's processes for the eventual solution of human problems, but Darwin held fast to his faith in the beneficent power of natural selection despite his growing doubts about evolutionary deism. "I could show fight on natural selection having done and doing more for the progress of civilization than you seem inclined to admit," he wrote to William Graham in 1881. "The more civilized so-called Caucasian races have beaten the Turkish all hollow in the struggle for existence. Looking to the world at no very distant date, what an endless number of the lower races will have been eliminated by the higher civilized races throughout the world."[14] For Darwin natural selection, aided and abetted by the inherited effects of mental and moral training, had become the guarantor of human progress, the hope of mankind.

More than three quarters of a century intervened between the publication of Darwin's *Origin of Species* and the general acceptance by biologists of the concept of natural selection as the centerpiece of evolutionary theory. In the interim, evolutionary theorizing was dominated by non-selectionist theories of orthogenetic, neo-Lamarckian, or saltationist-mutationist character. With the revival in the 1930s and 1940s of the idea of natural selection in the so-called "modern synthesis", however, there was an efflorescence of metaphorical language seeking to give value and meaning to evolutionary processes and to the science of evolutionary biology. Gone, for the most part, was the evolutionary deism that had sustained Darwin throughout much of his scientific career. Most of the champions of the modern synthesis were agnostics or atheists violently opposed to any suggestion of theism, vitalism, or teleology in nature or in natural science. For them the meaning of evolution had to be found in the evolutionary process itself, but without imputing any aim or purpose to that process. Scientific explanations, they insisted, must be "mechanistic".

Sir Julian Huxley's difficulties in pursuing this non-theistic, non-teleological search for meaning and value in evolutionary processes are described in a later essay.[15] Like Darwin, Huxley held that evolution was progressive in the long run, but whereas Darwin had been supported in this belief by nineteenth-century optimism, by the analogy of natural selection to artificial selection, and by faith in the beneficent effects of competitive struggle, Huxley could find no vindication of evolutionary progress in any of these sources. By the 1930s, after a world war, a great depression, and the advent of Fascism and Nazism, many people had come to doubt the inevitability of progress. The analogy between natural selection and plant and animal breeding had helped give rise to eugenics, but the eugenics movement had been rendered increasingly suspect by new discoveries in genetics and by Hitler's eugenic experiments. As for competitive struggle among individuals, tribes, nations, and races, Huxley had no stomach for *laissez-faire* political economy or for military and racial conflict. Biologists, he said, must give up the idea "that natural selection and the adaptations it promotes must be good for the species as a whole, for the good of the group undergoing adaptive radiation, or even that it must promote constant evolutionary progress."

> Natural selection [he concluded], though....like the mills of God in grinding slow and grinding small, has few other attributes that a civilized religion would call Divine. It is efficient in its way—at the price of extreme slowness and extreme cruelty. But it is blind and mechanical; and accordingly its products are just as likely to be aesthetically, morally, or intellectually repulsive to us as they are to be attractive.[16]

In this passage Huxley echoed Darwin's occasional misgivings about "the clumsy, wasteful, blundering, low, and horribly cruel works of nature", but whereas Darwin had been prepared to trust to natural selection and the inheritance of acquired characters for the eventual improvement of humanity, Huxley declared emphatically that the direction of evolution must be taken over by human beings, whose responsibility it was to develop "a rational applied biology".[17]

But if "natural selection" was no longer a satisfactory metaphor for the processes generating improvement in the organic world, what figures of speech were to be substituted in order to give meaning to evolutionary processes? The answer, Huxley discovered, was to personify life and to depict its adventures in the struggle with environing circumstances, its opening up of ever new possibilities, its growing independence and control of the environment, its gradual acquisition of self-consciousness, purpose, and rational control in its human phase.

> Living substance [wrote Huxley] demonstrates its improvement during evolution by doing old things in new and better ways, by acquiring new properties, by organizing itself in new forms, by increasing its efficiency and enlarging its variety.[8]

This personification turned out to be Huxley's basic figure of speech. He defines *improvement*, *advance*, *progress*, *higher*, and *lower* in terms of life's progressive realization of its inherent potentialities. Natural selection, he notes, "can only produce results which are of immediate biological advantage to their possessors...in relation to the particular situation of the moment, hence it often leads life into "blind alleys", from which there is no "evolutionary escape." Yet paradoxically, natural selection "operates with the aid of time to produce improvements in the machinery of living" which enable living substance to find its way onward and upward.[19] Thus, life achieves its triumphs and realizes its potentialities both *despite* the short-sighted operations of natural selection and *because* of them. Natural selection, writes Huxley, gives life increased efficiency in dealing with the "challenge" of the environment and thereby leads it into "regions of new evolutionary opportunity".

> Each new deployment, after steadily advancing over its new terrain, comes to an impasse. There is sometimes a path out of the impasse, but it is generally a devious one; it is through its twists and turns that life finds its way into a new field of maneuver; and this marks the beginning of another distinct step in progress.[20]

The religious thrust of Huxley's evolutionary biology became explicit in his popular exposition of evolutionary science entitled *Evolution in Action* (note the personification). Biological evolution was now linked to cosmic evolution at one end and to human evolution at the other to form a continuous chain of evolutionary progress, "a one-way process in time; unitary, continuous, irreversible; self-transforming; and generating variety and novelty in its transformations." Evolutionary science, the science of the entire process, was disclosing the destiny of man on earth, namely, "to be the agent of the world process of evolution, the sole agent capable of leading it to new heights, and enabling it to realize new possibilities."

I shall probably be attacked for going beyond the boundaries of science [Huxley added]. But I am sure that I have been right in formulating general conclusions of this sort. Only so can one hope to have them investigated, and general conclusions about man's origin and destiny are of importance, especially in an age of doubt and transition like the present.[21]

In Julian Huxley's writings the transition from evolutionary biology to a new secular religion styled "evolutionary humanism" was carried to completion.

Not all of the champions of the modern synthesis have been as open as Huxley in acknowledging the religious aspect of their devotion to evolutionary biology, but most of them, especially those who reject religious and philosophical approaches to the problem of human duty and destiny, manage to smuggle in by way of simile and metaphor the elements of meaning and value that their formal philosophy of nature and natural science excludes from consideration. Thus, Ernst Mayr, although he insists that evolution by natural selection is a "purely statistical phenomenon", describes the phenomenon in language suggesting direction, purpose, striving, success, and failure. Reproductive isolation between species is described as "a method guaranteeing evolutionary success". Natural selection, Mayr tells us, improves adaptation continually until it appears "as perfect as if it were the product of design". It "remodels" proteins "in order to improve interactions". It produces "ever increasing improvements in mechanical efficiency" and gives direction to evolution. It "does its best" to favor the production of programs that "guarantee behavior that increases fitness", but it can "fail" when the "right genes" are not available for selection.[22]

In like manner the paleontologist George Simpson portrays "life substance" as exploiting its opportunities, solving problems, inventing novel and successful types of organization, "trying out" every conceivable possibility, "pulling through" various crises in its history, and ultimately transcending itself by producing an animal, man, capable of undergoing a totally new kind of evolution guided by "interthinking" rather than by interbreeding. And Edward 0. Wilson, conceding that evolutionary naturalism, or "scientific materialism" as he calls it, is a form of mythology, a way of giving meaning, value, and direction to human activity, invites his readers to join him in unmasking rival mythologies (such as Christianity and Marxism), in strengthening the hold of the "evolutionary epic", and in plotting the future course of human evolution scientifically.[23] Mary Midgley was right, then, in saying that the theory of evolution is "not just an inert piece of theoretical science" but also "a powerful folktale about human origins", a dramatic world picture capable of influencing human thought and action for good or ill.

One would like to feel optimistic about the scientistic mythology that has grown up around the theory of evolution, but it is hard to do so. The myth is intellectually dishonest, employing teleological and vitalistic figures of speech to describe processes that are advertised as "mechanistic" and pretending to derive from evolutionary biology values that stem from classical, Judaeo-Christian, and Enlightenment sources. It deifies science, denigrates philosophy and religion, and panders to Western culture's penchant for regarding science and technology as the guarantors of indefinite progress toward some hazy but glorious future paradise on earth. Worse yet, it fosters dreams of genetic manipulation and control designed to reshape imperfect human nature according to some scientistic ideal.

The difficulty, I think, lies not with evolutionary biology itself but with unsound ideas about science and its relations to nature and to the rest of human culture. As Mary Midgley has indicated, there is in Darwin's writings, cheek and jowl with his ambivalent ideas and feelings about competitive struggle in nature and society, a sense of wonder at the variety, beauty, and interconnectedness of living things, at nature's "endless forms most beautiful and most wonderful," and also a sense of reverence for life and of fellow-feeling and responsibility for all the inhabitants of our globe. Here, if anywhere, is the place to look for the religious and moral elements in the theory of evolution. Here, indeed, Sir Ronald Fisher found them in his lecture *Creative Aspects of Natural Law* (1950), delivered at Cambridge University as the fourth Eddington Memorial Lecture.

The creative causes of evolutionary change, said Sir Ronald, are to be found "in the actual life of living things; in their contacts and conflicts with their environments, with the outer world as it is to them; in their unconscious efforts to grow, or their more conscious efforts to move. Especially in the vital drama of the success or failure of each of their enterprises." Equally important, he added, is "the creative action of one species on another."

> The timid antelope has played its part in the creation of the lion, and species long extinct must have left indelible memorials in their effects on species still surviving. Who knows if the mammals would ever have evolved, but for the creative activity of the dinosaurs?[24]

As a Christian, Fisher drew an analogy between the theory of natural selection and the doctrine of salvation by works: "Both views emphasize responsibility for our actions, and for their natural consequences." Science, through its technological applications, has been largely responsible for mankind's growing impact on the global environment, Fisher acknowledged, but it has thereby made human beings increasingly sensitive to their responsibilities toward other living things.

> We have come to expect kindness in the treatment of the domestic animals. We have come to deplore the irreplaceable loss of some of the species which ignorance and greed have exterminated. The future of some wild animals has occasioned sufficient anxiety for the provision of Parks and Nature reserves to be the normal policy of civilized peoples.[25]

Science, it appears, does not dictate what moral and religious conclusions must be drawn from its effort to describe the interconnectedness of things in terms of general laws and processes. That interconnectedness and the human mind seeking to discover it are pre-scientific. The scientist is both a part of that interconnectedness and, at the same time, an observer and admirer of it. But if he is wise, he (or she, as the case may be) will feel reverence and a sense of obligation to the source of that interconnectedness, realizing that the scientific way of grasping it is but one of many ways and that the aim of human existence is neither pure intellection nor the command of nature for human purposes but the shared harmony of life with life and with the source of all life and being.

NOTES

1. Mary Midgley, *Evolution as a Religion* (London: Methuen, 1985), pp. 3-4.

2. Alexandre Koyré, *From the Closed World to the Infinite Universe* (Baltimore: Johns Hopkins University Press, 1957), p. 2.

3. R. J. Forbes and E. J. Dijksterhuis, *A History of Science and Technology* (Middlesex, England: Penguin Books, 1963), I, 192.

4. As quoted in Gerald Holton, "Johannes Kepler's Universe: Its Physics and Metaphysics," *American Journal of Physics* 24 (1956), p. 250.

5. Charles Darwin, *The Foundations of the Origin of Species; Two Essays Written in 1842 and 1844*, Francis Darwin, ed. (Cambridge: Cambridge University Press, 1909), pp. 85-86.

6. Charles Darwin, *On the Origin of Species. A Facsimile of the First Edition with an Introduction by Ernst Mayr* (New York: Atheneum, 1967), p. 84.

7. Ibid., p. 121.

8. Charles Darwin to Charles Lyell, Ilkley, Yorkshire, October 25, 1859, in *The Life and Letters of Charles Darwin, Including an Autobiographical Chapter*, Francis Darwin, ed. 3 vols. (New York, 1898), I, 531.

9. Darwin, *Origin of Species*, p. 489.

10. Ibid., p. 79.

11. Charles Darwin to Charles Lyell, Down, April 27, 1860, in Darwin, *More Letters of Charles Darwin*, Francis Darwin, ed. 2 vols. (London: John Murray, 1903), I, 298.

12. Charles Darwin, *The Origin of Species.... and The Descent of Man....* (New York: The Modern Library, n.d.), p. 920.

13. Thomas Henry Huxley, *Selections from the Essays of T. H. Huxley*, Alburey Castell, ed. (New York: Appleton-Century-Crofts, 1948), p. 17.

14. Charles Darwin to William Graham, July 3, 1881, *Life and Letters*, I, 316.

15. See Chap. 4 in the present volume: "From Evolutionary Biology to Evolutionary Humanism: Science and World View in Sir Julian Huxley's Writings."

16. Julian Huxley, *Evolution. The Modern Synthesis* (New York and London: Harper & Bros., 1942), p. 485.

17. Ibid.

18. Julian Huxley, *Evolution in Action* (New York: New American Library, 1953), pp. 47-48.

19. Ibid., p. 101.

20. Ibid., p. viii.

21. Ernst Mayr, *Evolution and the Diversity of Life, Selected Essays* (Cambridge, MA and London: The Belknap Press of Harvard University Press, 1976), *passim*.

22. For quotations from George Gaylord Simpson and Edward 0. Wilson, see John C. Greene, *Science, Ideology and World View. Essays in the History of Evolutionary Ideas* (Berkeley and Los Angeles: University of California Press, 1981), pp. 168-179, 184-189.

23. Ronald A. Fisher, *Creative Aspects of Natural Law* (Cambridge: Cambridge University Press, 1950), pp. 18-19.

24. Ibid., p. 23.

3

DARWIN, HUXLEY & BALFOUR
AND
THE VICTORIAN CRISIS OF FAITH

Much of the recent literature on the Victorian crisis of faith has been devoted to explaining the development and character of that crisis in terms of British (especially English) social structure, institutional arrangements, economic conditions, political controversies, and professional ambitions. These writings make little, if any, attempt to view the crisis in the context of Western intellectual and cultural history.[1] This is not to say that nothing is to be gained by studying the influence of peculiarly English circumstances on the thought and action of Spencer, Huxley, Balfour, Stephen, and other protagonists—far from it—but only that these analyses should be balanced by some effort to portray the wider crisis in Western civilization precipitated by nineteenth-century developments in science and scholarship and the estimates of the nature of that crisis formed by British writers of the period.[1] To this end the present essay will endeavor to show (1) that Darwin, Huxley, and other champions of the new naturalistic world view had crises of their own to cope with, (2) that Arthur James Balfour, writing as a philosopher and as a Christian, called attention to a deeper crisis in Western civilization than many of his contemporaries envisaged, and (3) that the crisis he described is still with us, still unresolved, and becoming more urgent every day. But first we must sketch the outlines of the crisis as it presented itself to our nineteenth-century forebears.

The scientific challenge to traditional beliefs about the inspiration of the Bible was certainly an important factor in the crisis, for the Bible had long been regarded by Christians as the key to human origins, duty, and destiny. Exegetes could and did disagree as to the proper interpretation of the Biblical revelation, but all agreed that Scripture, properly interpreted, contained answers to the profoundest questions men and women could ask about their place in the cosmic scheme of things. If the authority of the Bible as the inspired word of God were called into question, one of the major bulwarks of Western civilization would be undermined, and millions of people would be set adrift in a sea of uncertainty. Darwin's writings were but one part of the scientific threat to this bastion of Christian belief. It was the entire advancing front of human knowledge—astronomy, geology, biology, archaeology, ethnology, comparative religion, Biblical criticism, and many other fields of inquiry—that had to be dealt with intellectually if Christian faith were to survive the onward march of science. The uproar provoked by the publication of *Essays and Reviews* (1860), a collection of essays examining the Bible "like any other book", is sufficient proof of that.

Equally menacing to Western peoples' view of the human condition were the implications of the mechanistic cosmology associated with modern science ever since its rise in the seventeenth century. Even in the static form postulated by Sir Isaac Newton the idea of nature as a lawbound system of matter in motion had serious implications for traditional ideas about the relations of nature, man, and God. Applied rigorously, as it was by the deists, it precluded the possibility of miracles, traditionally regarded as empirical proofs of the divine origin of Christianity, and raised doubts about the efficacy of prayer. Pushed even farther, it impugned the reality of human freedom, raising the spectre of Julien Offray de La Mettrie's *L'homme machine*. In René Descartes' radical "evolutionary" version, the mechanical philosophy undermined the static argument from design by deriving the present structures of nature from previous states of the system of matter in motion by the operation of natural laws.

In astronomy, this kind of speculation led from Descartes' mechanical explanation of the origin of stars, planets, and earth to Immanuel Kant's cosmic evolutionism and the Kant-Laplace nebular hypothesis respecting the origin of the solar system from a rotating mass of gas. In geology, it produced the geological uniformitarianism of the Count de Buffon, James Hutton, and Charles Lyell with its consequent vast time scheme. In natural history, it generated the evolutionary theories of Erasmus Darwin, Jean Baptiste de Lamarck, Charles Darwin, and Alfred Russel Wallace. In philosophy, it eventuated in Herbert Spencer's conception of the cosmic process, including life and human history, as "an integration of matter and concomitant dissipation of motion; during which the matter passes from an indefinite, incoherent homogeneity to a definite coherent heterogeneity; and during which the retained motion undergoes a parallel transformation, all by means of the laws of nature." The historical connection between Descartes and Spencer was made explicit by Thomas Henry Huxley when he laid it down as "the fundamental proposition of Evolution" that "the whole world, living and not living, is the result of the mutual interaction, according to definite laws, of the forces possessed by the molecules of which the primitive nebulosity of the universe was composed" and observed that this view of things was held in all its essentials by René Descartes, the spirit of whose *Principles of Philosophy* had been revived, said Huxley, in "the profound and vigorous writings of Mr. Spencer".[2]

This mechanistic picture of the cosmic process, however cheerfully Spencer and Huxley might speak of it in the 1860s, contained an ominous threat to human aspirations and values, as Huxley himself came to realize. The progress of science, he declared, "has in all ages, meant, and now, more than ever, means, the extension of the province of what we call matter and causation, and the concomitant gradual banishment from all regions of human thought of what we call spirit and spontaneity....And as surely as every future grows out of past and present, so will the physiology of the future gradually extend the realm of matter and law until it is coextensive with knowledge, with feeling, and with action. The consciousness of this great truth weighs like a nightmare...upon many of the best minds or these days."[3] If reality was to be reduced to the law-bound motions of matter, what room would be left for human freedom and for human ideas of justice, beauty, and truth?

These doubts about man's freedom and significance in a universe governed by ironclad laws were exacerbated by a third and final element in the Victorian crisis of faith, namely, the growing tendency to regard science as man's only means of gaining knowledge of reality. If one had asked Saint Thomas Aquinas about the kinds and degrees of human knowledge, he would have pointed to the knowledge revealed by God Himself in the Bible as the most certain and noble kind of knowledge and to metaphysical knowledge derived from self-evident first principles as next in certainty and dignity. Last of all would be the kind of probable knowledge achieved by induction from experience. But with the rise of modern science this hierarchy of the kinds and degrees of knowledge was slowly inverted. By the end of the eighteenth century scientific knowledge had come to be regarded in many quarters as the most reliable kind of knowledge; metaphysics and theology were increasingly viewed as pseudo-sciences incapable of yielding useful knowledge. In the nineteenth century this point of view was given a name, *positivism*, by Auguste Comte. Positivistic attitudes developed hand in hand with the triumphs of the sciences of nature, giving rise to the efforts to construct a science of society and history associated with the names of Comte, Karl Marx, Herbert Spencer, and their imitators. The fusion of positivistic conceptions of the sources of knowledge with mechanistic determinism and faith in science as the primary engine of human progress is admirably illustrated in T. H. Huxley's delineation of "the picture which science draws of the world" in 1860:

> Harmonious order governing eternally continuous progress—the web and woof of matter and force interweaving by slow degrees, without a broken thread, that veil which lies between us and the Infinite—the universe which alone we know or can know; such is the picture which science draws of the world....[4]

Huxley's portrait of nature-history and man's means of acquiring knowledge of it was all too obviously in conflict with the entire Western tradition stemming from Greek and Roman as well as Hebrew and Christian culture. According to a dominant view in that tradition, the things that are seen are temporal, but the things that are unseen—Plato's Ideas, Aristotle's forms and his Prime Mover, the Judaeo-Christian God, Hegel's Absolute Idea, and all other transcendent entities are eternal. In the new positivistic world of Comte, Spencer, and Huxley, however, entities transcending sense experience were reduced to figments of the human imagination or consigned to the realm of Immanuel Kant's *noumena* or Herbert Spencer's Unknowable. Natural science, it was becoming clear, dealt with interconnections in the realm of phenomena, of sense experience. It had no place in its conceptual framework for entities or purposes transcending nature or for ethical and esthetic judgments purporting to evaluate what *is* in the light of what ought to be. The dilemma from a positivistic point of view was clear: *Either* mankind could have no knowledge whatever concerning values and the meaning of human existence, *or* science itself would have to derive meaning and value from the processes of nature-history. As things worked out, some champions of the positivistic outlook chose one horn of the dilemma, some chose the other. In either case the dilemma was real, the crisis severe.

The elements of the Victorian crisis of faith were, then: (1) the challenge to belief in the divine inspiration of the Bible implicit in scientific discoveries and theories and in the mechanical philosophy and the positivistic epistemology associated with the progress of science, (2) the challenge to static natural theology and to the cosmic status of man implicit in the same evolutionized mechanistic cosmology, and (3) the challenge to the philosophical and religious foundations of Western moral and spiritual values implicit in the positivistic reduction of reality to the realm of sense experience. Let us now examine some of the ways in which Christians and non-Christians of the Victorian age responded to this crisis.

We begin, not with the Christians, but with the champions of the new faith in science and the cosmology and epistemology associated with it. These writers, too, had their crises of faith, as one discovers if one looks beneath the facade of confident optimism with which they confronted the critics of evolution and the world view associated with late nineteenth century science. Their optimism was compounded of nineteenth century faith in the progress of science, technology, and society and of evolutionary deism and its residues.

When the champions of evolution, from the time of Erasmus Darwin and Lamarck to that of Charles Darwin, Alfred Russel Wallace, and Herbert Spencer, abandoned Christianity they adopted in its place an evolutionary form of deism based on the belief that the Creator had so arranged the laws of nature that they would produce beneficial results in both nature and history. Even Spencer, in his early writings, believed that the Creator had implanted in man "desires for improvement, and aspirations after perfection, ultimately tending to produce a higher moral and intellectual condition of the world" and consequently that progress in nature-history was "not an accident but a beneficent necessity."[5] Later on, Spencer's Creator-God faded into a remote Unknowable hidden behind the veil of sense experience, and Spencer was forced to concede that the universal progress toward heterogeneity must eventually reverse itself, but he could still assert in 1861 that the present evolution of the world must end in "the most complete happiness."

A similar optimism, derived from similar sources, pervades Darwin's *Origin of Species*, where he depicts the processes of variation and natural selection as a system of secondary causes ordained by the Creator for bringing about adaptation and improvement in nature.[6] Alfred Russel Wallace was of the same opinion. It was, he declared, "simply a question of how the Creator has worked....I believe....that the universe is so constituted as to be self-regulating; that as long as it contains Life, the forms under which that life is manifested have an inherent power of adjustment to each other and to surrounding nature; and that this adjustment necessarily leads to the greatest amount of variety and beauty and enjoyment, because it does depend on general laws, and not on a continual supervision and re-arrangement of details."[7]

Huxley's deism was greatly attenuated by the time he converted to the evolutionary hypothesis, but he could still assure the Reverend Charles Kingsley that the operations of nature were entirely fair and just, even when they brought about the death of Huxley's son. And he could assure the public that "natural knowledge, seeking to satisfy natural wants, has found the ideas which can alone still spiritual cravings," adding that "natural knowledge, in desiring to ascertain the laws of comfort, has been driven to discover those of conduct, and to lay the foundations of a new morality."[8]

But underneath this show of triumphant belief in science and natural processes there was a good deal of uncertainty, anxiety, and, in Darwin's case, real pain. As early as 1856 Darwin confided to Joseph Dalton Hooker his dismay at the "clumsy, wasteful, blundering, low, and horribly cruel works of nature." And in 1860 he confessed to Asa Gray that he could not see as plainly as he wished "evidence of design and beneficence on all sides of us."

> There seems to me too much misery in the world [he wrote to Gray]....On the other hand, I cannot anyhow be contented to view this wonderful universe, and especially the nature of man, and to conclude that everything is the result of brute force. I am inclined to look at everything as resulting from designed laws, with the details, whether good or bad, left to the working out of what we may call chance.[9]

By the 1870s Darwin's confidence that the laws of nature implied the existence of a cosmic Designer had evaporated, and with it his hope that human reason might solve the riddle of existence. If man's mind had evolved from the mind of lower animals, what reason was there to think that its speculations about the ultimate nature of reality were at all trustworthy? "A dog might as well speculate on the mind of Newton," he wrote despairingly.[10] Yet to the end Darwin clung to the hope that the processes of nature-history were ultimately progressive, that natural selection and the inherited effects of moral and intellectual training would produce breeds of men who would look back on the men of Darwin's own generation as "mere Barbarians".[11] But over this hope there hung the menace of the ultimate extinction of life on earth when the cooling of the sun should have rendered sentient life impossible. "To think of millions of years, with every continent swarming with good and enlightened men, all ending in this, and with probably no fresh start until this our planetary system has been again converted into red-hot gas. *Sic transit gloria mundi*, with a vengeance...," Darwin wrote.[12] That these reflections were no laughing matter to Darwin is shown by the passages in his letters late in life in which he complains that life has become a burden to him: "I have everything to make me happy and contented, but life has become very wearisome to me."[13]

Herbert Spencer seems to have undergone no major crisis of faith, but even he began to question the ultimate beneficence of the lawbound processes of nature-history when the resurgence of German military power and the international competition for empire in the late nineteenth century threatened to reverse the supposedly inevitable trend of history toward the peaceful and purely voluntary forms of social organization depicted by Spencer in his *Social Statics* (1850) as the eventual outcome of social evolution. The progressive integration of simple societies into compound and doubly compound ones by military struggle had gone "as far as seems either necessary or desirable" he warned. Henceforth social progress would result from "the quiet pressure of a spreading industrial civilization on a barbarism which slowly dwindles."[14] But Spencer's confidence that barbarism would dwindle was plainly shaken.

Spencer stood his ground, but by this time Alfred Russel Wallace had abandoned the Spencerian-Darwinian camp in favor of spiritualism and socialism. To what extent his desertion was the result of an honest belief that the existence of a world of spirits had been scientifically demonstrated, to what extent it sprang from his conviction that human nature was not explicable in terms of natural selection, to what extent it stemmed from some internal spiritual crisis remains an unanswered question. In any case, it shows how unstable was the compound of evolutionary deism, mechanical determinism, and positivistic epistemology and faith in science that had united the champions of evolutionary science in the 1860s.[15]

T. H. Huxley's response to the Victorian crisis of faith was more complex than that of Spencer or Darwin or Wallace, but there can be little doubt that his pugnacious defense of Darwin, agnosticism, and the claims of science and the naturalistic world view he drew from it concealed a substantial amount of moral and metaphysical anxiety on his own part. He could avoid the grim implications of the mechanical cosmology by resorting to Hume's skeptical refutation of causal necessity, he could dismiss the question of teleology in nature with a casual "Why trouble oneself about matters which are out of reach, when the working of the mechanism itself, which is of infinite practical importance, affords scope for all our energies?", but the stubborn question of the basis of social ethics, of the validity of human values in a universe consisting of the "web and woof of matter and force interweaving by slow degrees, without a broken thread, that veil which lies between us and the Infinite" would not go away. By the 1890s his earlier confidence that ethics was summed up in learning to live in harmony with "the laws that govern men and things", serving as Nature's mouthpiece and interpreter while she acted as man's "ever beneficent mother"—that confidence had vanished. Huxley still believed that traditional ethical values were confirmed by experience, but he now saw the source of these values, not in science, not in the cosmic process, but in the insights of moral geniuses like the Old Testament prophet Micah. The cosmic process, he declared in his Romanes Lecture (1893), was something to be combatted, not to be imitated. "That progressive modification of civilization which passes by the name of 'the evolution of society'," he declared, "is, in fact, a process of an essentially different character both from that which brings about the evolution of species in the state of nature, and from that which gives rise to the evolution of [domestic] varieties in the state of art." Nor did he like the idea, just beginning to be suggested, that science might be able to improve the human race through eugenic planning and control. "I do not see how such selection could be practiced without a serious weakening, it may be the destruction of the bonds which hold society together," he warned. "That which lies before the human race [he concluded] is a constant struggle to maintain and improve, in opposition to the State of Nature, the State of Art, and organized polity; in which, and by which, man may develop a worthy civilization, capable of maintaining and constantly improving itself; until the evolution of our globe shall have entered so far upon its downward course that the cosmic process resumes its sway; and, once more, the State of Nature prevails over the surface of our planet."[16]

* * * * * * * * * * * * *

Christian responses to the Victorian crisis of faith were, inevitably, of a different kind. For the most part they were of two sorts. Conservative Christians, whether Catholic or Protestant, rejected evolution and the cosmology and epistemology associated with late nineteenth century science totally. At the Vatican Council of 1870 the Roman Catholic church turned its face against modernism in all its forms. Individual Catholics like St. George Mivart and Father John Zahm of the University of Notre Dame tried to reconcile Catholicism and evolutionism, but their efforts were repudiated by the Church. Not until the 1940s and 1950s did the Catholic Church begin to accommodate its teaching to evolutionary theory and the higher criticism of the Bible.[17]

On the Protestant side, biblical literalists adopted the anti-evolutionary stance to which they still adhere, rejecting all scientific theories that postulated a history of the earth and the universe different from that described in the early chapters of Genesis. For the most part, however, the Protestant denominations made their peace with evolutionary science before the end of the century, usually by regarding evolutionary processes as God's way of bringing about progress in nature and history. "There is still as much as ever proof of intelligent purpose pervading all creation," wrote Bishop Frederick Temple in 1884, borrowing an argument from the evolutionary deists. "The difference is that the execution of that purpose belongs more to the original act of creation [of matter and its laws], less to acts of government since. There is more of divine foresight, there is less divine interposition; and whatever has been taken from the latter has been added to the former."[18] The biblical revelation, too, could be viewed in evolutionary terms as a progressive human discovery of moral and spiritual truth under divine tutelage and inspiration. And so it was viewed by many Christians.

Some writers, however, were not willing to let the champions of science dictate the conception of nature and natural science to which Christians must accommodate their beliefs. In particular, Arthur James Balfour—philosopher, statesman, and eventually Prime Minister of Great Britain—took upon himself the task of proving that the mechanistic, positivistic, naturalistic world view advanced by Spencer, Huxley, Tyndall, and others as the certified "picture which science draws of the world" had no claim to be so regarded. Born in 1848, Balfour had a strong religious upbringing in the Church of Scotland and Church of England through the influence of his mother, a devout evangelical. At Cambridge University he studied philosophy under Henry Sidgwick and took his degree in modern philosophy and political economy. Generally conversant with the science of his day, he became personally acquainted with some of its leading practitioners, including Lord Rayleigh, Lord Rutherford, J. J. Thomson, John Larmor, and Sir Oliver Lodge, and became a strong supporter of the science education movement in Great Britain.[19] Devoted to both science and religion, he became increasingly distressed at the growing discord between the two and increasingly critical of the positivistic interpretations imposed on science by some of its self-appointed champions, and also of the tendency of Christian apologists to accept these interpretations of science and its relation to reality as the indubitable findings of science, to which they must adjust their religious beliefs.

In the mid-1870s, about the time he took his first steps toward a political career, Balfour undertook a philosophical examination of science and the cosmology and epistemology commonly associated with it, a project he had been thinking about ever since his Cambridge days. His conclusions, first set forth in *A Defense of Philosophic Doubt* (1879), were later amplified in his *Foundations of Belief*, a book which attracted much attention when it was published in 1895.

In the *Defense* Balfour announced his intention to undertake "a speculative inquiry into the nature and validity of the current scientific creed." He began by examining the conception of science and its relation to the world of nature expounded by John Stuart Mill, Herbert Spencer, and other British empiricists. Using arguments drawn from Bishop George Berkeley and David Hume, especially the latter, he called into question the view of Mill and others that physical science is based on reliable inductions from observations of the external world. He began by pointing out that the observation of particulars cannot yield general principles or laws unless one makes certain assumptions, such as the uniformity of the laws of nature and the idea of causation. But, even granting the postulate of uniformity, Hume had shown that the observation of regular successions of events gave no warrant for supposing that future events would follow the same pattern. Moreover, even if one granted for the sake of argument the reliability of our knowledge of laws connecting phenomena, one could still draw no reliable conclusions concerning events that happened in the past.

> In order...that a man may have any rational confidence in the history of the Cosmos as revealed in the teachings of science [Balfour wrote], he must be something more than an Agnostic. He must have very solid grounds for believing, not only that through the infinite past only one series of phenomena can be assigned capable of having produced the actual universe, but that nothing besides phenomena capable of acting on phenomena has ever existed at all—and these solid grounds...must not be drawn from history [since the existence of historical events is only an inference from present experience]; but, if derived from experience at all, must be derived from his own immediate observations.[20]

Balfour then withdrew the concession he had made for the sake of argument and proceeded to argue the unreliability of the two major assumptions on which the science of his day proceeded: (1) the persistence of the material universe, and (2) the law of universal causation. With regard to the first assumption Balfour drew on Bishop Berkeley's arguments to show that perception gives us no knowledge of anything except our own ideas or sensations. With regard to the second, he invoked Hume's demonstration that, on empiricist assumptions, one had no basis for believing in causal laws, or, indeed, in causes at all. Finally, he attacked Immanuel Kant's argument that certain ideas, such as those of permanence and causation are necessary *a priori* ingredients of any experience. Thousands of people, said Balfour, experience change every day without conceiving it in relation to permanence and causation.

Balfour then went on to argue that the picture of the world supposedly drawn by science was not coherent or intelligible. The external world of primary qualities postulated by modern science and its empiricist interpreters—a world of colorless, tasteless, soundless vibrating atoms acted on by forces—could no more be perceived or imagined, said Balfour, than the deity represented to mankind by theology: "in the first case, as in the second, we must content ourselves with symbolical images, of which the thing we can most certainly say is that they are not only inadequate but incorrect." "There is not a single particle of matter which we can either perceive or picture to ourselves as it really exists."[21] Nor would it help matters to argue that this postulated external world must be accepted because it had been arrived at by inference from directly observed facts, for Balfour had already shown how limited were the inferences that could validly be drawn from present observations. Finally, one could not argue that the picture of nature assumed by science was validated by the fact that predictions made on the basis of that picture were consistent with present observations. In so doing one would fall into the fallacy called "affirming the consequent", overlooking the possibility that the same present observations might be consistent with other hypotheses.

Having examined the premises, the inferences, and the conclusions of the science of his day, Balfour concluded as follows: "The first [the premises] are unproved; the second [the inferences] are inconclusive; the third [the conclusions] are incoherent."[22] The great prestige of science, he declared, rested on its practical successes rather than its internal logical coherence. As for the various positivistic-agnostic-naturalistic philosophical systems and world views claiming the sanction of science, they rested on even more precarious foundations. They were not really based on science, and, even if they were, science had been shown to have no firm logical and philosophical basis.

What, then, of the relations between science and religion? The answer to this question followed clearly from Balfour's foregoing arguments. The reconciliation of science and religion was to be accomplished, not by setting up the logic, method, and findings of science as the test of religious truth, but rather by recognizing that both science and theology were systems of belief resting ultimately on faith and that both were forced to represent to the human imagination in anthropomorphic language an ultimate reality transcending the power of human reason to grasp fully.

In his second book, *Foundations of Belief*, Balfour returned to these issues, but with an even deeper concern about the implications of evolutionary naturalism for the future of Western civilization. By this time he had adopted the word *naturalism* to designate the view of reality assumed by agnostics, positivists, and empiricists. The common element in all such views of reality, wrote Balfour, was the reduction of experience to sense perception and the insistence that the only knowledge human beings could achieve was knowledge of phenomena and the laws by which phenomena are connected. After Darwin, moreover, these views were linked to a conception of human nature that represented human beings as purely and simply products of natural processes—animals with a better brain than those from which they had descended.

Such a conception of human nature, Balfour argued, must have disquieting implications for traditional Western ideas concerning reason, morality, and the sense of beauty. From the point of view of evolutionary naturalism reason was a mere instrument for survival, an accidental product of unthinking natural processes. The passion for truth was an emotion with no foundation in the nature of things. Art and esthetics were no longer grounded in a search for immanent beauty but were "mere by-products of the great machinery of organic life". Morality was reduced to natural appetites. "Self-condemnation, repentance, remorse, and the whole train of cognate emotions, are...thus deprived of all reasonable foundation, and reduced, if they are to survive at all, to the position of amiable but unintelligent weaknesses."[23]

The overall result, Balfour concluded, was an "inner discord" between a world view claiming the sanction of science and the deepest intuitions, emotions, and spiritual yearnings of Western men and women. T. H. Huxley might describe the liberally educated man as "one who...is full of life and fire, but whose passions are trained to come to heel by a vigorous will, the servant of a tender conscience; who has learned to love all beauty, whether of Nature or of art, to hate all vileness, and to respect others as himself,"[24] but where was there a place for these moral and esthetic intuitions in Huxley's "web and woof of matter and force interweaving by slow degrees, without a broken thread, that veil which lies between us and the Infinite—the universe which alone we know or can know"? The exalted values of the champions of evolutionary naturalism, Balfour perceived, were derived from conceptions of reality and man's place in it that were totally incompatible with the picture of the universe they professed to draw from science:

> Their spiritual life is parasitic; it is sheltered by convictions which belong, not to them, but to the society of which they form a part; it is nourished by processes in which they take no share. And when those convictions decay, and those processes come to an end, the alien life which they have maintained can scarce be expected to outlast them.[25]

If naturalism prevailed, Balfour predicted, "the feeling and opinions inconsistent with naturalism must be fore-doomed to suffer change; and how, when that change shall come about, it can do otherwise than eat all nobility out of our conception of conduct and all worth out of our conception of life, I am wholly unable to understand."[26]

For Balfour, then, the essence of the Victorian crisis of faith was the inner discord between the values and intuitions associated with traditional Western conceptions of nature, man, and God and the implications of an evolutionary naturalism claiming the sanction of science. This discord, he predicted, would be resolved in one of two ways. Either evolutionary naturalism would be abandoned in favor of a philosophical and religious view of reality that recognized the essential similarity of the scientific and the theological ways of picturing reality and the need to postulate a rational Author of Nature as the source of the order, beauty, and goodness in the world, or Western culture would descend to a level consistent with Huxley's depiction of nature as "a realm of matter and law...co-extensive with knowledge, with feeling, and with action."[27]

Balfour's *Foundations of Belief* did not suffer the general indifference which greeted his first book. Defenders of positivism, empiricism, rationalism, and agnosticism rushed to the defense of their positions: Frederic Harrison for Comtean positivism, Karl Pearson for rationalism and empiricism, and Thomas Henry Huxley, now approaching the end of his days, for agnosticism. Writing in the *Positivist Review* for May 1895, Harrison argued convincingly that Balfour's delineation of naturalism did not fit Comtean Positivism conceived as "the religion of humanity resting on the philosophy of human nature."[28] To this Balfour replied that what he had had in mind was not Comtean positivism but rather the "Positive Philosophy" described by John Stuart Mill: "We have no knowledge of anything but Phenomena; and our knowledge of Phenomena is relative, not absolute.... The laws of Phenomena are all we know respecting them. Their essential nature and their ultimate causes, whether efficient or final, are unknown and inscrutable to us."[29]

Karl Pearson's slashing attack on Balfour's book accused Balfour of identifying naturalism, science, and rationalism (despite Balfour's dissociation of science from any necessary connection with naturalism) and rejected completely Balfour's argument that science presupposes the independent existence of a material world.

> Science [Pearson maintained] is sometimes popularly supposed to deal with an outside world of phenomena—it can only deal with what is content of the human mind. Sense-impressions have left stored sense-impresses, and these by extension, association, and comparison have become concepts and ideas before the reason is applied and we reach anything that can be fairly called knowledge....Science only begins with the classification and comparison of concepts.[30]

Like Huxley, Pearson believed that human beings can know nothing of existences behind "the veil of sense-impressions". Theology might pretend to know something of such existences, but science confined itself to concepts based ultimately on sense impressions, the only source of real knowledge.[31] In the words of Ernest Nagel:

> Pearson subscribed to an essentially instrumentalist conception of the function of scientific theory; and he maintained that theories are simply convenient tools for predicting the course of events, and ultimately for achieving success in man's struggle for existence. On the other hand, Pearson's empiricism was controlled by the psychological assumptions he took over uncritically from the major tradition of British philosophy. He thus accepted the view that the ultimate data of knowledge are individual

sense impressions, occurring atomistically at the nerve endings of the brain.[32]

Thomas Henry Huxley's reply to Balfour was to have been published in two successive issues of *The Nineteenth Century*, but he died shortly after the first part appeared. As might be expected, Darwin's bulldog was in no mood to accept Balfour's definition of naturalism or his views concerning the crisis in Western civilization. In Huxley's view, naturalism was simply the sensible alternative to supernaturalism. Agnosticism, in turn, was nothing more than the Socratic attitude of learned ignorance. Natural science was a method of investigation and discovery not limited to the world given by sense perception, as Balfour thought, but embracing the whole range of mental activities as well.

> It is really better to leave these Natural Science people alone [he warned]; or the day may come when they will put forward a claim to History and Art, in both of which provinces Archaeology has already planted their flag; to Ethics, where Evolution has even now something to say; nay, perhaps (terrible to reflect), over Theology, where a close ally of Natural Science, the "Higher Criticism", is already ravaging the hinterland.[33]

As for the crisis in Western civilization, Huxley had his own quite different view of that development. For him the history of the West had been, and still was, a "struggle for mastery" between the scientific spirit (originating in Greek philosophy) and the opposing spirits of post-prophetic Judaism and of "that prophetic Judaism, already colored by Hellenism, which bore the name of Christianity." Today, Huxley declared:

> Judaism stands substantially where it did; while the simple Christian faith of the second century has been overlaid and transmuted by Hellenic speculation into the huge and complex dogmatic fabric of Ecclesiastical Christianity. Finally, the scientific spirit, freed from all its early wrappings, stands in independence of, and for the most part in antagonism to, its ancient rivals. Its cosmology, its anthropology, are incompatible with theirs; its ethics are independent of theirs.

> That...is in broad outline the state of affairs among us; and the future of our civilization as certainly depends on the result of the contest between

Science and Ecclesiasticism which is now afoot, as the present state of things is the outcome of the former strife.[34]

A starker contrast in assessments of the Victorian crisis of faith can scarcely be imagined. On the one hand Balfour viewed the crisis, not as the outcome of an irremediable conflict between science and religion, but as the result of a clash between a world view based on an incoherent and inadequate philosophy of science and a Christian apologetics grounded in the same philosophical misconceptions. What was needed, Balfour believed, was a complete rethinking of the foundations of belief in both science and theology. Only thus could the inner discord between the reigning "creed of science" and the ideas and values undergirding Western civilization be dissolved and the slow descent to a sensual and materialistic culture consistent with naturalism be avoided. For Huxley, on the other hand, the issue was not the philosophy of science but the threat posed by organized religion to the triumph of the scientific spirit in every domain of human thought and action. What was needed, and under way, was a New Reformation based on scientific attitudes and discoveries.[35]

One thing is clear. The issue between Balfour and Huxley has by no means been laid to rest. Balfour was right in believing (1) that much of the Western cultural tradition was based on the belief, partly Platonic and partly Pauline, that "the things which are seen are temporal, but the things which are unseen are eternal", (2) that this tradition had been gradually undermined by positivistic attitudes generated by the success of the sciences in explaining natural phenomena by means of observation, experiment, and theoretical models postulating entities and events that were in principle, if not always in fact, detectable by some mode of sense perception, (3) that the values held dear by Huxley and other advocates of naturalism were derived in considerable part from cultural traditions they no longer regarded as valid sources of knowledge, and (4) that the naive realism which regarded the models of theoretical science as valid pictures of an external reality would not go unchallenged by philosophers of science. On this last point the modern English philosopher Mary Midgley quotes with approval Ivan Tolstoy's dictum in *The Knowledge and the Power*:

We have had to change our ideas of what understanding consists in. As [Niels] Bohr said, 'When it comes to atoms, language can only be used as poetry. The poet, too, is not nearly so concerned with describing facts as with creating images.' The same is true of cosmological models, curved spaces and exploding universes. *Images and analogies are the key...we* must learn to ignore our preconceptions concerning space, time and matter, abandon the use of everyday language and resort to metaphor.[36]

Balfour would agree!

Balfour was less prescient, however, in envisaging the future course of the "inner discord" he perceived in Western culture. He lived to see Alfred North Whitehead construct a metaphysics designed to embrace both the scientific and the moral and esthetic ways of apprehending reality within a theistic framework, but he also witnessed the rise and spread of logical positivism and of the logical empiricism of Bertrand Russell and his followers. In our own day the philosopher of science Mary Hesse has adopted a position reminiscent of Balfour's. Writing in the *New York Times* for October 22, 1989, she argues:

We must reject the notion that theoretical science is that highly successful methodology that eventually discovers the essences and true causes of the world, and can therefore be expressed in consistent and unambiguous and exact language amenable to logic....Science is successful only because there are sufficient local and particular regularities between things in space-time domains where we can test them. These domains may be very large but...there is an infinite gap between the largest conceivable finite number and infinity.

Clearly the whole imperialist aim of theoretical science to be the royal and single road to knowledge has been a profound mistake...scientific theory is just one of the ways in which human beings have sought to make sense of their world by constructing schemes, models, metaphors and myths. Scientific theory is a particular kind of myth that answers to our practical needs with regard to nature. It often functions as myths do, as persuasive rhetoric for moral and political purposes.[37]

But, on the same page with Hesse's statement, the physicist Sheldon Glashow advances a contrary view under the title "Cosmic Catechism":

We believe that the world is knowable, that there are simple rules governing the behavior of matter and the evolution of the universe. We affirm that there are eternal, objective extrahistorical, socially neutral external and universal truths and that the assemblage of these truths is what we call physical science. Natural laws can be discovered that are universal, invariable, inviolate, genderless and verifiable....This statement I cannot prove, this statement I cannot justify. This is my faith.[38]

With respect to the moral and religious dimensions of Balfour's "inner discord", too, the passage of a century has settled nothing. The rethinking of doctrines of revelation and inspiration envisaged by Balfour has taken place, sometimes along the lines he himself suggested,[39] but the proliferating fundamentalist sects, far from adopting Balfour's stance with respect to the relations of science and religion, have rejected the findings of evolutionary science and cosmology root and branch and have claimed the sanction of science for an unyielding Biblical literalism. At the other end of the spectrum, Julian Huxley, George Gaylord Simpson, Edward O. Wilson and others have tried to derive traditional Western values from science itself.[40] Strange to say, concern for human rights is more widespread than ever, although bereft of its traditional Lockean-Jeffersonian basis in Judaeo-Christian creationism. The question whether Western civilization is to rise phoenix-like from its Graeco-Roman and Judaeo-Christian bed of ashes or whether, instead, it will move off in some new direction consistent with the total denial of transcendence, as in Aldous Huxley's *Brave New World*, remains unanswered.

NOTES

1. Compare, for example, the mode of analysis employed in the present essay with that used by L. S. Jacyna in "Science and the Social Order in the Thought of A. J. Balfour," *Isis* 71 (1980), pp. 11-34. See also John C. Greene, *Darwin and the Modern World View* (Baton Rouge, La.: Louisiana State University Press, 1963). In the same intellectual tradition as Greene are Bernard Lightman, *The Origins of Agnosticism. Victorian Unbelief and the Limits of Knowledge* (Baltimore and London: The Johns Hopkins University Press, 1987) and Frank Miller Turner, *Between Science and Religion: The Reaction to Scientific Naturalism in Late Victorian England* (New Haven: Yale University Press, 1974).

2. Thomas Henry Huxley, "Evolution in Biology", in *Darwiniana: Essays* (New York: D. Appleton, 1908), p. 206. First published in 1878.

3. Thomas Henry Huxley, "On the Physical Basis of Life," in Alburey Castell, ed., *Selections from the Essays of Thomas Henry Huxley* (New York: Appleton-Century-Crofts, 1948). First published in 1868.

4. Thomas Henry Huxley, "The Origin of Species," in *Darwiniana: Essays*, p. 58. First published in 1860.

5. See Spencer's article in *The Nonconformist*, II (1842), p. 700, and his "Progress: Its Law and Cause" in *Illustrations of Universal Progress; A Series of Discussions* (New York: D. Appleton, 1878), p. 58.

6. Charles Darwin, On the Origin of Species. A Facsimile of the First Edition with an Introduction by Ernst Mayr (New York: Atheneum, 1967), pp. 488-489.

7. Alfred Russel Wallace, "Creation By Law," in *Contributions to the Theory of Natural Selection* (London and New York: Macmillan, 1870), pp. 267-268.

8. Thomas Henry Huxley, "On the Advisableness of Improving Natural Knowledge," in Castell, ed., *Selections*, p. 9. First published in 1866.

9. Charles Darwin to Asa Gray, May 22, 1860, in Francis Darwin, ed., *The Life and Letters of Charles Darwin*, 3 vols. (London: John Murray, 1888), II, 311-312.

10. Charles Darwin to William Graham, Down, July 3, 1881, in ibid., I, 316.

11. Charles Darwin to Charles Lyell, Down, April 27, 1860, in Francis Darwin, ed., *More Letters of Charles Darwin*, 2 vols. (London: John Murray, 1903), II, 30.

12. Charles Darwin to Joseph Dalton Hooker, Down, February 9, 1865, in *More Letters*, I, 260-261.

13. Charles Darwin to Alfred Russel Wallace, Down, July 12, 1881, in James Marchant, ed., *Alfred Russel Wallace: Letters and Reminiscences* (New York and London: Harper & Brothers, 1916), p. 261.

14. Herbert Spencer, *The Principles of Sociology*, 3 vols. (New York, 1877), II, 663-664.

15. For a summary of the world view on which Spencer, Darwin, Huxley, and Wallace converged in the 1860s see John C. Greene, *Science, Ideology, and World View: Essays in the History of Evolutionary Ideas* (Berkeley, Los Angeles, London: University of California Press, 1981), pp. 128-157.

16. Thomas Henry Huxley, *Evolution and Ethics and Other Essays* (London: Macmillan, 1895), pp. 36-37, 44-45, 82-83. For a discussion of Huxley's change of views respecting Spencerianism, ethics, and evolution see M. S. Helfand, "T. H. Huxley's 'Evolution and Ethics': The Politics of Evolution and the Evolution of Politics," *Victorian Studies* 29 (1977), pp. 159-177. See also Greene, *Science, Ideology and World View*, pp. 141-143, 158-160.

17. For a discussion of Christian responses to Darwin's writings, especially in regard to natural theology and the doctrines of revelation and inspiration, see Greene, *Darwin and the Modern World View*, chaps. 1-2. See also James R. Moore, *The Post-Darwinian Controversies: A Study of the Protestant Struggle to Come to Terms with Darwin in Great Britain and America, 1870-1900* (Cambridge: Cambridge University Press, 1989).

18. Frederick Temple, *The Relations of Religion and Science* (London, 1884), pp. 122-123.

19. See Kenneth Young, *Arthur James Balfour. The Happy Life of the Politician, Prime Minister, Statesman and Philosopher, 1848-1930* (London: G. Bell and Sons, Ltd, 1963), especially chaps. 3, 8.

20. Arthur James Balfour, *A Defense of Philosophic Doubt, Being an Essay on the Foundations of Belief* (London: Hodder and Stoughton Ltd, 1926), p. 284. Original edition 1879.

21. Ibid., pp. 245, 250.

22. Ibid., p. 293.

23. Arthur James Balfour, *The Foundations of Belief, Being Notes Introductory to the Study of Theology*, 8th ed. (London, New York, Toronto: Longmans, Green and Co., 1933), p. 27. Original edition 1895.

24. Thomas Henry Huxley, "A Liberal Education," in Castell, ed., *Selections from the Essays of T. H. Huxley*, p. 18.

25. Balfour, *Foundations of Belief*, pp. 87-88.

26. Ibid., p. 87. For an excellent account of the Victorian agnostics Balfour was attacking, see Lightman, *Origins of Agnosticism* (Footnote 1).

27. Huxley, "On the Physical Basis of Life," in Castell, ed., *Selections*, p. 21.

28. Balfour, *Foundations of Belief*, p. 7. See also Frederic Harrison, The *Philosophy of Common Sense* (Freeport, N. Y.: Books for Libraries Press, 1968 (1907)), chap. 19, "Mr. A. Balfour's Foundations of Belief," pp. 314-324.

29. Balfour, *Foundations of Belief*, p. 7, citing John Stuart Mill, *Auguste Comte and Positivism* (London: N. Truebner, 1865), p. 79. Many of the British reviews carried commentary on Balfour's book. See, for example, William Wallace, "Mr. Balfour's 'Foundations of Belief'," *Fortnightly Review* 57 (April 1895), pp. 540-550; C. Lloyd Morgan, "Naturalism," *Monist* 6 (1895), pp. 76-90; Andrew Pringle-Pattison, "The Term 'Naturalism' in Recent Discussion," *The Philosophical Review* 5 (1896), pp. 576-584. See also Pringle-Pattison, *Man's Place in the Cosmos and Other Essays* (New York: Charles Scribner's Sons, 1897), pp. 226-308; John Passmore, *A Hundred Years of Philosophy* (London: Gerald Duckworth & Co. Ltd, 1957), p. 100; Young, *Arthur James Balfour*, chap. 8.

30. Karl Pearson, "Reaction! A Criticism of Mr. Balfour's Attack on Rationalism," in Pearson, *The Chances of Death and Other Studies in Evolution*, 2 vols. (London and New York: Edward Arnold, 1897), I, 184. (First published as a pamphlet in 1895.) Pearson mentions Ernst Mach, Gustav Robert Kirchoff, William R. Clifford, and T. H. Huxley as scientists who would reject Balfour's description of the scientist's implicit philosophy of science. For a mid-twentieth-century view of the philosophy of science somewhat similar to Pearson's but eventuating in a quite different conception of the relations between science and religion, see Herbert Dingle, "The Scientific Outlook in 1851 and in 1951," in W. Warren Wagar, ed., *European Intellectual History Since Darwin and Marx* (New York, Evanston, and London: Harper & Row, 1966), pp. 159-183. Dingle describes the mid-Victorian view of science as an inquiry into an independently existing, causally connected material world in language similar to Balfour's. He then rejects that view in favor of a philosophy of science similar to Pearson's, but he criticizes Pearson's bias in favor of sense impressions as compared to other forms of experience.

> From the modern point of view [Dingle writes], from which experience appears as the starting-point, the initial datum of our considerations, and not as a derivative of an imagined real material world, the experiences that have given rise to the physical and biological sciences are seen to be different from, but, for scientific purposes, co-equal with, those that have given rise to the faiths for which men have died. The correlation of the former, though by far the more advanced, has not yet come within sight of conceptions sufficiently generalized to be capable of embracing the latter (pp. 180-181).

31. Pearson, "Reaction!" p. 214.

32. Ernest Nagel, "Introduction," in Karl Pearson, *The Grammar of Science* (New York: Meridian Library, 1957), p. viii.

33. Thomas Henry Huxley, "Mr. Balfour's Attack on Agnosticism," *The Nineteenth Century* 37 (1895), p. 539. The second half of Huxley's reply to Balfour was published in Houston Peterson's *Huxley, Prophet of Science* (London, New York, Toronto: Longmans, Green and Co., 1932), pp. 315-327.

34. Ibid., p. 350.

35. For a stimulating and informative discussion of the idea of a "New Reformation" among anti-Establishment intellectuals in England in the second half of the nineteenth century, see James R. Moore, "Crisis Without Revolution: The Ideological Watershed in Victorian England," *Revue de Synthèse* 107 (janvier-juin, 1986), pp. 69-75. See also Lightman, *Origins of Agnosticism*, pp. 123-125.

36. As quoted in Mary Midgley, *Science as Salvation* (London and New York: Routledge, 1992), p. 213. The italics are Midgley's. The Tolstoy quotation is from Ivan Tolstoy, *The Knowledge and the Power: Reflexions on the History of Science* (Edinburgh: Canongate, 1990), pp. 15-16.

37. Mary Hesse, "Models, Metaphors, and Myths," *New York Times*, October 22, 1989, Section E, p. 24.

38. Sheldon Glashow, "We Believe That the World Is Knowable," *New York Times*, October 22, 1989, Section E, p. 24.

39. See Greene, Darwin and the Modern World View, chap. 1.

40. See the next two essays in the present volume; also Greene, *Science, Ideology, and World View*, chap. 7.

4

FROM EVOLUTIONARY BIOLOGY TO EVOLUTIONARY HUMANISM:

SCIENCE AND WORLD VIEW IN SIR JULIAN HUXLEY'S WRITINGS

When Arthur James Balfour predicted the shipwreck of Western values if evolutionary naturalism were to prevail, he overlooked the possibility that the advocates of that point of view might try to derive traditional Western values from evolutionary biology. But that is precisely what happened. Less than two decades after Balfour threw down the gauntlet to Thomas Henry Huxley in *Foundations of Belief* (1895) Huxley's grandson Julian began defining a world view based primarily on Darwinian biology with the deliberate aim of uniting mankind under the banner of evolutionary humanism and displacing forever the creeds and dogmas he believed had retarded the progress of civilization in past ages. No one was more convinced than he that human beings crave and need a picture of reality that makes them feel at home in the universe and gives them a purpose in life. Huxley himself felt this need deeply. Strongly idealistic, yet torn by conflicting impulses toward self-assertion and self-doubt, he yearned for inner peace and self-assurance. Grandson of the man known as "Darwin's bulldog", he felt a strong obligation to excel as a scientist and an even stronger calling to take the lead in what his grandfather had sometimes called the New Reformation, a movement of individual and social regeneration based on science instead of revelation. But whereas his grandfather had experienced great difficulty in reconciling the positivistic, mechanistic science of his day with his deeply felt moral and esthetic intuitions, young Huxley was determined to unite the physical, the mental, the moral, and the spiritual in one gospel of evolutionary progress grounded in Darwinian biology. Darwin, he told his fellow undergraduates at Cambridge University, was "the greatest scientist, and perhaps even the greatest man of the XIXth century." Science, which had had to fight for her life in earlier centuries, had now won an assured place in society. "What we want now," he continued, "is a linking of Science and Life in general."[1] To that endeavor Julian Huxley devoted his life.

Huxley's contributions to science were made along three lines: (1) the study of the courtship rituals of birds in relation to theories of sexual selection and animal behavior, (2) the experimental study of growth rates, dedifferentiation, and other aspects of ontogeny, and (3) synthesizing the leading results of investigations in genetics, systematics, and paleontology to create a neo-Darwinian picture of evolution based squarely on the theory of natural selection. This last project, culminating in his book entitled *Evolution. The Modern Synthesis*, Huxley considered his most important contribution because it laid the foundation for a world view which would guide and inspire mankind in its onward march of progress. To his writings on evolution we must look, therefore, if we would throw light on the interaction of science and world view in his career as a scientist.

We begin with the concept of nature set forth in his books and articles. Huxley was deeply dissatisfied with the picture of the universe and man's place in it derived from the physical science of his time. Physics and chemistry yielded a "materialistic and somewhat gloomy Weltanschauung," he declared. They presented "a world of matter hostile or at least neutral to our humanity," a universe gradually running down.[2] Evolutionary biology, on the other hand, described a world of life moving slowly and erratically, but steadily in the long run, toward results that seemed admirable from a human point of view: toward increasing intensity of mental power, of emotion, of consciousness and will. Again, evolutionary biology vindicated the idea of progress, an idea that had suffered greatly, and in Huxley's view unjustly, in the disillusionment following World War I. Moreover, it showed that mind, which appeared to be a mere epiphenomenon in the physicist's world, was an important aspect of reality, playing an efficacious role in the struggle for existence and becoming more and more dominant over the inorganic world in the course of evolution. If man was a part of nature, mind was a part of nature, and the principles of uniformity and unity in the cosmos required that the mental aspect of things be carried down the scale of nature to the lowest organisms and beyond them to the realm of inanimate matter. The best working hypothesis, said Huxley, was "to assume that physicochemical properties and properties of the same nature as those that we call mental are both inherent in what, at present, we can only call the common stuff of the universe.

> The assumption is...that organic has arisen from inorganic. Organic consists of world-stuff [and] has two sets of properties—physico-chemical (or objective) and mental (or subjective).[3]

Given these assumptions, Huxley continued, it might be possible to construct a graph displaying the course of evolutionary progress in both its objective and subjective aspects, the X axis representing the passage of time and the Y axis biological progress. He even sketched a graph designed to compare the curves of progress of the physico-chemical and the mental properties of life, the "critical point" Q marking the stage in the history of life when, with the emergence of man, mental organization became biologically more important than bodily organization. "A direction towards mind is visible," wrote Huxley. "More and more of matter is embodied in living organisms, more and more becomes subservient to life."[4]

Huxley's strategy in this line of argument was clear. Faith in human progress was to be given an "external justification" in biological progress, which, in turn, was to be defined in terms of qualities valued by human beings, namely, increasing intensity of mental, emotional, and volitional power yielding ever greater control and independence of the environment. Biology would bolster faith in the possibility and actuality of human progress, and human value judgments would provide the criteria of biological progress. The course of evolution could then be depicted by analogy to human progress as the record of life's experiments, successes and failures, victories and defeats in the struggle to achieve ever higher levels of awareness and control. Finally, biology, which had been the Cinderella of the sciences before Darwin, would assume its rightful place as the queen of the sciences, with psychology, the science of mind, at her right hand.

But there were difficulties in this strategy. To represent life as struggling to attain ever greater dominance of mind over matter was to use vitalistic, teleological language proscribed by the conceptions of nature and science to which Huxley gave allegiance. Science, he believed, was "simply a scrutiny and a putting together of scrutinized facts."[5] It could say nothing about values or purposes. Likewise nature, apart from human beings, was devoid of purpose. How, then, could Huxley's central doctrine of biological progress be defended scientifically? How was the charge of vitalism and teleology to be refuted?

Huxley's strategy in countering these objections was complex. He began by asserting that biological progress was a scientific fact. It was a fact, he argued, that in the course of evolution certain qualities of organisms, both physical and mental, had increased—for example, size of the units and their aggregations, duration of life, complexity involving division of labor, self-regulation yielding greater independence of environmental changes, memory in various forms, and, finally, intensity of faculties of knowing, feeling, and willing. Not all evolutionary change had been in these directions, he admitted, but "the *upper* level of these properties...has been continually raised, their average has continually increased...and this tendency...is what we sum up and generalize...as the law of biological progress."[6]

In these passages Huxley oscillated between properties of organisms, such as size, which were capable of biological definition and properties, such as intensity of willing, feeling, and knowing, which were difficult to define biologically but which were valued for their own sake by human beings. On the whole, however, he picked out those developments in the history of life that seemed valuable from a human point of view and made them the main trend. From this point of view the evolution of plants was uninteresting, a dead end. The *important* movement of evolution, Huxley insisted, was "movement towards a realization of the things judged by the human mind to have value," towards "increase of power, of knowledge, of purpose, of emotion, of harmony, of independence," towards "the embracing of ever larger syntheses by the organism possessing them."[7]

But why should these trends be considered important and valuable? Huxley was face to face with the question of the role of values in science. Ever since the seventeenth century science had excluded value judgments from its domain, or at least had tried to do so. But evolutionary biology had reintroduced the idea of levels of being into science, although not without considerable ambivalence and uneasiness arising from the difficulty of defining terms like "higher" and "lower" scientifically. Advocates of the theory of natural selection vacillated between regarding the organisms that survived and reproduced as "fit" only in the sense that they happened to have characteristics suited to local circumstances and viewing them as somehow better than, improved upon, their less successful rivals. The latter point of view seemed natural to them as human beings, but they had difficulty reconciling it with the traditional conception of science as excluding value judgments. The evolutionary process, Huxley wrote, hinged on survival and the production of offspring, "but even these ends" were only apparent ends or purposes—"the machinery is in reality blind".[8] One might distinguish, as Huxley did, between "biological values" and "spiritual values", but in Huxley's universe all values were human values. Science could discern a direction in organic evolution, but the judgment that this trend constituted "progress" lay outside of science unless the idea of science was radically revised.

As we have seen, Huxley was not prepared to undertake any such revision. Science was for him "simply a scrutiny and a putting together of scrutinized facts". How, then, was the scientist to evaluate the trend Huxley thought he had discerned in organic evolution? Huxley's solution to this problem had all the characteristics of a *tour de force*. In *The Science of Life*, a book written in collaboration with H. G. and G. P. Wells, Huxley and his co-authors wrote:

If one wants to analyze purely objectively it is best to leave values out. On
the other hand, if we want something fuller and more warming than
detached analysis, if we want to build from the multitudinous facts a vision
of Evolution as an imposing whole, there is nothing to stop our putting
them in.[9]

Huxley and the Wellses were definitely after something "fuller
and more warming" than science could provide. In their opinion, "to
shirk questions of feeling and will because they did not admit of the
hard precision of a purely objective treatment would be to rob our
Science of Life of half its interest and two-thirds of its practical
value."[10]

But if values and purposes could not be derived from science,
where did they come from? On this question the authors of *The
Science of Life* were ambivalent. On the one hand, they accepted
many of the traditional values of Western civilization—e.g.
"trustworthiness, frankness, fairness, willing helpfulness, charity,
devotion to the common weal". On the other hand, they plainly
believed it important to give these traditional values a solid
grounding in a picture of the universe derived from modern science.
Biology, in particular, must "ratify" the "higher and more intuitive
developments of religious thought".[11] It must not only ratify them; it
must provide the inspiration necessary to make them effective in
human conduct.

For this latter purpose vitalistic figures of speech involving the
personification of life were indispensable. Huxley's works, both
popular and scientific, were replete with figures of this kind, lending
considerable credence to Lord Zuckerman's and Francis Huxley's
characterization of him as a vitalist.[12] To rebut the suspicion of
vitalism Huxley relied on two lines of argument. First, he pointed
out that he attributed no special properties to living matter. "Living
matter is but a special arrangement of ordinary matter." Second, he
stressed that his "mechanism" of evolutionary change, natural
selection, was non-vitalistic. Natural selection was not a mysterious
inner drive but a force, "a constant biological pressure (to use a term
which, though still symbolic, a mere analogy, is less misleading and
question-begging than *élan vital*) tending to push some of life on to

new levels of attainment, new steps in progress, because any variations in that direction will have selection value, a selection value above the ordinary."[13]

Thus, even in attempting to refute the charge of vitalism Huxley could not refrain from using language implying purpose. For him, natural selection was not simply a matter of differential survival and reproduction; it was a "method" of bringing about progress by realizing life's potentialities. "Progressive" characteristics were selected, not because they were progressive from a human point of view, but because they were of competitive advantage to the organisms concerned. They could only be *known* to be progressive after the fact, when judged to have carried life forward in the direction of producing human beings.

Given this anthropocentric definition of the situation, it made sense to compare the progress produced by competition among biological organisms with technological progress in human affairs. "There," wrote Huxley, "although the ways in which variations arise, and the way they are transmitted, are different from those of organic evolution, yet the type of 'pressure', the perpetual struggle, and the advantage of certain kinds of variation therein—these are in essence really similar."[14] This way of looking at things, in turn, made human progress a continuation of biological progress, but one involving different "methods" of advance. The "method" of natural selection had "achieved" admirable results, Huxley observed, but at a terrible cost. It was time for human beings to take command of the process and guide it more efficiently in a direction it did not know it was going but which, from a human point of view, seemed the right way to go.

Thus, human beings were at one and the same time the crowning achievement of the process of natural selection and the tribunal before which those processes were judged to be clumsy, cruel, and obsolete. Regarded scientifically, man was but the latest product of the blind evolution of living matter, which, in turn, was but a "local eddy" in the larger but equally blind cosmic evolution.[15] And yet, as a valuing, self-conscious thinker and moralist, man was ready to declare himself, his reason, and his values the highest "achievement" of life on earth and to assert his right and duty to control the future course of evolution, both human and non-human, as "trustee" for the blind processes that had produced him.

Thus Huxley moved back and forth between opposite views of science, nature and man. On the one hand, science was objective analysis, a scrutiny and putting together of scrutinized facts without value judgments; on the other, it yielded a world view ratifying the traditional values of Western civilization and generating a scientific attitude and a scientific style of behavior.[16] On the other hand, nature was a complex of blind, unconscious processes exhibiting no trace of purpose or value orientation; on the other, organic evolution was a directional process achieving, however unintentionally, a gradual increase in mental capacity culminating in human thought, feeling and willing, "the highest expression yet attained". On the one hand, man was "an inhabitant of a thin rind on a negligible detached blob of matter belonging to one among millions of stars in one among millions of island-universes," dwarfed into spatial and temporal insignificance by the processes of nature; on the other, he was the crowning achievement of life's upward thrust toward rationality, the trustee of evolutionary progress sitting in judgment on the processes of nature and bearing on his shoulders the awful responsibility for controlling his own and cosmic destiny.[17]

The connecting link between biology and the highest human values, Huxley believed, would be the nascent science of psychology, especially the psychology of the unconscious, which revealed how the sexual instinct could be sublimated to produce great science, great art, and religious ecstasy. Evolutionary biology and the new psychology, Huxley asserted, would yield "a religious system basing itself on scientific method." Inorganic nature might be hostile or indifferent to human values, but organic evolution disclosed a trend in the same direction as human desires and ideals and thereby gave an "external sanction" for man's hopes. Human mental activity, in turn, had changed the course of evolution by the substitution of new methods of making progress for old, by introducing values ultimate for the human species, and by generating an interplay of conscious and unconscious thought and feeling yielding "ideas apparently infinite, emotions the most disinterested and overwhelming." Here, said Huxley, was a view of the universe and man's place in it which could "support the distressed and questioning minds and be incorporated into the common theology of the future."[18]

Here, too, it may be remarked, was a world view, which could blend the disparate elements of Huxley's own psyche into a satisfying whole. It was evolutionary and Darwinian in the tradition his grandfather had defended. It was scientific without being mechanistic and deterministic in the manner of the physical sciences. It employed the language of Bergson's vitalism without conceding an unbridgeable gap between the organic and the inorganic or casting doubt on the omnicompetence of discursive reasoning. It utilized Freudian psychology without accepting Freud's gloomy assessment of human nature and prospects. It exalted spiritual values and the dignity of man without separating man from nature. It vindicated the idea of progress and the political stance of liberals committed to intelligent planning as the key to social progress. It cleared the path to a brighter future for mankind by discrediting the supernatural sanctions claimed by defenders of existing institutions and behavior patterns. Through Darwin, science had liberated the human mind, life's last, best creation, for new and more glorious conquests in the progressive triumph of mind over matter. And Julian Huxley—scientist, moralist, philosopher, poet, and lover of nature—would be the prophet of the new religion, evolutionary humanism.

* * * * * * * * * *

So much for Huxley's general ideas about nature, man, science, and society. In what ways did these ideas shape or influence his work as a scientist? In particular, how did they affect his effort to integrate researches in the various fields of biology in order to achieve an evolutionary synthesis based on Darwinian principles? In the first place, these ideas provided the impetus towards a synthesis. For Huxley, particular researches in biology were incidental to the larger purpose of constructing and disseminating a world view that would inspire and sustain the progress of civilization. During his years of teaching and research at Oxford University (1919-1927) he preached and practiced what he called "philosophical biology," much to the dismay of some of his scientific colleagues who thought that scientists should stick to science and leave philosophical and religious questions to philosophers and theologians. In 1927 Huxley resigned his chair in zoology to collaborate with H. G. Wells and his son on a book for the general public intended not simply to inform readers about the latest developments in biology but also to propagate a world view conducive to human progress. And when, in 1936, Huxley outlined his evolutionary synthesis before the Zoological Section of the British Association for the Advancement of Science, he entitled his address "Natural Selection and Evolutionary Progress" and in his concluding remarks congratulated his fellow zoologists for having together made "a fundamental contribution" to human thought, namely, "the demonstration of the existence of a general trend which can legitimately be called progress, and the definition of its limitations."[19] In Huxley's view, the idea of biological progress was not an afterthought, an extraneous addition to biological science, but the heart and soul of evolutionary biology.

The centrality of the idea of progress in Huxley's evolutionary synthesis is apparent not only in his 1936 address but in the elaborate version of that address published in 1942 under the title *Evolution. The Modern Synthesis*. Ostensibly only the last two chapters of this book were devoted to the discussion of progress in evolution, the first eight chapters being concerned with evolutionary change at or below the species level. But Huxley's overriding concern with evolutionary progress was evident throughout the work. Although he discussed at length the various processes involved in the production of what he called "minor systematic diversity," he clearly considered these developments of lesser importance as having no bearing on the main course of evolution; they were, he said, "a mere frill of variety superimposed upon its broad pattern." The biologist, he declared, must study evolution in all its varied forms, but his main concern must be to discover the overall pattern of development in macroevolution and to indicate its significance for the future progress of mankind.[20]

Having made the concept of progress central to his synthesis, Huxley faced the problem of defining it in a manner acceptable to his fellow zoologists and of relating it to the theory of natural selection. Was evolutionary progress simply a fact demonstrated by the fossil record independently of theories of organic change, or was it a necessary implication of the theory of natural selection, or both? Huxley vacillated somewhat on this question, but in general his answer was "both". In *Evolution. The Modern Synthesis* he relied mainly on the fossil record, arguing that paleontology disclosed a succession of dominant forms, the later forms displaying increased biological efficiency as measured by the degree of control over and independence of the environment they exhibited. In other works, however, he echoed Darwin's argument that the theory of natural selection implied long-run improvement in the organic world, since the organisms successful in the struggle for existence would necessarily be improvements on less successful forms and would have to undergo still further improvement if they were to survive in the ongoing competition with still other forms. Huxley adopted Darwin's term "improvement" alongside his own term "progress" and eventually tried to distinguish various kinds and degrees of improvement, designating them by such terms as "improvement," "advance," and "progress" according to their presumed degree of importance. Thus, biological specialization was an improvement giving competitive advantage in the short run, but it might lead to extinction in the long run by foreclosing other lines of development needed for survival in new circumstances. Hence specialization was "one-sided progress," making no necessary contribution to "all-around progress". "All-around progress" yielded increasing control over and independence of the environment through increases in "size, and power", mechanical efficiency, increased capacity for self-regulation and more efficient avenues of knowledge and of methods for dealing with knowledge.[21] By these criteria the evolutionary development of wings was a mere specialization, enabling certain organisms to inhabit the air but foreclosing other developments such as placental reproduction that were essential to the emergence of intelligent, self-conscious, purposive organisms. Birds, said Huxley, were "ruled out" in those developments because they had deprived themselves of "possible hands" in favor of "actual wings". Conceptual thought could arise only in a monogamous mammal of terrestrial habit, but arboreal for most of its mammalian ancestry."[22] Viewed thus, evolution was a series of "blind alleys" except for the lineage leading to man. In Huxley's biology, man was the measure of all things, including biological progress. Plant evolution, although worthy of study by biologists, had no intrinsic importance when judged in terms of Huxley's man-centered criteria of progress. Plants had evolved in tandem with animals, but plant evolution had failed to produce organisms possessing efficient avenues of knowledge and of methods for dealing with knowledge.

The influence of Huxley's world view on his evolutionary theorizing is equally apparent in his ambivalent attitude toward natural selection. On the one hand, the theory of natural selection was essential to him as the mainstay of the Darwinian legacy he believed he had inherited from his grandfather and as a polemical weapon in the battle against theistic, vitalistic, and teleological interpretations of evolution. Huxley was well acquainted with developments in genetics, including the work of Ronald Fisher and J. B. S. Haldane in population genetics, and he made good use of this knowledge in constructing a picture of evolutionary change as a product of "a series of small multiple allelo-morphic changes in the genic background."[23] The argument from probability, which had been used by Bergson and others against the theory of natural selection, Huxley used in its favor in explaining the origin of adaptive structures by a series of modifications:

> ...when two or more steps are necessary, it becomes inconceivable that they shall have originated simultaneously. The first mutation must have been spread through the population by selection before the second could be combined with it, the combination of the first two in turn selected before the third could be added, and so on....The improbability is therefore enormous that they can have arisen without the operation of some agency, which can gradually accumulate and combine a number of contributory changes; and natural selection is the only such agency that we know.[24]

But although Huxley argued effectively for the efficacy of natural selection, at least in cases involving successive small changes, he was plainly unhappy with natural selection as an agency for producing biological progress.

All that natural selection can ensure is survival [he wrote]. It does not ensure progress, or maximum advantage, or any other ideal state of affairs. A type may survive by deceiving its enemies...just as well as by some improvement in digestion or reproduction, by degenerate and destructive parasitism as much as by increased intelligence.[25]

Intra-specific competition, which Darwin had regarded as the main source of evolutionary change and improvement, seemed to Huxley of dubious value from the standpoint of evolutionary progress. He conceded that intraspecific competition was more common than interspecific competition among abundant species, but he was inclined to agree with Haldane that it was, on the whole, "a biological evil".

The effects of competition between adults of the same species....[quoting Haldane] 'render the species as a whole less successful in coping with its environment. No doubt weaklings are weeded out, but so they would be in competition with the environment. And the special adaptations favored by intra-specific competitions divert a certain amount of energy from other functions.'[26]

For Huxley, as for Haldane, this argument was especially important in refuting the claims of those who invoked Darwin's theory of natural selection to justify unrestrained competition in the economic and political worlds. It refuted, said Huxley, "the notion, so assiduously rationalized by militarists and *laissez-faire* economists, that all man needs to do to achieve further progressive evolution is to adopt the most thoroughgoing competition." Natural selection, Huxley insisted, was "blind and mechanical," "efficient in its way—at the price of extreme slowness and extreme cruelty."

Both specialized and progressive improvement are mere by-products of its action, and are the exceptions rather than the rule. For the statesman or the eugenist to copy its methods is both foolish and wicked. Not only is natural selection not the instrument of God's sublime purpose: it is not even the best mechanism for achieving progress.[27]

As this passage suggests, Huxley's ultimate concern was with human progress. Biological progress was important only insofar as it validated faith in the progress of mankind. The theory of natural selection, however useful it might be in undermining theism, vitalism, teleology, and the social and political institutions claiming their sanction, was a two-edged sword, capable of doing much damage if applied directly to human affairs. It must be safely sheathed as a once potent, but now outmoded, method of achieving progress. The struggle for existence must give way to the struggle for fulfillment. Intelligent eugenic planning must supersede the cruel and haphazard method of natural selection.

In the decades following the publication of his *Evolution. The Modern Synthesis* Huxley, although no longer a practicing scientist, continued to read widely in the literature of evolutionary biology and to champion the idea of biological progress both in his popular writings and in his contributions to scientific journals and symposia. Against geneticists like Theodosius Dobzhansky who defined "Darwinian fitness" solely in terms of the contribution made by organisms to the gene pool of succeeding generations without any reference to improvement or progress Huxley argued that natural selection resulted in "a higher total and especially a higher upper level of evolutionary fitness, involving greater functional efficiency, higher degree of organization, more effective adaptation, better self-regulating capacity, and finally more mind." When Dobzhansky replied that, although natural selection sometimes produced those results, a definition of fitness in those terms was hopelessly vague and mathematically unmanageable, Huxley responded by proposing a distinction between reproductive selection and survival selection, the former typified by sexual selection and other forms of intra-specific competition, the latter involving "increased potentiality of long-term survival and multiplication of a strain, species, or type."

> In many cases [Huxley explained]...the two processes go hand in hand....
> Yet in general they are distinct; reproductive selection may readily favour short-term ends, which, in the long run, are injurious for the continued evolutionary improvement of the species or type, notably in difficult conditions. This is precisely what it is doing now in industrially advanced nations.[28]

In Huxley's view, "fitness" must involve some substantive excellence in what survives. To measure fitness simply in terms of the number of surviving offspring in succeeding generations was to rob the theory of natural selection of all inspirational value by overlooking the valuable results natural selection had produced in the long run. It would also make nonsense of eugenics, which derived much of its impetus from the conviction that the less fit members of industrial societies were proliferating more rapidly than the truly fit members.

Huxley also championed the idea of improvement, or progress, in relation to the classification of animals. In 1957, in a contribution to the journal *Nature*, he made what his biographer called "the startling suggestion" that the traditional classification of animals in terms of morphological differences should be complemented by a quite different classification based on the degrees of improvement which they exhibited. This suggestion was elaborated in Huxley's paper at the Stockholm symposium on taxonomy in 1958. In this paper Huxley rejected the earlier (1934) dictum of Save Soderbergh that biological classification should be purely phyletic, aimed at delimiting natural phyletic groups, arguing that a purely phyletic system would not take account of the trends these groups exhibited or provide a terminology for the stages through which they passed in geological time.

> ...it [the purely phyletic system] classifies the products of cladogenesis but neglects those of anagenesis [Huxley wrote]. To take proper account of both processes, we need a two-way grid system, with two sets of terms cutting across each other, one for anagenetic advance, the other for cladogenetic divergence of monophyletic units.[29]

"Anagenesis" was a term Huxley had adopted to give a scientific cast to his favorite idea, the idea of improvement, or progress. Animals were to be classified not only in *clades*, i.e. in terms of morphological divergence, but also in *grades*, according to the degree of biological improvement they exhibited. Improvement, said Huxley, "covers detailed adaptation to a restricted niche, specialization for a particular way of life, increased efficiency of a given structure or function, greater differentiation of functions, improvement of structural and physiological plan, and higher general organization. At all levels it is the direct consequence of natural selection." Biological improvement, Huxley added in language reminiscent of Darwin's *Origin*, involves the substitution of new types for old, "a new and more improved type (of any degree of magnitude) partly or wholly *replacing* an older and less improved type."

> The rise and success of a new type is evidence that it has attained a higher degree of improvement than its predecessor. This not a circular argument [Huxley added], but a simple deduction from neo-Darwinian principles.[30]

Unfortunately Huxley did not explain how neo-Darwinian principles exonerated his argument from the charge of circularity. Survival and proliferation could not be the criterion of improvement unless he was prepared to regard newly evolved parasitic forms as improvements on their ancestors and rivals. The whole point of his criticism of Dobzhansky's criterion of fitness was that survival in increasing numbers was not a sufficient criterion of fitness. How, then, could it be proof of improvement? Huxley had been on safer ground when, in his earlier writings, he had acknowledged that biological progress was defined in terms of human value judgments incapable of validation by science.

As an example of his proposed double-barreled system of classification, Huxley instanced the classification of man. In terms of customary phylogenetic classifications, he noted, the hominids were "merely one phyletic clade (the family Hominidae) of the higher tailless Primates or Anthropoids." Viewed anagenetically, however, they deserved to be classified as a distinct grade-group, the Psychozoan, described by Huxley as "a radically new and highly successful dominant group, evolving rapidly by the new method of cultural transformation." The Hominidae were so successful and unique, said Huxley, that they should be considered "equivalent in magnitude to all the rest of the animal Kingdom." They constituted, he declared, "an entirely new Sector of the evolutionary process, the psycho-social."[31]

For a view of Huxley's outlook on evolutionary biology in relation to world view in the mid-1950s we turn to his introductory chapter to a volume of essays in his honor published in 1954 and titled *Evolution as a Process*. In this essay Huxley abandoned his earlier emphasis on the multiformity of evolution and chose instead to depict it as a unitary process—unitary because it was the result of "a single basic mechanism," natural selection, and because it displayed the same kinds of long-term trends in all evolving groups. Whereas in 1942 he had assigned an important, but not exclusive, role to natural selection he now declared: "Evolutionary change is almost always gradual and is almost wholly effected through selection." Genetics, which had played a leading role in Huxley's 1942 synthesis, was now declared to have nothing new to say about evolution: "...genetics has given its basic answer and evolutionary biologists are free to pursue other problems."[32]

Among the other problems Huxley considered important were the concepts of improvement and progress. Improvement, he explained, included "any increase in the efficiency of living organisms, regarded as machines for carrying on the business of living and reproducing themselves in the environment provided by this planet." So defined, biological improvement was analogous to technological improvement in the human realm. In the "dialectic of evolution," selective pressures making for improvement were the thesis, the shortcomings or limitations of natural selection in producing improvement were the antithesis, and evolutionary progress was the higher synthesis resulting from the dialectic. What, then, was evolutionary progress? It was, said, Huxley, "biological improvements which permit or facilitate further improvements." Most biological improvements eventually reached a condition of maximum efficiency beyond which no further improvement could be made. Only one line of improvement, namely that leading to conceptual thought, was susceptible of indefinite improvement. With the emergence of man, life had evolved a new method of making progress to which no limit could be assigned. In man, said Huxley, the evolutionary process "has for the first time become aware of itself, is studying the laws of its own unfolding, and has a dawning realization of the possibilities of its future guidance or control. In other words, evolution is on the verge of becoming internalized, conscious, and self-directing."[33] Little wonder, then, that Huxley wrote an adulatory introduction to Père Teilhard de Chardin's *The Phenomenon of Man* when that appeared in English translation in 1959. For both men evolution was the story of the triumph of mind over matter, but in Huxley's case without the aid of a divine final cause.

What, then, shall we say of Huxley's lifelong effort to ground Western values—his own values and those of his grandfather—in Darwinian biology? To many it will seem a noble effort, worthy of emulation. To others it will seem foredoomed to failure by Huxley's insistence on restricting science to the scrutiny and putting together of scrutinized facts. To leave values out, Huxley felt, would be to rob the science of life of "half its interest and two-thirds of its practical value." But how were values to be included if the scientist, as scientist, was confined to putting together scrutinized facts? Perhaps non-scientists, some of them at least, would be willing to impose Western values on the facts willy-nilly, but Huxley's fellow biologists were in no mood to do so. The vast majority of them, nurtured on ideas of science and nature inimical to the notion of levels of being, either rejected outright Huxley's effort to graft "improvement" and "progress" onto evolutionary theory or hedged their bets by placing terms like "higher, "lower," "improvement," and "progress" in quotation marks. Evolutionary biologists, it seemed could neither live with nor live without the idea of progress.

NOTES

1. Julian Huxley, "Darwin and His Work," Election '04, Huxley MSS, Fondren Library, Rice University.
2. Huxley, MS on teaching biology to school children, Box 59 (ca. 1921-1922), Fondren Library, Rice University, p. 16.
3. Huxley, "The Idea of a Critical Point in Evolution," MS in Huxley Papers (Box 59:12), Fondren Library, Rice University.
4. Huxley, "Biology and Sociology," in *Essays of a Biologist* (Books for Libraries Press, Freeport, N.Y., 1970), pp. 75-76. First printed in 1923.
5. H. G. Wells, Julian Huxley, and G. P. Wells, *The Science of Life*, 2 v., (Doubleday, Doran and Co., Inc., Garden City, N.Y., 1931), II, 1411.
6. Huxley, "Progress, Biological and Other," *Essays*, pp. 21, 32. Ibid., p. 58.
7. Huxley, *Essays*, "Preface," p. xi.
8. Huxley, Wells and Wells, *The Science of Life*, II, 793.
9. Ibid., II, 1390.
10. Ibid., II, 1407.
11. Statements by Lord Zuckerman and Francis Huxley in discussing papers read at the Huxley Symposium held at Rice University, September 25-26, 1987.
12. Huxley, "Progress, Biological and Other," *Essays*, pp. 35-36.
13. Ibid., pp. 36-37.
14. Huxley, Wells and Wells, *The Science of Life,* I, 646.
15. Ibid., II, 1407.
16. Ibid., II, 1473.
17. Huxley, "Rationalism and the Idea of God," *Essays*, p. 220.
18. Huxley, "Natural Selection and Evolutionary Progress," Presidential Address, Section D, in *Report of the Annual Meeting, 1936*, British Association for the Advancement of Science (London, 1936), p. 100.
19. Julian Huxley, *Evolution. The Modern Synthesis* (New York: Harper & Bros., 1943), 389.
20. Huxley, "Natural Selection and Evolutionary Progress," p. 96.
21. Ibid., p. 98.
22. Ibid., p. 83.
23. Ibid., p. 88.
24. Ibid.
25. Ibid., p. 95.
26. Ibid., p. 96.
27. Huxley, Letter to the Editor, *Eugenics Review*, 55(1963), p. 130.

28. Huxley, "Evolutionary Processes and Taxonomy With Special Reference to Grades," *Uppsala Univ. Arsskr.* (1958), 26. See also Huxley, "Three Types of Evolutionary Process," *Nature* 180 (Sept. 7, 1957), pp. 454-455.

29. Ibid., p. 21.

30. Ibid., p. 36.

31. Huxley, "Evolution as a Process," in Gavin de Beer, A. C. Hardy, and Julian Huxley, eds., *Evolution as a Process* (London: George Allen and Unwin Ltd., 1954), 4.

32. Ibid., p. 13.

33. Ibid., p. 13.

5

DEBATING DOBZHANSKY:
AN EPISTOLARY EXCHANGE

NOTE: As indicated in the opening essay, my first meetings with Theodosius Dobzhansky were at the Darwin centennial celebrations in Philadelphia and Chicago in the spring and fall of 1959. Our correspondence commenced soon after the Chicago meeting and quickly became focussed on the figures of speech evolutionary biologists use in describing evolutionary processes, a topic I had been interested in for many years. The following are excerpts from our letters, which were published in full in *Biology and Philosophy* (11: 445-491, 1996) with the permission of the American Philosophical Society and are excerpted here with the permission of Kluwer Academic Publishers.

December 6, 1959

Dear Dr. Greene:

I had hoped that we might have a good unhurried conversation while in Chicago, but as usual on occasions like that celebration one sees too many people and one sees nobody in particular.

What I wanted to say to you is, in brief, this: You should seize the initiative from Julian Huxley and his like. By "You" I mean scientifically informed philosophers. We, research scientists, can help you, but we cannot do it alone. A negative attitude is not enough. I take it that you are not a fundamentalist, and accept the fact that science is here to stay. I mean it is here to stay not as a collection of knowledge how to make gadgets only, but as a part of man's view of himself and of the universe. A mere grudging acceptance of this fact by Christians is not enough. We need a synthesis. Scientific activity should become a charismatic activity. I realize that this is asking a lot, but it seems to me that nothing less will do. You have to write a sequel to the "Death of Adam"! How does modern evolution look to you with old Adam dead?

Cordially,
Th. Dobzhansky

August 30, 1960

Dear Professor Dobzhansky:

....The first lecture on "Darwin and the Bible" [of my Rockwell Lectures at Rice University, later published by the Louisiana State University Press as *Darwin and the Modern World View*] is in pretty good shape now, and I have just completed what I hope will be the penultimate draft of the second on "Darwin and Natural Theology." I send the latter along as a partial answer to your request of last December....As you will see, I am baffled, astounded, and perturbed by the vocabulary, which you, Simpson, Huxley, and others use in talking about evolution. It seems to me totally at war with your philosophical postulates. You should either abandon the vocabulary or revise your postulates. I put this very baldly, as if I was sure of my own views of the matter. Actually, I am not at all clear on many of the issues involved, but I do feel strongly that many biologists are trying to have their cake and eat it on the subject of teleology in evolution. I know that you distinguish your views from those of Huxley, but from the point of view of the intellectual historian you both seem to be in the same general camp....

Sincerely yours,
John Greene

September 17, 1960

Dear Professor Greene:

I wish I could convince you that the "vocabulary" which Huxley, Simpson, and myself are using does not mean to us what it means to you (or rather to the old fellows who used it long ago). Even more I would like to convince you that Huxley, Simpson, and myself are not "in the same general camp" as far as our philosophical attitudes are concerned. Huxley is militantly and virulently anti-religious. Simpson can, I think, fairly be described as an agnostic. I happen to be a Christian....Personally, I think that evolution (cosmic + biological + human) is God's method of creation (not a very original view, I realize). But this does not oblige me to say that God manipulates the segregation of the genes or the nerve impulses in human brains....

Sincerely yours,
Th. Dobzhansky

Nov. 13, 1961

Dear Dr. Greene:

I have just finished reading your very meaty book on Darwin [*Darwin and the Modern World View*], and I have an uncomfortable feeling that I must be misunderstanding something quite simple and elementary. Why should biologists shun such words as "creativity," "improvement," "trials and errors," etc.? By God, this is what they observe happening or infer having happened. Should they translate these things into Greek so they would sound unfamiliar? Why does "a natural creative process" make no sense without "a creative ground capable of envisaging the possibilities"? Even so simon pure a "scientist" as my colleague Ernest Nagel permits biologists to speak of purposes....Certain evolutionary processes are "creative" because they bring about (a) something new, (b) having an internal coherence since it maintains or advances life, and (c) may end either in success or in a failure. One of the notable successes, let us say the greatest success, was the origin of man. Now, you and I are "creative grounds" capable of envisaging these possibilities, post factum. As I see it, nothing would be gained were I to assert that another "creative ground" caused the genes to change to achieve certain possibilities. But it does make a difference whether one follows Julian Huxley in saying that all "creative grounds" are superstitions, or follows Birch and Teilhard in saying the opposite....

Sincerely,
Th. Dobzhansky

November 17, 1961

Dear Professor Dobzhansky:

I appreciate your recent letter greatly....I am sure we do not understand each other very well. You will remember that....you objected to my lumping you and others with Julian Huxley. Accordingly, I took pains in the revision of the manuscript to distinguish between biologists who acknowledged some creative principle, element, or ground (whatever you like) in the processes of nature and those who did not. I said that, in my opinion, the former group had some philosophical justification for speaking of the "achievements," "successes," "failures," etc. of organic evolution, whereas the latter group had no such philosophical (i.e. rational) justification. I included you and Birch[1] and Teilhard de Chardin[2] in the former group.

In your recent letter, however, you seem to take a position more like Huxley's than like Birch's or Teilhard de Chardin's (as I understand them). Both of the latter seem to recognize what I have called a creative ground or principle in evolution. Teilhard calls it Omega and identifies it with the Christian God. Birch is less explicit, but since he appeals to Whitehead, I presume he adopts something like Whitehead's "principle of concretion" and his general idea of the "envisagement" of the realm of possibility by this element of the cosmic process. The word "envisagement" is Whitehead's.

You, on the contrary, seem to incline to Huxley's view that the creativity of nature requires no explanation, no creative ground. Evolution is a "natural creative process," and that's all there is to it. I must say that this makes no sense to me. We have to ask ourselves the question: what must the universe be like to have produced and still be producing improvements, higher forms of life, new levels of being, etc.? Surely you would agree with me that Thomas Henry Huxley's rhapsody about blind force producing conscious intellect and will is unintelligible. We simply cannot conceive how such a thing could happen. It does not help matters to say that the cosmic process is "naturally creative" or that it "transcends itself." An enigma rephrased in poetic language is still an enigma. What would you say to a physicist who told you that it was a natural property of matter or matter-energy to transcend itself? You concede that you and I are "creative grounds." How did such creatures come to be? Did a process devoid of intelligence, of direction, of will, etc. produce beings possessing all these things? You may answer that here we are as a matter of fact—we *have been* produced. I agree, but that only proves that the process that produced us is not devoid of intelligence, aim, etc. Whether the intelligence is immanent in the process or whether it in some sense also transcends the process (doctrine of creation) is an issue between Christians and, say, Whiteheadians, but this is a secondary question.

As to "success" and "failure," "trial and error," etc. these expressions make no sense unless you assume that something or someone is trying to go somewhere or accomplish something. Success without a succeeder, trial and error without an experimenter, etc. makes no sense whatever. In Huxley's writing the agent who succeeds, fails, experiments, etc. appears to be "living substance," or, in cases where the origin of life is concerned, "world substance." But what could be more ridiculous than this unless one assumes that matter really does strive to achieve new forms, an assumption totally incongruous with Huxley's formal philosophical position. Apparently, he does on occasion impute some elements of will, intelligence, etc. to the lowest forms of matter to help him solve the problem of the origin of new levels of being. That is, in his saner moments he realizes that it solves nothing to talk about "self-transcendence" or matter as "naturally creative."

Do not misunderstand me. I am not trying to fasten Huxley's views on you. I simply do not understand where you stand. If you are a Whiteheadian, like Birch, you should not object to my demand for some creative principle in the cosmic process or to the idea of "envisagement." I believe you told me once that you are a Christian. If so, what is God's relation to nature, and how do you interpret the

Christian doctrine of creation? You seem to fear that admitting a creative intelligence in or in-connection-with nature will involve you in saying that this intelligence causes the combinations of genes in certain ways, etc. This does not necessarily follow. In Whitehead's philosophy there is an element of "subjective aim" in every "occasion of experience" (not just human experience), hence a kind of *nisus* or striving in nature. In Christian terms, however, one could, if one chose, regard the causation involved in evolutionary developments as purely a matter of secondary causes....But this is not to abandon the argument from design or teleology more generally. One still has to face the questions: why is there anything at all, and why do the things that exist act in regular and uniform ways instead of haphazardly? Whence the order in the universe? In order for there to be evolution there must be something to evolve and this something must have definite characteristics....

Much of the inability of biologists to discern purpose in nature springs from their assumption that nature is "going somewhere," i.e. progressing. If God is thought of as trying to produce the modern horse from Eohippus, then he must be branded as a slow, clumsy, inefficient workman. But why should we regard the modern horse as better than Eohippus? I would think the two creatures were equally happy and equally precious in the sight of God. "Better" in evolutionary lingo is somewhat like "better" in modern advertising—the indefinite comparative. Our product is "better". Better than what? Better for whom?

Lastly, there is the whole question whether science can or should admit value concepts into its theoretical structure. The usual assumption in modern times has been that it should not. You will remember Boyle's objection to the Aristotelian-medieval habit of regarding some elements as "nobler" than others. But modern evolutionary vocabulary is loaded with expressions that imply value judgments in their ordinary usage—"higher," "lower," "success," "failure," "progress," etc. Now it may be that all these terms can be defined in a "purely scientific" way, so as to eliminate any value implication. Darwin attempted to do so by invoking the criterion of survival-in-the-long-run..., but he ran into serious difficulties. So has everyone else, in my experience, who has tried to empty these words of their value content.

What conclusion do I draw from this? The following: either biologists should eliminate these words from the language of biology, *or* they should recognize frankly that biological theory requires concepts that can only be defined in terms of a general philosophy of nature, a philosophy of nature in terms of which these value-loaded expressions make sense. If the biologist follows the first course, he will talk about *change*, but not about *progress*. He will speak of a change in the average character of populations, but not about *improvement* in their character. He will, in short, adopt the ethically neutral attitude we associate with physical science. He may feel as a human being that these changes constitute progress in the long run, but he will ignore this because he cannot deal with it *as a scientist*. If, on the contrary, he insists that these concepts and expressions are absolutely indispensable to the biological enterprise, he will have to ask himself philosophical questions: what do I mean by progress, improvement, higher, lower, etc., and what must the universe be like to produce ever new levels of being, etc?

On the whole I think the latter course is more rational, because it seeks understanding in the broadest terms and does not close its eyes to apparent facts because they cannot be dealt with in the current language of science....

I must come to an end....In the meantime, please do not take anything I have said as implying the slightest degree of hostility toward you or toward science. I am delighted to have someone to discuss these matters with, and I am doing my best to increase my pitifully small acquaintance with natural science....

With great esteem,
John Greene

New York, Nov. 23, 1961

Dear Greene:

Let me assure you that I am grateful to you for your detailed reply....Even if we find ourselves in rather basic disagreement, let us drop the titles of "professors", and let us discuss things, even though this is very difficult in letters and we have not an opportunity to do so in any other way.

You say you do not understand where I stand. Let me remove all doubts about this. I am a Christian, hence I stand with my good friend Birch, and you, and Teilhard, and certainly not with Huxley, although his is very much a majority opinion among at least the natural scientists. I am not a Whiteheadian, and so differ from Birch, who likes Whitehead, which to me is a rather meaningless philosophy.

It is hard to go much beyond these sweeping statements, but let me try. You and I will agree that the world is not a "devil's vaudeville" (Dostoyevsky's words), but is meaningful. Evolution (cosmic + biological + human) is going towards something, we hope some City of God. This belief is not imposed on us by our scientific discoveries, but if we wish (but not if we do not wish) we may see in nature manifestations of the Omega, or your creative ground....or simply of God.

But let us face the problem of how the creative ground creates. I think it is here that your view is weak. You yourself say that if God was trying to make an Equus out of an Eohippus, then "He must be branded as a slow, clumsy, inefficient workman." Well, this is the crux of the whole matter. Nothing makes sense if you suppose that God makes a special intervention to direct evolution. I refuse to believe in "direction" in any other sense than that the Alpha and Omega of evolution are simultaneously present in God's eyes (like to Laplace's universal intelligence). To direct evolution in any other sense, God must induce mutations, shuffle the nucleotides in DNA, and give from time to time little pushes to natural selection at critical moments. All this makes no sense to me (nor to Birch, Teilhard is unclear on this). I cannot believe that God becomes from time to time a particularly powerful enzyme.

I see no escape from thinking that God acts not in fits of miraculous interventions, but in all significant and insignificant, spectacular and humdrum events. Pantheism, you may say? I do not think so, but if so then there is this much truth in pantheism. The really tough point is, of course, in what sense can God's action be seen in all that happens. I am not foolish enough to think that I can solve this. Perhaps Teilhard had a hint, very obscurely expressed.... But look, if everything that happens is in some sense "trial and error," then it is merely redundant to say that "someone" is trying to accomplish something in particular in one place but not in another. But I refuse to abstain from talking about progress, improvement, and creativity. Why should I? Some extreme "scientists" would eliminate expressions such as that the eye is built so that the animal can see things. Perhaps extremes converge, and you would join these mechanistic purists? In evolution some organisms progressed and improved and stayed alive, others failed to do so and became extinct. Some adaptations are better than others—for the organisms having them; they are better for survival rather than for death. Yes, life is a value and a success, death is valueless and a failure. So, some evolutionary changes are better than others. Yes, life is trying hard to hang on and to produce more life. I see no need *at this point* to say that some creative ground is trying to get better adaptations and better values and more living substance. For one thing, this creative ground is only very slowly learning how to do it, and is even now clumsy and inefficient about it, as you yourself admit! Your surprise at the fact that a process devoid of intelligence and will has produced beings that have intelligence and will is for me hard to understand, I cannot follow you in saying that this *proves* that this process itself is (and was?) not devoid of these things. Evolution, biological and especially human, is a process which generates novelties. Very remarkable indeed; but not a proof of the action of a creative ground shuffling genes. I feel really shocked—arguing with you I have to sound like a Huxley, something I do not like at all.

"The Death of Adam" showed clearly that to you evolution is something unwelcome though unavoidable. Your new book and your letter underscore this. To me, like to Birch and Teilhard, evolution is a bright light. But it does not follow that evolution is a source of natural theology and a "proof" of the existence of God. I am driven to the view of such a conservative as [Karl] Barth which you quote on page 57 of your recent book (although otherwise I have no stomach for the neo-orthodoxy).* I am groping for a tolerable selfconsistent Weltanschauung but do not claim having found one. Teilhard seemingly did, but perhaps not unexpectedly his book only hints at it and is unable to spell it out. Let me try to say this—evolution should be eventually understood *sub specie religionis* and religion *sub specie evolutionis*. But neither is deducible from the other. Both have to be somehow integrated in one's philosophy of "ultimate concern." I hope this is what you are struggling to do, but I submit that your attempt to view evolution as being actually propelled by a "creative ground" is no more satisfactory than all finalistic theories of evolution (popularized or rather vulgarized by Lecomte de Noüy).

I fear the above sentences may be misunderstood—I do not doubt that at some level evolution, like everything in the world, is a manifestation of God's activity. All I say is that *as a scientist* I do not observe anything that would prove this. In short, as scientists Laplace and myself "have no need of this hypothesis," but as a human being I do need this hypothesis! But I cannot follow your advice and put these things in watertight compartments, and see only "change" and no "progress," only change and no "trial and error." For as a scientist I observe that evolution is on the whole progressive, its "creativeness" is increasing, and these findings I find fitting nicely into my general thinking, in which your "creative ground" is perfectly acceptable.

Well, this is a very long letter, and I fear not succeeding to explain what I would like to explain....But this is the best I can do in a letter. And I still hope that some day in a future not too remote we may find an opportunity to spend a good long evening...over glasses of wine if you use it or over cups of coffee if you don't, discussing, these things....

Sincerely yours,
Th. Dobzhansky

---

* Barth: "The world gives us no information about God as the Creator....He is to be sought and found by us in Jesus Christ." *(Dogmatics in Outline* [Harper, 1959], p. 51)

December 1, 1961

Dear Dobzhansky:

Many thanks for your interesting letter of November 23rd....

It seems to me that the crux of our misunderstanding and disagreement is the question of the relations of science and philosophy rather than of science and religion. Whether a natural theology is possible and, if so, of what kind is a question on which I have not made up my mind. I find Catholic natural theology and some Anglican natural theology interesting and to some extent persuasive, but I have not read extensively enough in either to have a firm grasp of what they are arguing, much less whether it is convincing....In any case, Christian faith does not depend on the possibility of a demonstrative natural theology. I think we are agreed on this.

The point where we seem to disagree is on the extent to which the "facts," propositions, and theories of evolutionary biology are scientific and the extent to which (degree in which) they involve philosophical presuppositions, and hence require explicit philosophizing if we are to be clear what we mean. You say, for example, that "evolution (cosmic + biological + human) is going towards something." I am not clear whether you regard this as a scientific fact, a philosophical interpretation, or as an affirmation of religious faith. In your next sentence you say "This belief is not imposed on us by our scientific discoveries," but it is not clear whether you mean by "this belief" the statement that evolution is going somewhere or your subsequent statement that "we may if we wish (but not if we do not wish) see in nature manifestations of the Omega, or your creative ground, or simply God."

As I read Huxley, he seems to feel that the statement that evolution (cosmic, etc. etc.) is going somewhere is a statement of scientific fact, simply a matter of observation. But surely this is not true, certainly not on the cosmic level. Quite apart from the controversies between advocates of the expanding universe and the steady-state universe, our knowledge of the existence of life, etc., in other parts of the universe is too scant to be dignified by the name of knowledge. In the eighteenth century (and 17th too) it was pretty generally assumed that all of the stars must have solar systems inhabited by intelligent beings; otherwise, said Huygens, etc. they would have been created in vain. Modern scientists shrink from such an *a priori* argument, but it seems plain to me that Huxley, [Harlow] Shapley, etc., make what assumptions they have to make about "cosmic evolution," life on other worlds, etc. in order to give some basis to their assertions about man's importance, dignity, responsibility, etc. etc....At the same time they overlook the enormous difficulties involved in defining what one means by "going somewhere." Such an idea involves notions of "perfection," "improvement," etc., which don't make sense in a mechanistic philosophy of nature. Let me quote to you in this connection a passage from Alexander Koyré's brilliant book *From the Closed World to the Infinite Universe* [1958]: "This scientific and philosophical revolution [of the 17th century]...can be described roughly as bringing forth the destruction of the Cosmos, that is, the disappearance, from philosophically and scientifically valid concepts, of the conception of the world as a finite, closed, and hierarchically ordered whole (a whole in which the hierarchy of value determined the hierarchy and structure of being, rising from the dark, heavy, and imperfect earth to the higher and higher perfection of the stars and heavenly spheres), and its replacement by an indefinite and even infinite universe which is bound together by the identity of its fundamental components and laws, and in which all these components are placed on the same level of being. This, in turn, implies the discarding by scientific thought of all considerations based on value-concepts, such as perfection, harmony, meaning and aim, and finally the utter devalorization of being, the divorce of the world of value and the world of facts."

Koyré is not alone in this analysis of the ultimate implications of the mechanistic philosophy that took hold of the Western mind in the 17th century. Whitehead and Charles Peirce had much the same thing to say: there is simply no intellectual room in the Newtonian universe for ideas of perfection, meaning, aim, higher and lower, etc. There is only change, the motions of valueless matter in infinite space. In *The Death of Adam* I undertook to show how these implications worked themselves out in natural history, and how

Darwin found himself caught between biological facts which seemed to cry aloud for interpretations involving concepts of value, direction, aim, etc. and the pitiless logical implications of the mechanistic philosophy of nature. His attempt to define "progress," higher and lower, etc. in terms of survival was a desperate effort to make sense of the facts without abandoning the mechanistic philosophy. It seems to me that you, as well as Huxley and many others, are caught in this same dilemma. You say, for example: "In evolution some organisms progressed and improved and stayed alive, others failed to do so and became extinct. Some adaptations are better than others—for the organisms having them; they are better for survival rather than death. Yes, life is a value and a success, death is valueless and a failure. So some evolutionary changes are better than others. Yes, life is trying hard to hang on and to produce more life." This way of talking doesn't make sense to me. All organisms die eventually. What, then, becomes better—the variety? the species? Life? But these things are mere abstractions. Individual organisms may try to survive (both Lamarck and Darwin said they did—perhaps even plants), but a *species* does not struggle to survive. "Life" does not struggle to survive; it has no concept of better and worse. I can't make philosophical sense of this language, *much less scientific sense.* Is it a scientific truth that "life is a value and a success, death is valueless and a failure?" The whole thing smacks of vitalism, Lamarckism, and other things which are supposed to be hideous to modern biologists. These personifications of varieties, species, life, etc. are not necessary for scientific purposes; they obfuscate science. They are only desperate attempts to make a mechanistic world meaningful.

I have not touched the questions you raise about the concept of a creative ground. That must be reserved for another letter. Suffice it to say for the moment that you seem unnecessarily to restrict the alternatives: *either* I must believe that some kind of anthropomorphic deity shuffles the genes, etc. *or* I must concede that nature is a self-contained mechanism which, apart from man, grinds out its products without aim, etc. (yet, surprisingly enough, it "makes progress"). I refuse to accept these as the only alternatives.

I note near the end of your letter...the following statement: "...as a scientist I observe that evolution is on the whole progressive, its 'creativeness' is increasing," etc. I don't believe you. You know as well as I do that the community of biological scientists has no generally shared understanding of terms like "progressive" and "creative." The fact that you put creativeness in quotation marks shows that its meaning is ambiguous. Most biologists, as a matter of fact, would strenuously deny that concepts of this sort belong in biological science. Or, to put the matter another way, when you define what you mean by words like these in some way that biologists generally (or even a substantial number of them) find scientifically meaningful, then I will believe you when you say that you observe all this as a scientist....

Sincerely yours,
John Greene

December 6, 1961

Dear Greene:

I have to admit you being right that my phrase "evolution (= cosmic + biological + human) is going toward something" confuses religious affirmation with scientific fact. In my letter I intended it to be the former, as the following sentence indicated. But I still insist that scientific generalization (which is, of course, a bit more than mere "fact") leads to results *compatible* with this affirmation, and such *compatibilities* are what make scientific research exciting. Look, if life began with some sort of autotrophic viruses, and eventually led among other things to higher plants, insects, vertebrates, and man, then the fact that this change did not stop at viruses must be described somehow, and the word "progressive" is used; granted, attempts to define what is "progressive" and what is not (including my own attempt) have not given quite satisfactory results, but I dare say that certain changes that occurred almost everybody will agree were progressive and certain others were not. Similarly it is as hard fact as you can ask that certain structural and functional features bring about organisms surviving and reproducing, and absence of these features increases the probability of non-survival and non-reproduction. Such features are called adaptations, and it is a perfectly honest theory that adaptations may arise through natural selection, and that evolution leads very frequently, though not always, to adaptation retained, improved, or to new adaptations arising. You may protest that scientists should either close their eyes to all this or say that they observe the operation of a creative ground (with or without Capital letters). I fear you will have a hard time convincing scientists...that they "obfuscate" science when they say that individuals, populations, and species struggle to survive. They most certainly do struggle to survive. Surely one may find some circumlocution to say the same thing without using the words which offend you; for example, "oxygen consumption stops in individuals of the genotype A sooner than in those of B". But I say this is mere pedantry which adds nothing to my understanding of what I describe. And I just do not see why saying that the species mammoth has failed to survive, while the species man has succeeded in so doing "personifies" the species. Please, note that species of sexual organisms are not mere congeries of individuals but *organized* genetic *systems*. To some extent they are "personified," and this is again a generalization of hard facts (of course, "personified" being a bad word in scientific writings, I do use another, and if you wish more pedantic word "integrated").

Now, if the above makes me sound to you like another Julian [Huxley], I will next agree with you that an "honest philosophical analysis of problems deeply embedded in the structure of evolutionary theory" and "rethinking fundamental concepts" is badly needed, and this is where *you* can be most helpful.... But I fear you will be on the wrong track if you will propose to do it by forcing biologists to stick to a simon-pure inorganic phraseology, instead of what you call "metaphorical vocabulary." Please do not conclude that I am a pompous ass not realizing my philosophical ignorance. Let me repeat that "metaphorical vocabulary" has, properly disinfected, a blessing of Ernest Nagel, whom nobody suspects of being a theology monger and not a purest scientist. So, I am wholeheartedly in favor "of understanding (in cooperation with philosophers) a reconstruction of the philosophy of nature." But...

let me implore you, that to do it you need biologists giving you this biological fact in their metaphorical vocabulary, so that you can take it and demonstrate its *compatibility* with the idea of the Creative Ground. I hope that I misinterpret you, but reading your books (which I claim to have honestly read, not merely skimmed) I have an uncomfortable impression that in them there are some overtones of feelings that if the old Charles Darwin had not invented this business of evolution then philosophy and religion would have been a lot better off. I ascribe this to the wholly justified irritation with Julian Huxley's use of evolution as a weapon to combat religion. For this reason, in every letter that I write to you I stress that Huxley is not the only biologist, there also exist Birch, and Teilhard, and even myself.

Cordially,

Th. Dobzhansky

January 5, 1962

Dear Dobzhansky:

I turn now to our discussion of the concept of progress in evolutionary biology. You take your stand on a common sense view of progress: "...if life began with some sort of autotrophic viruses, and eventually led among other things to higher plants, insects, invertebrates, and man, then the fact that this change did not stop at viruses must be described somehow, and the word 'progressive' is used; granted, attempts to define what is 'progressive' and what is not have not given very satisfactory results, but I dare say certain changes occurred which almost everybody will agree were progressive and certain others not." I certainly agree that from a common sense point of view the fossil record seems to disclose a definite if somewhat erratic and haphazard "progress" of living forms. But this common sense view of earth history involves common sense value judgments, common sense ideas of levels of being, "higher" and "lower," with (as Darwin noted) an implicit assumption that man is the highest form of being on earth. The question then immediately arises whether this common sense view of progress (or any philosophically refined version of it) can be used by the biologist and, if so, in what way?

Our modern concept of natural science holds that value-judgments and notions of levels of being (the "nobility" of natural objects) are excluded from science. Perhaps this notion is wrong. Perhaps we shall be forced to change it and go back to some concept of science which requires and admits ideas of this kind. Perhaps the overthrow of the mechanical philosophy of nature will result in the overthrow of the concept of natural science associated with it. If, however, you adhere to the modern concept of science (and I get the impression that you do), then I think you must concede that the common sense idea of progress cannot be made a part of biological theory. The most that could be done could be to say that, *if* we accept the value judgments and notions of levels of being implicit in the common sense view of progress as valid (though we cannot prove them so scientifically), then we can reach some conclusions as to whether evolutionary processes are progressive. The precise definition and refinement of the concept of progress would be a philosophical undertaking, in which the biologist-as-philosopher might cooperate with professional philosophers. Economists frequently resort to some such strategy with respect to value judgments. That is, they say: if we assume that such-and-such ends are to be desired, then we must act in such-and-such a way. But they do not pretend *as economists* to be able to determine whether given ends are or are not to be valued.

The other alternative, if the biologist feels that the concept of progress is indispensable to his work and is not satisfied with the approach just described, is to attempt a "purely scientific" definition of terms such as "progress," "higher," "lower," etc. By "purely scientific" one would mean presumably a definition that did not involve a value judgment and was not dependent for its meaning on a general philosophy of nature—some kind of "operational" definition. Many efforts along this line make *survival* the key to the definition of progress. Those organisms and types of organisms are "highest" and "most progressive" that are most capable of surviving and leaving progeny to remote generations. [J. M.] Thoday's discussion of biological progress [1953] is of this nature. Darwin attempted something of the kind in his discussion (in letters) of the evolution of competitive fitness, where the test of fitness was survival in a kind of endless tournament, in which the survivors in one geographical theater were sooner or later brought into competition with the survivors in another theater, etc.

In practice, however, this approach to the definition of "progress" tends to break down, tends to become infiltrated with value judgments derived from the common sense view of progress. In the first place, there is an implicit value-judgment in favor of survival. It is better to be than not to be, as you yourself observe. Quite true, but this is not a scientific conclusion, nor even one which is indisputable from a philosophical point of view. In the second place, the survival criterion becomes subtly infected with value-elements that do not properly belong to it. If we adhered strictly to the "purely scientific" approach, we should have to say that organisms that have greater awareness of their environment, greater independence of it, greater control of it, are higher *only because* their chances of having descendants in the remote future are better than those of other organisms. But no one really believes this. If we knew that the human race would become extinct in one hundred years, would we accept the conclusion that other terrestrial forms that would not become extinct are higher than man? Simply because the dinosaurs disappeared from the face of the earth, are they to be ranked lower than amoebas? Implicitly we assume that greater awareness of the environment, greater independence and control of it, are valuable quite apart from their effects on the chances of survival. We feel that it is better and nobler to be capable of moral choice and perish by choosing badly than to be incapable of moral choice.

I am convinced that when biologists talk about "the problems connected with the element of progress in evolution," or problems connected with macroevolution, they are drawing on the common sense view of progress, with all its implications about levels of being. I do not say that there are no circumstances in which progress could be defined in a simple, unambiguous way for limited purposes, but the generally progressive character of terrestrial evolution as a whole, to which you allude, cannot be so defined, certainly not in terms of mere survival.

The fundamental dilemma of the modern evolutionary biologist seems to me to be the following. He approaches nature either consciously or unconsciously with a mechanistic philosophy of nature (and a corresponding definition of natural science) derived from Newtonian physics and cosmology. In his philosophy of nature, when pushed to its logical conclusion, there is no room for levels of being, for progress, for higher and lower. There are simply displacements in uniform space of particles of valueless matter. Every state of the self-contained system of matter in motion is predictable by mathematical rule from the previous states. But the fossil record which the paleontologist studies presents a different picture. It seems to reveal not simply change but progress, the emergence of new levels of being. Evolutionary theory cannot operate without concepts of this kind. But these concepts are forbidden in the mechanical philosophy. Unwilling or unable to revise his philosophy of nature, the biologist attempts to have his cake and eat it, asserting the mechanical philosophy as his formal philosophical position, yet introducing words such as "progress," "higher," "lower," etc. into the language of his science and oscillating between the effort to define them "purely scientifically" and the temptation to import into these concepts value-judgments which his formal philosophy does not permit him to introduce, but which the facts seem to require.

I now broaden the discussion to include not only the idea of progress but also such expressions as "trial and error," "opportunistic," "evolutionary loopholes," "errors in self-replication," evolutionary "success and failure," "blind alleys," etc. You seem to defend this language vigorously. Why? Do you feel that it is indispensable or even convenient in biological science? We are not talking here of metaphors like "natural selection" which are a convenient shorthand for a complex interweaving of natural processes. A cautious use of such metaphors is certainly permissible. But the expressions I have just alluded to serve no such function. You yourself state the facts with admirable clarity without resorting to them when you want to: "...certain structural and functional features bring about organisms surviving and reproducing, and absence of these features increases the probability of non-survival and non-reproduction. Such features are called adaptations, and it is a perfectly honest theory that adaptations may arise through natural selection, and that evolution leads very frequently, though not always, to adaptation retained, improved, or to new adaptations arising." This certainly is an honest description. Why obfuscate it with talk about "trial and error," nature's "opportunism," evolutionary "success and failure," etc. That which does not *try* cannot be said to succeed or fail or to involve "trial and error." Genes cannot make "mistakes" or "errors" in self-replication unless they *try* to copy themselves. "Opportunism" implies the entertainment of ends. These expressions add nothing to biological science. Their main function seems to be to create an impression that evolution is going somewhere, that some kind of travail is slowly but surely producing things of higher and higher value, that nature does not act in vain. They make evolution seem exciting, dramatic, worth while. Now, if one actually believes that nature strives to accomplish worthwhile things and does, in the long run, actually accomplish them, then this language is perhaps permissible in a treatise of the kind Father Teilhard de Chardin wrote [1963], though of dubious value in an ordinary scientific paper. But if one *expressly denies* striving, aim, etc. in nature (apart from man), this metaphorical language is ridiculous. It serves no scientific function, and its philosophical tendency is hopelessly at odds with the philosophy of nature held by most modern biologists. Its psychological function is to allow one to have his cake and eat it—to deny that nature acts for any purpose and to assert metaphorically that nature does not act in vain.

I skip over various other topics to comment on your twice-mentioned impression that I would be happier if Charles Darwin had never lived and evolutionary theory had never been propounded. This is most unexpected. Whitehead and Koyré both think that enormous damage was done by the philosophical interpretation placed on the 17th century revolution in physics. Does this mean that they wish Galileo, Descartes, Huygens, and Newton had never lived and never written. Of course not. I think great damage has been done and is being done by some philosophical interpretations (some of them masquerading as "science") of evolutionary biology, and by some of the attempts to carry the concepts of biology bodily into "social science" (you yourself have deprecated the latter), but I have no desire to hinder in any way the pursuit of truth, or to be shielded from the truth once known. The essential question is: what is the truth about evolution? I would not bother to investigate the intellectual history of the subject if I did not entertain the hope that what I wrote and said on the subject might help in ascertaining the truth, both scientific and philosophical. I suspect that biological science itself suffers from the intellectual confusion that lies hidden in the undergrowth of metaphors and implicit metaphysics. Doubtless biology will survive these confusions and march on to new intellectual triumphs, but whether our civilization can survive confusion about the nature of science and its relations to philosophy, religion, art, politics, etc. is quite another question.

With warmest personal regard,

John Greene

January 11, 1962

Dear Greene:

First of all, my wife and myself hope to see you on the afternoon or evening of February 9th (Friday)....Naturally, we shall dine together, family style. Since we hope to have you all for ourselves, we shall not invite anybody else. And so, I may postpone the discussion of the illegitimate language in which biologists indulge until we meet. Just one "shot." Yes, I think anybody reading "The Death of Adam" will feel that if Darwin never lived, or occupied himself as a country gentleman of his day was normally expected to be occupied, this would be a wiser and happier world. I fully believe that you did not intend this. Maybe it is "subconscious"? Now, I like to be an optimist, and to think that Darwin was a good boy; you are evidently more pessimistic. This reminds me of the definitions of optimist as one "who believes that this the best of all possible worlds," and of pessimist as one "who is afraid that the optimist is probably right."

Well, and so till Friday after!

Cordially,

Th. Dobzhansky

July 19, 1962

Dear Dobzhansky:

I send you herewith a copy of my review of your *Mankind Evolving*, to be published eventually in *Technology and Culture*. The book was a liberal education to me, for you handle a whole series of complex and highly controversial subjects with the greatest ease and clarity and erudition. The tone of the book, like that of your conversation and letters, is judicious and humane, but never dull.

I probably ought to have indicated more fully my admiration for the book in my review of it, but I usually find myself looking for a chance to argue when I write a review. The points I agree with don't have the same interest for me as those I disagree with. As to the latter, it seems to me that you oscillate (without warning) between conceiving the "evolutionary process" in scientific terms (mutation, recombination, isolation, selection) and conceiving it in philosophical terms (the cosmic process transcending itself, etc.). Thus you give the reader the impression that your generalizations on the latter level have the same standing as your generalizations on the former. I am sure that you do not think that culture is *simply* a means of adaptation to the environment, but your language often suggests that you do. As to the word *nature*, I do not pretend to philosophic clarity in using it. But I find great difficulty in the idea of nature contemplating nature contemplating nature. I do not see how one can avoid some concept of the "trans-natural" (or whatever word you choose) in speaking of the mental and moral activity of human beings. The objects Darwin studied were part of nature, but his theory of evolution (a cultural product) is scarcely a part of nature. It is more like what Whitehead called an "eternal object." So is the concept of the dinosaur and the idea of man. I think we get into logical and semantical difficulties if we try to speak of cultural evolution as "natural" in the same sense that organic evolution is a natural process. This is the truth that underlies the oft repeated expressions about man being "little lower than the angels," etc., a link between the brutes and the divine. He is both a part of nature and not a part of nature.

Cordially,
John Greene

July 31, 1962

Dear Greene:

Just back from Europe, and your letter and copy of the review are on my desk. Many thanks for the review....In your review, my only complaint is that your objections to my regarding human evolution as "a part of nature" are stated so briefly that, I fear, most readers will not know what are our respective stands. In other words, I think, or I hope, that if the difference were explained more fully, most readers would probably be on my side, not on yours. Of course any reader who has read carefully your "Death of Adam" will know what you mean, but is it fair to assume that they have done so?....

Sincerely,
Theodosius Dobzhansky

NOTES

1. Dobzhansky met the Australian zoologist Charles L. Birch during a six months stay in Australia in 1960. For an example of Birch's views see C. L. Birch, "Creation and the Creator," *Journal of Religion*, 37 (1957), 85-104.

2. Dobzhansky was much taken with the book of the Jesuit paleontologist Father Pierre Teilhard de Chardin entitled *The Phenomenon of Man* (London: Collins, 1963).

II

FROM ARISTOTLE TO DARWIN AND BEYOND:

A DIALOGUE WITH ERNST MAYR

NOTE: The essays in this section, drafts of which were submitted to Professor Mayr for his comments, elicited strong criticisms from him and initiated a lively dialogue in published works and in correspondence, as indicated in the following pages.

JOHN AND ELLEN GREENE WITH ERNST MAYR (L) AT THE MAYR
FARM IN NEW HAMPSHIRE, 1992

6

THE HISTORY OF EVOLUTIONARY IDEAS REVISITED

In an essay entitled "Objectives and Methods in Intellectual History," published in 1957, I proposed that the field of study known as the history of ideas, or intellectual history, be defined as a search for (a) the most general presuppositions of thought in a given age and (b) the factors responsible for bringing about changes in those presuppositions in the course of time.[1] By way of illustrating this approach to the history of ideas I undertook to delineate (1) what I conceived to be the dominant view of nature in the eighteenth century, (2) a formerly dominant but now (in the eighteenth century) subdominant view centered on the notion of decline from original perfection, and (3) an incipient view of nature as a law-bound system of matter in motion. I then tried to suggest some of the historical developments responsible for making the once-incipient view of nature the dominant view by the end of the nineteenth century. By that time the static view of nature as a framework of rationally contrived structures fitted as a stage for the activities of intelligent beings had been replaced by a view that represented all the structures of nature—stars, solar systems, mountain ranges, species, etc.—as products of the operations of a law-bound system of matter in motion, the only permanent structures being the atoms, the ultimate particles of the system.

As to the factors which helped to produce this change in presuppositions concerning nature, I suggested the following: (1) new discoveries in astronomy, geology, and paleontology suggesting that the seemingly permanent structures of nature might be more mutable than had been suspected, (2) the tendency of speculative thinkers like Descartes, Immanuel Kant, Erasmus Darwin, Laplace, and Lamarck to draw out the idea of universal mutability implicit in the mechanical view of nature by seeking to derive the present structures of nature from some previous, more homogeneous state of the system of matter in motion, (3) the use of the mechanical view of nature as an ideological weapon (by the *philosophes* and by Marx and Engels) in attacking the established institutions of society, (4) technological, social, economic, and political transformations accustoming the Western mind to the idea of constant change.

In short, I proposed a study of the interaction of science, ideology, and world view in modifying the general presuppositions of thought in the modern Western world, the basic idea being that in the short run the scientific enterprise was shaped and conditioned by prevailing ideas about nature, science, man, and God but that in the long run scientific discoveries and theories altered these ideas. In its first aspect, that of delineating the presuppositions of thought in given periods, my conception resembled Michel Foucault's concept of an archaeology of ideas, but whereas Foucault offered no explanation whatever of the transition from one set of presuppositions to another in the course of history, I tried to suggest some of the influences involved, and I worked some of these out in my book *The Death of Adam. Evolution and Its Impact on Western Thought* (1959).[2] In contrast to the Marxians, I did not suppose that science, ideology, and world view were all part of the ideological superstructure of capitalist society and hence determined in their nature by the capitalist mode of production. Instead, I viewed these three factors as interdependent variables interacting with each other and with other variables in Western civilization. Science I viewed as grounded partly in intellectual curiosity, the desire to know for the sake of knowing. Ideology I conceived as oriented toward programs of social action. World view I thought of as a set of assumptions (accompanied by feeling tone), sometimes explicit but generally implicit in figures of speech, concerning reality. Unlike Thomas Kuhn and Ernst Mayr, I did not believe that ideology and world view became less influential in scientific thought as the sciences became more "mature." On the contrary, I suggested that my mode of analysis could be applied to twentieth century developments in science, although not without difficulties arising from the historian's immersion in twentieth century thought.

So much for the schema set forth in 1957. What modifications and elaborations of it did subsequent years of research and reflection produce? First, when I began to explore the origins of the dominant static view of nature and of the rival view of nature as a lawbound system of matter in motion, I discovered that each of them had a history reaching back to one or more schools of thought in antiquity. The static view of nature and natural history presupposed by John Ray, Carl Linnaeus, Georges Cuvier, and others was in many respects a Christianized Aristotelianism, or so it seemed to me. The forms of the species, which for Aristotle were eternal, were now regarded as having been created "in the beginning"; in either case they remained stable and unchanged. The adaptation of structure to function and of organism to environment, which Aristotle attributed to nature's purposiveness, its immanent teleology, was now attributed to the wisdom of the Creator and hence regarded as absolutely perfect—something Aristotle had not claimed. Aristotelian logic dominated the taxonomic enterprise of naming, classifying, and describing the plants and animals of the world. Aristotle's physics and cosmology had been overthrown, but his biology persisted in a suitably Christianized form, not to be overthrown until Darwin published his *Origin of Species*.

As for the mechanical view of nature that replaced Aristotle's physics and cosmology, it was compounded of Christianized Platonism and Christianized atomism—a strange combination if there ever was one. The Bible contained no science, but it did contain the idea of an omnipotent, omniscient, benevolent Creator who had fashioned the material world and man in wisdom and who regarded his creation as good. The atomism of Leucippus and Democritus yielded little in the way of science because it postulated no ordering principle, but it contributed the atomic hypothesis and the doctrine of primary and secondary qualities. Plato's mathematicism, building on the Pythagorean idea that all things are made according to number and proportion, produced some excellent work in mathematics, optics, statics, and astronomy, but it was precluded from arriving at the concept of a general mathematical physics by its derogation of sense experience, its doctrine that material objects were but imperfect copies of ideas laid up in heaven, and its belief that the principle of reason in nature is not omnipotent.

The fusing of these quite disparate conceptions of nature required centuries. Some evidences of a Christianized Platonism were evident in the Middle Ages alongside the dominant Christianized Aristotelian physics and cosmology, but it was not until the seventeenth century that creationism and Platonism were united in the work of men like Kepler, Galileo, Descartes, and Newton. In Kepler's writings, the Pythagorean-Platonic idea that mathematics is the key to understanding reality is presented in Christian terms: "....God, who founded everything in the world according to the norm of quantity, also has endowed man with a mind which can comprehend these norms," Kepler wrote to Michael Maestlin. "Those Laws [which govern the material world] lie within the power of understanding of the human mind; God wanted us to perceive them when he created us in His image in order that we may take part in His own thoughts...." The mathematical harmonies in nature, said Kepler, are "not an image of the true pattern, but the true pattern itself."[3] Thus, the marriage of Biblical creationism and Pythagorean mathematicism produced a world view in which a mathematical physics was not only possible but inevitable. Matter was no longer, as for Aristotle, an abstract capacity for taking on form. It was a concrete stuff created by God and structured and set in motion according to number and proportion.

Galileo, too, chose to conceive matter as a tangible stuff with mathematical properties imposed on it by the "divine Artificer." He then went beyond Kepler in adopting the Atomists' distinction between primary and secondary qualities, stripping nature of all qualities but shape, size, motion, and other mathematical properties. Isaac Newton took the final step in fusing the Biblical with Platonic and Atomist world views when he speculated in the *Optics* that "God in the Beginning form'd Matter in solid, massy, hard, impenetrable, moveable Particles of such Sizes and Figures, and with such other Properties, and such Proportion to Space, as most conduced to the end for which he form'd them."[4]

It was René Descartes, however, who grasped the implication of universal mutability implicit in the mechanical cosmology and proposed, in his famous vortex theory, to derive the present structures of nature from previous states of the system of matter in motion by the operation of natural laws. Newton was horrified at this "mechanick theism" pretending to derive the present beautiful world from chaos by "a slight hypothesis of matter so and so mov'd." He preferred to think that the same God who created the atoms of matter with their mathematical properties had ordered them in such a way as to produce the present universe. Newton's universe was no self-regulating, self-sufficient machine. God was ever active in it; electricity, magnetism, gravitational force, and the like were modes of divine activity. (In this view, Richard S. Westfall has suggested, Newton drew on the alchemical tradition[5]).

Thus, the mechanical view of nature was not a monolithic, indivisible whole. Its component elements were fused in different ways by different seventeenth-century thinkers. In its Newtonian form, as in the Christianized Aristotelianism that prevailed in natural history, it was a highly static conception of nature linked to a static natural theology. In its Cartesian form, however, it was subversive of that static view and the accompanying argument from design. Newton's physics was destined to prevail over Cartesian physics in a relatively short time, but Descartes' project of deriving the present structures of nature from previous states of the law-bound system of matter in motion through the operation of natural laws was fated to bring about the eventual collapse of the static universe of Newton and John Ray.

The process of undermining and overthrowing the static view of nature and natural science was not a simple one, however. Within the static view itself some changes took place in the course of time, notably the emergence of a Platonic rival to the Christianized Aristotelianism of Linnaeus and Cuvier: namely, the Naturphilosophische conception of nature as a manifestation of Spirit or Idea—a rivalry dramatized in the famous debate between

Georges Cuvier and Étienne Geoffroy Saint-Hilaire in 1830. This rival view, derived in considerable part from the philosophical idealism of Immanuel Kant and Friedrich Schelling, challenged the Aristotelian functionalism of Cuvier but not the underlying static view of nature and natural history. Nor was the gradual discovery of facts seemingly inconsistent with belief in the immutability of the structures of nature—e.g., organic remains of creatures not known to have living counterparts—sufficient to shake the hold of the static view. These discoveries could be explained away in one way or another, for example by postulating a series of successive creations to account for the succession of forms disclosed in the fossil record. Only when these anomalous facts were viewed with a Cartesian disposition to derive the existing structures of nature from the operations of a law-bound system of matter in motion did they become subversive of the static view of nature. The speculative temptation implicit in the mechanical cosmology led directly from Descartes to Buffon, Kant, and Laplace in astronomy, to the geological uniformitarianism of James Hutton and Charles Lyell, to the transformist ideas of the Count de Buffon, Erasmus Darwin, and Jean Baptiste de Lamarck, and eventually to the all-embracing cosmic-biological-social evolutionism of Herbert Spencer. T.H. Huxley summed this development up succinctly when he laid it down as "the fundamental proposition of Evolution that "the whole world, living and not living, is the result of the mutual interaction, according to definite laws, of the forces possessed by the molecules of which the primitive nebulosity of the universe was composed," adding that this view was held in all its essentials by René Descartes, the spirit of whose *Principles of Philosophy* had been revived (said Huxley) in "the profound and vigorous writings of Mr. Spencer."[6] What better evidence could a historian of ideas demand as demonstrating the gradual replacement of the once-dominant static view of nature by the once-incipient mechanical view? Indeed, Spencer declared his ultimate objective to be "the interpretation of all concrete phenomena in terms of the redistribution of matter and motion." Robert Boyle's *Origin of Forms and Qualities*, which explained the qualities of inorganic substances as resulting, not from their forms, but from a "concourse of accidents" in the atomic world, found its nineteenth-century counterpart in Charles Darwin's *Origin of Species*, a long essay on the origin of forms and qualities in the organic world. To a considerable extent Spencer, Darwin, and Huxley thought of themselves as simply extending to the world of life and history the conception of nature (now nature-history) as a law-bound system of matter in motion. The mechanical cosmology, which had overthrown Aristotelian physics and cosmology in the seventeenth century, had now overthrown the Christianized Aristotelianism of Linnaeus and Cuvier and the Christianized Platonism of Naturphilosophie as well!

A neat hypothesis, but things were not that simple. The extension of the mechanical view of nature to the realms of biology and history introduced ideas incompatible with that view, ideas capable ultimately of forming the basis of quite different views of nature. The first of these ideas was the idea of progress, the notion that the operation of the law-bound system of matter in motion could produce not only changes in the configurations of inorganic matter but also living organisms capable of evolving into higher and higher forms of life. But this notion of levels of being was foreign to the mechanical cosmology, which, as Alexandre Koyré observed, discarded "all considerations based upon value concepts." But theories of evolution, from the time of Erasmus Darwin and Lamarck onward, incorporated the idea of progressive improvement, partly because the fossil record seemed to indicate that the "lower" forms of life had preceded the "higher" and partly because the growing belief in progress in the human world infected thinking about the natural world. From that time to the present day the idea of progress has played an incongruous and ambivalent role in evolutionary theory. Evolutionary biologists could not live with it because they could not define it without introducing value concepts prohibited by their idea of science. But neither could they live without it, partly because the fossil record seemed to require it and partly because, as human beings, they needed to give meaning and value to the study of evolutionary biology.

Closely related to the idea of progress was a second idea equally incompatible with the mechanical view of nature, namely, the idea that mind is a part of nature. From Galileo onward nature had been conceived as a law-bound system of material particles possessing only mathematical properties such as size, shape, and motion. All other qualities—color, taste, sound, etc.—were "in the mind," generated there by the impact of the particles of matter on the human sense organs. Mind and matter were totally incommensurable, said Descartes. The motions of matter could never produce mind. Yet this was exactly what evolutionary theory asserted: the motions of matter had given rise to one-celled organisms which, in their interactions with each other and with the inorganic environment, had evolved into thinking beings. Mind was now a part of nature, but nature was still conceived by Darwin, Huxley, and Spencer in terms of concepts derived from the mechanical cosmology of the seventeenth century. (Darwin repeatedly compared his theoretical achievement to Newton's, and Huxley, as we have seen, thought of his and Spencer's views as an extension of Cartesian ideas). Huxley might rhapsodize about "Nature's great progression from the formless to the formed—from blind force to conscious intellect and will,"[7] but how was this possible? Neither Newton nor Descartes would have been able to make any sense of such a progression.

A third evolutionary idea that fit badly with the mechanical view of nature and the conceptions of science associated with it was the idea of competitive struggle as the source of order, harmony, and progress in nature. This idea seems to have been peculiarly British and to have been closely linked to the development of British political economy and to the competitive ethos of British society. It was entirely foreign to the world view of *Naturphilosophie*—nature as a manifestation of Idea or Spirit—and equally incompatible with the French obsession with the problem of order, a problem posed by successive political revolutions. One can scarcely imagine August Comte, preoccupied as he was with this problem, suggesting competitive struggle as its solution. From Adam Smith onward, however, British thinkers were fascinated by the idea of competitive struggle. In Smith's *The Wealth of Nations* (1776) the idea appeared in its sunny, optimistic guise. The "system of natural liberty," if left to operate according to the law of supply and demand, would insure, "as if by a divine hand," that everyone in the market place got his due as the wealth of nations increased. In Thomas Malthus's *Essay on the Principle of Population* (1798), however, the darker, pessimistic side of *laissez-faire* political economy became manifest. The tendency of human populations to increase geometrically produced a struggle for existence, especially among the laboring poor, driving wages down to the subsistence level, Malthus argued.

Given this view of things and British predominance in the rivalry of nation states for colonies and empire, it is not surprising that all of the thinkers who came forward with some idea of natural selection in the first six decades of the nineteenth century were British, mostly English. One thinks of William Wells, Patrick Matthew, Herbert Spencer, Charles Darwin, and Alfred Russel Wallace, all of whom had read Malthus's *Essay* and taken it seriously. British interest in overseas colonization and in scientific breeding of plants and animals also helped to produce theories of natural selection, and British natural theology enabled the men who produced these theories to view the competitive struggle as ultimately beneficial in its results. "As natural selection operates only by and for the good of each being," wrote Charles Darwin, "all corporeal and mental endowments will tend to progress towards perfection."[8]

Closely linked to the idea of the beneficial effects of competition was another idea incongruous with the mechanical cosmology: the idea that chance plays an important part in nature. The essence of the law-bound system of matter in motion was that it was bound by natural laws to produce exactly what it did produce, so that, as T. H. Huxley (drawing on Laplace) put it:

> ...the existing world [we now behold] lay, potentially, in the cosmic vapour; and...a sufficient intelligence could, from a knowledge of the properties of the molecules of that vapour, have predicted...the state of the Fauna of Britain in 1869 with as much certainty as one can say what will happen to the vapour of the breath on a cold winter's day.[9]

Darwin, too, thought that everything was governed by fixed laws—"laws impressed on matter by the Creator," as he called them in the *Origin of Species*—but his theory of natural selection was a probabilistic theory about the chances of survival and reproduction among organisms varying at random with respect to their organic needs. The "laws" Darwin specified in the "Conclusion" to the *Origin* were processes rather than laws of nature in the traditional sense:

> These laws, taken in the largest sense, being Growth with Reproduction; Inheritance which is almost implied by reproduction; Variability from the indirect and direct action of the conditions of life, and from use and disuse; a Ratio of Increase so high as to lead to a Struggle for Life, and as a consequence to Natural Selection, entailing Divergence of Character and the Extinction of less-improved forms.[10]

Darwin's theory, Charles Sanders Peirce noted, was simply "the consequence of a theorem in probabilities."[11] Yet this essentially statistical process, devoid of any principle of order, was now called upon to account not only for the exquisite adaptation of organ to organ and of organism to environment but also for the gradual emergence of higher and higher levels of organization, mentality, and purpose in nature. The theory of natural selection purported to explain how functionally integrated organisms were modified by a process of differential survival and reproduction, but it offered no explanation as to how they came to be functionally integrated in the first place. This problem was pushed back into the evolutionary past in an infinite regress leading ultimately into the inorganic realms of nature.

Closely related to the conception of evolution as a statistical process was another idea equally difficult to reconcile with the mechanical cosmology—the idea of the uniqueness, the individuality, of every organism. The atoms and molecules of the physical sciences might have different properties depending upon whether they were atoms or molecules of hydrogen or oxygen or copper, but the atoms or molecules of any given substance were thought of as essentially identical. Their individuality, if any, was negligible so far as science was concerned. But the organisms comprising a species of plant or animal were all different from each other in some respects, and it was these individual differences that determined the organism's chances of survival and reproduction and, concomitantly, the direction which organic evolution would take.[12]

Thus, the triumph of the Cartesian program of deriving the present structures of nature from previous states of the law-bound system of matter in motion produced a world view containing ideas inconsistent with the mechanical cosmology which had helped to give it birth. These new ideas—progress and the concomitant idea of levels of being; mind as a part of nature; the functional unity and interdependence of organisms; struggle, chance, and individuality as real factors in nature—rested in uneasy tension alongside conceptions of nature and natural science derived from seventeenth century physical science. The tension was apparent in Darwin's oscillation between rejecting "necessary progression" in evolution and asserting "natural improvement" as a general consequence of natural selection; between discoursing about higher and lower organisms (including human races) and swearing never again to use the terms "higher" and "lower"; between viewing the course of evolution as entirely dependent on combinations of circumstances devoid of direction or aim and viewing it as the outcome of laws impressed on matter by the Creator insuring that in the long run all corporeal and mental endowments would tend to progress toward perfection; between asserting that everything was governed by fixed laws and acknowledging that natural selection was a statistical process; between emphasizing competitive struggle as the *sine qua non* of progress in nature and history and shuddering at "the clumsy, wasteful, blundering, low, and horribly cruel works of nature;" between seeking to ground ethics and esthetics in natural and sexual selection and accepting Victorian standards of beauty, truth, and goodness as valid for mankind. Clearly the Darwinian world view, compounded of mechanistic determinism, belief in evolution by competitive struggle and survival of the fittest, and the idea of nature-history as a single continuum undergoing progressive change in accordance with fixed laws discoverable by science, was not a seamless fabric fashioned for all time but an unstable compound of old and new ideas whose incompatibility must eventually become apparent with the progress of science and speculation.

As in the case of the Newtonian world view, however, the Darwinian world picture required about seventy-five years to gain general acceptance in the scientific community and even then did so only in a modified form. Newton's law of universal gravitation and his conception of atoms moving in empty space under attractive and repulsive forces were not accepted by Continental scientists until the 1740s and then only with important qualifications and additions borrowed from the Cartesian-Huygensian-Leibnizian tradition. So, too, with Darwinism. The idea of organic evolution caught on rapidly after the publication of the *Origin of Species*, but the Darwin-Wallace theory of natural selection as the "mechanism" of evolution found no widespread acceptance among biologists before 1930. Evolutionary theories invoking Lamarckian and neo-Lamarckian factors, "mutation pressure," and the like proliferated until, in the 1930s and 1940s, the protagonists of the "modern synthesis" made the theory of natural selection the centerpiece in their synthesis of the results of several decades of research in genetics, systematics, and paleontology. Only then can a truly Darwinian evolutionary biology be said to have emerged triumphant.

On the scientific battlefield the chief enemy of the champions of the neo-Darwinian synthesis was not static creationism, as it had been for Darwin, but rather various forms of evolutionary theory that postulated some directive principle or tendency in nature other than natural selection. In some respects the arguments were purely scientific. Was the inheritance of characters acquired during the life of an organism scientifically credible? Could a series of mutations in a given direction produce a new species without the aid of natural selection? In other respects, however, the attack on the theories of orthogenesis, nomogenesis, aristogenesis, and neo-Lamarckianism incorporated elements of world view. These theories were rejected in part as "metaphysical" resurgences of vitalism and finalism, as unscientific ideologies incompatible with a truly scientific and mechanistic view of evolution.

Elements of world view came to the surface in the writings of nearly all of the founders of the neo-Darwinian synthesis. Julian Huxley's *Evolution: The Modern Synthesis* (1943) was as much concerned with vindicating the idea of evolutionary progress and laying the groundwork for a secularized evolutionary humanism as it was with showing that the theory of natural selection, revised in the light of discoveries in genetics, could unify the science of biology.[13] In like manner Ernst Mayr, George Gaylord Simpson, and G. Ledyard Stebbins appealed to mechanistic and positivistic conceptions of science and nature to discredit creationism, vitalism, and teleology while, at the same time, stressing the organic character of living things by way of refuting the reductionism of "laboratory mechanists" and creating a space for biology as an autonomous science.[14]

As scientists, most of the founders of the neo-Darwinian synthesis were primarily concerned with evolution at or below the species level, with "microevolution." But as philosophical biologists, as members of the human community concerned with political and social issues, as individuals seeking to find meaning and value in their scientific work, they looked to evolution on the grand scale for answers to the age-old problem of human duty and destiny, answers grounded in ideas of nature, man, science, society, and history. For this purpose microevolution was of little use. One must grasp the broad outlines of the evolution of life on earth, discover the processes that had generated and shaped it, and draw lessons concerning human nature, duty, and destiny.

It turned out, however, that the lessons to be drawn were prescribed in advance by preconceived ideas concerning nature, science, mankind, and reality in general. Ontologically, nominalism was prescribed: "only individual phenomena have reality." Epistemologically the outlook was positivistic, opposed to "any mixing of philosophy and science" and dismissing vitalism and finalism as "nonscientific ideologies" involving "unverifiable theological or metaphysical doctrines." Scientific explanations must be mechanistic and causal. Teleological explanations were rejected as "noncausal"; causes must be "material" and "not in the future."[15]

Unfortunately, these mechanistic and positivistic maxims, however useful they might be in refuting creationists, finalists, and vitalists, became an embarrassment when the champions of the modern synthesis turned to meet challenges from the advocates of

mutation pressure, neutralism, and molecular genetics. Against the
laboratory mechanists the field naturalists adopted a very different
line of argument. Evolutionary biology, said Ernst Mayr, was "more
like archaeology and linguistics than like physics." Computer
simulations of evolutionary processes were invalid because
biological organisms, unlike atoms and molecules, were unique. For
that reason the study of evolution could not yield general laws but
only generalizations possessing statistical validity. Evolutionary
biology was "incurably historical." Prediction was difficult in both
microevolution and macroevolution, and causal explanations of past
biological events were often "unspecific and purely formal." Above
all, living things possessed a quasi-teleological functional unity;
their activities were "goal-directed."[16]

Obviously this line of argument, if pressed to its logical
conclusion, would undermine the positivistic, mechanistic critique
of creationism, finalism, and vitalism essential to the new
Darwinism. Somehow or other the "overall harmony of the organic
world" and the "perfection of adaptation" in that world must be
explained without recourse to any "outside agency" or any inner
perfecting principle in nature. The apparent purposiveness and goal-
directedness of organisms must be shown to be an illusion
explicable on "good mechanistic principles."

Pressing the analogy to machines, the neo-Darwinians
analogized improvements in organisms to improvements in the
motor car, projecting technological language onto the evolutionary
process and thereby introducing a cryptic teleology into the
description of evolution. Progressive evolution was said to produce
"ever-increasing improvements in mechanical efficiency," but
efficiency is always defined with respect to some end. What end?
Survival and reproduction? Qualitative improvement? The efforts of
living matter to "exploit" the environment? In a truly mechanistic
view of nature there are no ends. There are only effects, such as
survival and reproduction or non-survival and non-reproduction.
Nor is there any room for "qualitative improvements" of any kind.
Human beings may feel that certain products of evolutionary
processes are "higher" and "better" than others, but evolutionary
biology in the "mechanistic" Darwinian context has no criteria for

making such qualitative judgments. The mechanistic world view, as Alexandre Koyré observed, involved

> ...the discarding by scientific thought of all considerations based upon value concepts, such as perfection, harmony, meaning and aim, and finally the utter devalorization of being, the divorce of the world of value from the world of facts.[7]

But the founders of the modern evolutionary synthesis refused to live in a world stripped of meaning, harmony, perfection, and value. As field naturalists, they were keenly aware of the harmony of living things, of the perfection of adaptation, of the qualitative differences between the life of an amoeba and the life of a human being. They had to make room for these intuitions, and if the conception of nature and natural science in which they were reared left no such room, simile and metaphor must be called upon to give evolutionary biology a meaning and value that could not be supplied by the positivistic, mechanistic conceptual framework of neo-Darwinism.

By the mid-twentieth century, then, important changes had taken place in the Darwinian world view. Natural selection continued to be regarded as the primary agent of both microevolution and macroevolution, but it was now conceived statistically rather than as a competitive struggle for existence. Such a struggle seemed less admirable and hopeful, after two world wars and the horrors of the Nazi death camps, than it had in Darwin's time. As for the idea of progress, it continued to play a highly ambivalent role in Darwinist biology. Efforts to define progress scientifically and prove its existence from the fossil record found little support in the scientific community, yet the idea kept cropping up again and again in the language biologists used to describe evolutionary processes, and always with the tacit assumption that human beings were the highest product of those processes.[18] Man was still regarded as a purely natural being, but the effort to conflate nature and human history in a single continuum governed by natural laws foundered on the growing realization that the future course of evolution on the planet Earth depended primarily, not on the impersonal operation of laws of nature-history, but on human choices dictated by value attitudes foreign to nature and by visions of the ideal possibilities of human nature. Despite the effort to sink man into nature and explode his pretensions to a special status, the evolutionary picture became more and more anthropocentric.

Indeed, the concept of nature presupposed by Darwin and his contemporaries was disintegrating. At the level of physical research the mechanical world view lay in ruins. Heisenberg's principle of indeterminacy gave the *coup de grâce* to T. H. Huxley's vision of Evolution unrolling ineluctably from the properties characterizing the molecules comprising the primitive nebulosity of the universe. Statistical mechanics showed that the so-called laws of nature were merely condensed descriptions of how things were observed to behave, no different in kind from statistical generalizations concerning human behavior. Atomic research exploded Newton's Christianized atomism; the atoms were not only divisible but generable and dissoluble. Quantum mechanics shattered what was left of the mechanistic universe, posing baffling problems concerning the ultimate nature of reality.

Meanwhile the champions of the modern synthesis, although they continued to invoke the mechanistic and positivistic maxims of nineteenth-century physics against creationists, finalists, and vitalists, began at the same time to reject the philosophy of science associated with modern physics as adequate or normative for biology, stressing the uniqueness and functional unity of organisms, the presence of levels of integration in nature, and the "incurably historical" character of evolution. Physicists, wrote George Gaylord Simpson, seek to find principles of increasing generality applicable to all material processes, but this leads them to falsify nature and ignore the complexity of living things. It would be better, said Simpson, to unify the sciences by studying phenomena to which all principles, not just the principles of physics, apply. It would then be seen that biology, not physics was " the science that stands at the center of all science."[19]

Other advocates of the modern evolutionary synthesis, wrestling with the problems raised by sinking man into nature and thus making mind a part of nature, were driven to various forms of panpsychism, as may be seen from the essays by Bernhard Rensch and Sewall Wright in *Mind in Nature* and from Julian Huxley's *Evolution in Action*. In Wright's view:

> Emergence of mind from no mind at all is sheer magic. We conclude that the evolution of mind must have been coextensive with the evolution of the body. Moreover, mind must already have been there when life arose and indeed must be a universal aspect of existence.

Again:

> Reality clearly consists primarily of streams of consciousness. This fact must take precedence over the laws of nature of physical science in arriving at a unified philosophy of science, even though it must be largely ignored in science itself.[20]

But instead of contrasting the uniqueness and hierarchic structure of organisms with the homogeneity and lack of hierarchic structure in atoms and molecules (as Ernst Mayr did) Wright found individuality and hierarchic structure throughout nature.

> The crucial point was that a living organism is more comparable to a molecule or atom among inanimate things than to a mere unorganized aggregation of materials like a stone. Conversely a molecule or atom might seem much like a little organism if we could observe the incessant activity which the physical scientists now attribute to them.[21]

Meanwhile the concepts of nature and science taken for granted by the advocates of neo-Darwinism were subject to increasing attack within the biological community. On the one hand, structuralist biologists like A. J. Hughes and D. M. Lambert assailed the functionalism and reductionism of neo-Darwinian evolutionary theory, resurrecting Étienne Geoffroy Saint-Hilaire's call for "a pure morphology uncontaminated by functional considerations" and rejecting the neo-Darwinian genotype-phenotype and organism-environment dichotomies. Darwinian functionalism, they asserted reduced organisms to collections of traits and then called upon natural selection to explain every aspect of organic form, attributing quasi-teleological creative powers to it. The true method, they argued, was to abandon the concept of biological adaptation ("a subset of environmental functionalism") and explain the evolution of whole organisms in terms of structural laws, providing "explanations of the actual as realizations from a constrained set of possibilities defined by intrinsic principles of physical order." Reductionist genetic determinism must be replaced by biological determinism at a higher level. "The absolutely fundamental question," Hughes and Lambert concluded, "is whether the *real* world can best be interpreted from a functionalist or a structuralist perspective."[22]

Marxist biologists, on the other hand, were not content with suggesting a new "way of seeing" the facts of nature. Instead, they set out to show that the Darwinian and neo-Darwinian views of evolutionary change were reflections of bourgeois society. Darwin, said Richard Levins and Richard Lewontin in their book of essays entitled *The Dialectical Biologist*, performed a valuable service by substituting "real, material entities" (individual organisms and populations) for the ideal forms of species and explaining organic change by "real forces among real existing objects." But, bourgeois Victorian that he was, Darwin was led astray by Cartesian reductionism, the prototypical scientific reflex of a social order that regarded society as a collection of individuals. Accordingly, Darwin and his followers reduced organisms to collections of traits and viewed natural selection as selecting among those traits to produce ever more perfect adaptation to an environment that changed without reference to the needs and purposes of organisms.

It is the organism as the alienated *object* of external forces that marks off the Cartesianism of Darwin from the dialectical view of organism and environment as interpenetrating so that both are at the same time subjects and objects of the historical process.[23]

In neo-Darwinian theory, Levins and Lewontin add, the Cartesian approach has produced a population genetics capable of describing mathematically the endless reshuffling of the basic units of DNA but incapable of accounting for qualitative change; an ecology that ignores the impact of organisms on their environments and imposes on nature concepts of efficiency, waste, maximum return on investment, etc. borrowed from bourgeois political economy; and a sociobiology that reduces organisms to collections of traits and then explains those traits as determined by genes.

To replace the "mechanistic materialism" of bourgeois evolutionists Levins and Lewontin recommend Friedrich Engels' dialectical view of nature—purged, however, of its Lamarckian assumptions. In this view "motion" becomes synonymous with change, as it was for Aristotle. It comprehends "all changes and processes occurring in the universe, from mere change of place right up to thinking."[24] For Levins and Lewontin, as for Spencer and Julian Huxley, "evolution" embraces cosmic and social as well as biological evolution; they are all part of the universal dialectic of nature. "Parts and wholes evolve in consequence of their relationship and the relationship itself evolves."[25] The "materialism" of this view seems to consist in the authors' insistence that explanations must involve only "real forces among real existing objects" (ideal entities are not "real"; individual organisms and populations are real, but whether species, genera, classes, etc. are real is not clear).

Despite their rejection of mechanistic materialism, Levins and Lewontin resort to the language of mechanics in describing the operation of the "forces" of natural selection arising out of the struggle for existence:

> Once it is assumed that evolutionary change is the result of the conversion of variation among individuals into variation among species and of successive alterations of species over time, it is necessary to identify the force for that conversion and to describe the mechanism by which that force converts the variation. That is, we need a dynamics and a kinematics.[26]

Unfortunately, these authors add, modern evolutionary theory provides only a kinematics of the evolution of abstract genotypes without any dynamics of organism-environment interaction capable of explaining the transformation of quantitative into qualitative change. Until such an "exact theory" is attained, they conclude, ideas of evolutionary order and direction must continue to be dictated by ideological commitments.[27]

It seems evident, then, that concepts of nature and science are in flux. The ideas thereof which Darwin and his contemporaries took for granted are no longer viable, although they linger on in the biological community as convenient sticks with which to beat creationists, finalists, and vitalists. New views of nature and science, of man and society, of reality in general are in the making. What dominant view of nature and man's place in it (clothed in appropriate figures of speech) will emerge in the twenty-first century only future historians of ideas can tell.

NOTES

1.   John C. Greene, "Objectives and Methods in Intellectual History," *Mississippi Valley Historical Review* 4 (1957), pp. 58-74. Reprinted in J. C. Greene, *Science, Ideology and World View: Essays in the History of Evolutionary Ideas* (Berkeley, Los Angeles, London: University of California Press, 1980), pp. 9-29.

2.   John C. Greene, *The Death of Adam. Evolution and Its Impact on Western Thought*, (Ames, Iowa: Iowa State University Press, 1959).

3.   As quoted in Gerald Holton, "Johannes Kepler's Universe: Its Physics and Metaphysics," *American Journal of Physics* 24 (1956), p. 350. See also Winifred Lovell Wisan, "Galileo and God's Creation," *Isis* 77 (1986), pp. 473-486.

4.   Isaac Newton, *Opticks....*, 4th ed. (London, 1730), p. 376.

5.   Richard S. Westfall, *Never at Rest: A Biography of Isaac Newton* (New York: Cambridge University Press, 1980). p. 299 ff.

6.   Thomas Henry Huxley, "Evolution in Biology," in *Darwiniana: Essays* (New York: D. Appleton and Co., 1908), p. 206. This essay was first published in 1878 in the *Encyclopedia Britannica*, 9th ed., VIII.

7.   Thomas Henry Huxley, *Man's Place in Nature and Other Anthropological Essays* (New York: D. Appleton & Co., 1898), p. 151.

8.   Charles Darwin, *On the Origin of Species....*Facsimile of the First Edition with an Introduction by Ernst Mayr (New York: Atheneum, 1967), p. 489.

9.   T. H. Huxley, *art. cit. supra* n. 6, p. 206.

10.   Darwin, *On the Origin of Species*, pp. 489-490.

11.   As quoted in Philip P. Wiener, *Evolution and the Founders of Pragmatism* (Cambridge: Harvard University Press, 1949), p. 81.

12.   This line of argument is developed by Ernst Mayr in his *Evolution and the Diversity of Life: Selected Essays* (Cambridge: Harvard University Press, 1976), chap. 6.

13.   Julian Huxley, *Evolution: The Modern Synthesis* (New York: Harper & Bros., 1943).

14.   See Vassiliki Betty Smocovitis, "Unifying Biology: The Evolutionary Synthesis and Evolutionary Biology," *Journal of the History of Biology* 25 (Spring 1992), pp. 1-65.

15.   Ernst Mayr, *op. cit. supra* n. 12, *passim*.

16.   Ibid., Part IV.

17. Alexandre Koyré, *From the Closed World to the Infinite Universe* (Baltimore; Johns Hopkins University Press, 1957), p. 2.

18. See John C. Greene, "Progress, Science, and Value: A Biological Dilemma," *Biology and Philosophy* 6 (1991), pp. 99-106.

19. George Gaylord Simpson, *This View of Life. The World of an Evolutionist* (New York: Harcourt Brace, 1964), p. 107.

20. Sewall Wright, "Panpsychism and Science," in *Mind in Nature: Essays on the Interface of Science and Philosophy*, John B. Cobb, Jr. and David R. Griffin, eds. (Washington, D. C.: University Press of America, 1977), p. 82.

21. Ibid., p. 80.

22. A. J. Hughes and D. M. Lambert, "Functionalism, Structuralism, and 'Ways of Seeing'," *Journal of Theoretical Biology* 3 (1984), 787, 789, 794-797. See also Stephen J. Gould and Richard C. Lewontin, "The Spandrels of San Marco and the Panglossian Paradigm: A Critique of the Adaptationist Programme," *Proc. Roy. Soc. Lond.*, B 205 (1979), pp. 581-598.

23. Richard Levins and Richard Lewontin, *The Dialectical Biologist* (Cambridge, Mass.: Harvard University Press, 1985), p. 4.

24. Ibid., p. 11.

25. Ibid., pp. 3-4, 31.

26. Ibid., p. 31.

27. Ibid., pp. 16, 64.

7

THE DEATH OF DARWIN?

by Ernst Mayr

In 1957 John Greene wrote *The Death of Adam*. In recent years he has seemed to want to prove the death of Darwin, as indicated by the preceding essay and other recent writings. Is there any substance to Greene's endeavor to demonstrate the obsolescence of Darwin's theories and ideas? A Darwinian reading Greene's arguments is overcome by a feeling of frustration. There we have labored for the last 50 years to make Darwin's thought better known, and have documented how brilliantly Darwin has overcome all the objections raised against his work so that we are now closer to Darwin's basic ideas than biologists have ever been since 1859. It is discouraging to find out how completely Greene ignores this argumentation and instead arrives at conclusions that reveal quite conclusively how little he understands Darwin's thought.

Ghiselin, myself, and many of the recent Darwin scholars have emphasized what a revolutionary innovator in philosophy Darwin was. Without referring to any of that literature, Greene treats Darwin as a man hopelessly entangled in the now obsolete concepts of the Galilean motion. He altogether fails to mention that Darwin has liberated us from the philosophy of everything in nature being due to matter in motion. Darwin's emphasis on variation, populations, chance, and pluralism started a new era in the philosophy of nature, an insight that can no longer be ignored even though there are still some philosophers who only read each other's writings or the literature of the physical sciences. How little Greene understands Darwin's thought is well documented by the fact that he always brackets him together with Spencer, two writers whose ideas had remarkably little in common, as has been demonstrated by recent writers.

Even though Darwin, in the fashion of his period, talked a good deal about laws, it is quite evident, and Greene also recognizes this, that they were not the God-given laws of the deists but rather simple facts or what Greene calls processes. Since Darwin did not believe in fixed laws, natural selection for him was a statistical process. This went over very poorly with the deterministic physicists, and this is why Herschel maligned natural selection as the law of the higgledy-piggledy. To describe Darwin's entirely new way of interpreting nature as an adherence to the Cartesian matter-in-motion principle is totally misleading.

Greene seems to think that he can document Darwin's uncertainties and inconsistencies particularly well by his treatment of progress. When dealing with progress in the world of life, one must make a clear distinction between the progression in the complexity of types of organisms in the long geological history of the Earth, and the teleological interpretation of the causes of such progress. Through the researches of the last 25 years, we now know that life on Earth after its origin about 3.5 billion years ago remained extremely simple for about 2 billion years, and that such evolutionary innovations as warm-bloodedness and highly organized central nervous systems are a product of only the last couple of hundred million years. The term *evolutionary progress* is highly inappropriate when ascribed to teleological or finalistic forces. But both Darwin (Mayr, 1983) and Julian Huxley rejected such a usage. Yet to designate as progress the series of changes from the simplest prokaryote to a large angiosperm tree or a primate, is descriptively legitimate. How else could we designate the successive, innovative acquisitions of photosynthesis, eukaryoty (development of a nucleus), multicellularity (metaphytes, metazoans), diploidy, homeothermy, central nervous systems, and parental care (Mayr, *The Growth of Biological Thought. Diversity, Evolution and Inheritance*, Cambridge Mass., the Belknap Press of Harvard University Press, 1982, p. 532)? Greene finds it impossible to reconcile this evolutionary progression "with the mechanistic view of nature". Yet, as Darwin said so clearly, the combined forces of competition and natural selection leave no other alternate but either extinction or evolutionary progression. The analogy between evolution and industrial development is quite legitimate. Why are modern motor cars so strikingly better than those of 75 years ago? Because all manufacturers constantly experimented with various innovations, while competition through customer demands led to enormous selection pressure. Neither in the automobile industry nor in the world of life do we find any finalistic forces at work, nor any mechanistic determinism. Hence when J. Huxley described progressive evolution in figures of speech borrowed from the progress of human technology, he did not in the least fall "into an implicit vitalism and teleology and undermined the idea that human beings are part of nature" as Greene accuses him.

How little Greene understands variational evolution is documented by his statement that there is a conflict between "competitive struggle as the sine qua non of progress in nature and history and admiring the wonderful adaptedness and interdependence of organic beings". But that is of course exactly the core concept of natural selection. Of course an essentialist, and Greene writes like an essentialist, has trouble understanding what consequences the selective survival of certain uniquely different individuals in a large population will have on the genetic endowment of future generations. Incidentally, competition was not quite as strictly a British concept as claimed by Greene. It was well appreciated on the Continent, as documented in the writings of Herder and de Candolle. These authors, however, being essentialists, were unable to use competition in a theory of natural selection.

Greene, the historian, is very much of an externalist, and seems inclined to ascribe all changes in scientific theory to ideological forces. When evolutionists (during the evolutionary synthesis) rejected orthogenesis and neo-Lamarckism, they did so, thinks Greene, because these theories were considered "metaphysical". A closer look at the literature, however, shows rather clearly that these theories were rejected for three reasons: first, numerous facts were in clear violation of these theories; and secondly, all efforts to find biological mechanisms that would make orthogenesis or an inheritance of acquired characteristics possible were unsuccessful; and thirdly, all the relevant facts could be explained quite readily by natural selection. I found no evidence in the literature that these hypotheses were rejected as being "metaphysical". They simply did not stand up against a proper scientific analysis.

Greene's failure to understand Darwinian thought is well illustrated by his detailed analysis of the thought of Julian Huxley. In fact he devotes nearly 30 percent of his essay to an analysis of these views, particularly as presented in *Evolution: the Modern Synthesis* (1943). Actually, Huxley's views although upholding the main thesis of Darwin, were not at all typical of those of the architects of the synthesis. Huxley's strong support of evolutionary progress, his definition of progress by criteria that would establish Man as the highest, best adapted organism, his claim that evolution at the species level was ultimately irrelevant as far as evolutionary trends are concerned, and several other claims made by Huxley were criticized by Simpson, Dobzhansky, Mayr, and other evolutionists long before Greene. In order to evaluate J. Huxley, one must remember that his background was in experimental biology and that he never worked in population biology or systematics. What he said on these subjects was derived from the literature and did not always reflect the best contemporary thinking. It must also be remembered that, like his grandfather, Huxley excelled in popular presentation and that he lectured far and wide to the general public. His concern for these audiences clearly colored his writings.

In many of his objections against Darwinism, Greene argues like a teleologist, with this word being used in its classical sense, in the same sense as it was by Darwin's adversaries Sedgwick and K. E. von Baer. Indeed his teleology seems to have the same ideological basis. From all of his writings it is evident that Greene is a devout Christian. Apparently he cannot adopt Darwinism because he sees God's hand in everything in nature. The evolutionary progression from the simplest prokaryotes to Man is for him clear evidence of the workings of the mind of the Creator. Any attempt at a purely materialistic explanation would cause an insoluble conflict.

Evidently Greene is unable to see any difference between teleonomic and teleological. That organisms are entirely different systems from inanimate matter is something Greene evidently fails to understand. The fact that the genetic program is coded information, that it contains instructions, and that it behaves in most ways very much like a program in a computer, somehow seems to make no sense to Greene. That it was convenient for the evolutionist to take over some of the computer terminology in view of the far-reaching equivalence of the two systems is for Greene simply a "highly anthropomorphic projecting onto a nonhuman process the technological aims and terminology of human engineering". Aristotle more than 2000 years ago already understood remarkably well that a program of instruction is needed for the development of an egg, as recently shown by Aristotle scholars, and molecular genetics has discovered the nature of this program. To do away with these developments as "anthropomorphism" is a remarkably ingenuous solution.

How simplistic Greene's understanding of evolution is, is well expressed by his question: "How, then was he [J. Huxley] to avoid the Scylla of finalism and vitalism without steering into the Charybdis of a mechanical determinism that reduces biology to physics and chemistry?". As if Darwin had not found in natural selection exactly the way by which the stated dilemma can be avoided.

In a curious argument which, frankly, I was quite unable to follow, Greene accuses the Darwinians of having brought telos into the world and to have placed "anthropocentrism once more in the driver's seat". He ridicules the fear expressed by J. Huxley that "the fate not only of mankind but also of life in the planet Earth... was now seen to depend...on human decisions for good or ill". Has Greene never heard of the heart-rending destruction of the tropical forests and the inevitable extermination of quite literally millions of species of animals and plants, has he never heard of the thousands of sterile acid lakes, or of the dying of a large part of the European forests, or of the desertification of the Sahel and other savannah regions aggravated by overgrazing, or the greenhouse effect, not to mention the threatening nuclear winter? It is a real mystery to me how anyone in this day and age can still ignore the fatal impact of human decisions on the life occupying the planet Earth.

Philosophers of science have always emphasized that all major research traditions (Kuhn's paradigms) are a mixture of old and new, with inconsistencies and even outright contradictions as well as unopened black boxes. Darwin's paradigm was no exception, and evolutionary biologists have worked for the last 125 years to explore the black boxes and to remove inconsistencies. Would it be justified to claim that this revisionary process has led to a refutation of Darwinism, or is it rather true that it merely resulted in its clarification and purification? Greene insists on the former, we evolutionists on the second alternative. The only way to decide who is right is to look at the set of theories of which Darwin's paradigm is composed, and see whether or not they are still considered valid.

Was Darwin right about proclaiming evolution? Certainly, except that he called it a theory, while the modern biologist has such overwhelming evidence for evolution that he simply considers it a fact, as much of a fact as that the Earth moves around the Sun rather than the reverse.

Was Darwin right about common descent? Certainly. The last link in the chain of evidence was the demonstration by molecular biology that all organisms have the same genetic code. There is a historical unity in the entire living world which cannot help but have a deep meaning for any thinking person and for his feeling toward fellow organisms.

Was Darwin right about the gradualness of evolution? Yes, provided gradualness is properly defined. Darwin opposed typological saltation as well as any special creation by the "introduction" of new species in the form of single individuals. We now understand that evolution is a populational process, consisting of the gradual—slow or rapid—genetic reordering of populations. To be sure there is also polploidy, a process able to produce new species instantaneously, primarily among plants. But this had not led to any macroevolutionary consequences different from populational evolution. All other speciation is populational, even in the theory of punctuated equilibria.

Finally, what about natural selection? Darwin realized that selection could not work unless it had unlimited variation at its disposal. But he had no idea where this variation came from. So he thought that use and disuse, and other forms of inheritance of acquired characters, might contribute to the production of variability. We now know that in this he was wrong. He was also wrong in thinking that at least some inheritance was "blending", that is that it would lead to a complete fusion of paternal and maternal characters. Otherwise, Darwin was remarkably astute. He clearly saw (better than Wallace and most other contemporaries) that there were two kinds of selection; such for general viability leading to the maintenance or improvement of adaptedness, and this he called natural selection, and such other selection that leads to greater reproductive success.

Where we differ from Darwin is almost entirely on matters of emphasis. Darwin was fully aware of the probabilistic nature of selection, but the modern evolutionist emphasizes this even more. Chance events play an important role in evolution as it is seen by modern evolutionists. Nor would we be prepared to say that "selection can do anything" (neither did Darwin ever say this). On the contrary, there are very numerous constraints on selection. And appallingly often selection is for various reasons unable to prevent extinction.

How different is this interpretation of the evolutionist from Greene's ultimate conclusions? They are embodied in such sentences as "the concept of nature presupposed by Darwin and his contemporaries took for granted is no longer viable"; in other words, Darwin is dead!

Actually, the basic Darwinian paradigm is as well and as alive today as it was in Darwin's day. Some of the peripheral ones of Darwin's ideas such as inheritance of acquired characters and blending inheritance, had to be discarded. But this actually only strengthens his theory. All of Darwin's more basic principles are far more firmly established today that they were in Darwin's lifetime.

Greene might answer that he is not interested in technical details of evolutionary biology, but in the more basic conceptual framework that controlled Darwin's thinking. But here also the philosophical revolution brought about by Darwin is more firmly established than ever. What Darwin rebelled against were a number of dominant beliefs of his day. One was the assumption of natural theology that the world had been designed by the Creator and that everything in the world of life was the result of the wise and benign thought of the Creator. How decisively Darwin emancipated himself from this belief of his youth has been excellently described by Gillespie (1981). In connection with this Darwin once and for all refuted another dominant belief of his period, that there is an immanent teleology in this world that will lead to ultimate perfection or whatever telos the Creator had in mind. Darwin eliminated any reliance on supernaturalism and provided the explanatory models that made this possible. Equally important was his refutation of essentialism and its replacement by population thinking. It established a new emphasis on variation, on a potential for change, and on the uniqueness of individuals. It was this population thinking that made the theory of natural selection possible. Philosophers have not yet quite caught up with the consequences of these revolutionary new ideas.

Contrary to Greene's assertions, these most basic ideas are not only still alive, but they are infinitely better established than they were in Darwin's own day. One hundred and twenty-five years of unsuccessful refutations have resulted in an immense strengthening of Darwinism. Whatever attacks on Darwinism are made in our age are made by outsiders, jurists, journalists, etc. The controversies within evolutionary biology about such matters as the occurrence of sympatric speciation, the existence or not of cohesive domains within the genotype, the relative frequency of complete stasis in species, the rate of speciation, and whatever other arguments there are these days, all take place within the framework of Darwinism. The claims of certain outsiders that Darwinism is in the process of being refuted are entirely based on ignorance. To repeat, the basic Darwinian principles are more firmly established than ever. Paraphrasing Mark Twain, we are justified in saying that the news of "the death of Darwin" is greatly exaggerated.

Ernst Mayr,
Harvard University

8

LETTER TO THE EDITOR OF THE *JOURNAL OF THE HISTORY OF BIOLOGY* IN RESPONSE TO MAYR'S "THE DEATH OF DARWIN?"

July 28, 1988

Dear Everett:

In reading Professor Ernst Mayr's latest volume, *Toward a New Philosophy of Biology*, I was surprised to find reprinted therein his commentary on my article "The History of Ideas Revisited," which appeared in the *Revue de Synthèse* in the July-September issue 1986 accompanied by five commentaries. I was surprised because I had written to Professor Mayr explaining that he had misunderstood and misrepresented my views about Darwin and Darwinism, the relations of science and world view, the impact of modern technology on the global environment, and other topics as well, and I had felt reassured by his reply indicating that "your letter...tells me far better what your real thinking is than your recent essay."

Since the readers of Professor Mayr's excellent new book will be many and since most of them will have had no occasion to read my article in the *Revue de Synthèse* (and hence will have no reason to question Professor Mayr's representation of my views), I am sending you a copy of my letter of June 4, 1986, explaining my true views to Professor Mayr after I had received an advanced copy of his commentary. I send it in the hope that you will publish it and the present letter in your journal by way of setting the record straight. I know of no better way to reach a large number of readers likely to have read Professor Mayr's commentary, and I cannot imagine that he would have any objection to my making this request of you. I value his friendship highly, and I would certainly not want to mar that friendship in any way.

Sincerely yours,

John C. Greene

June 4, 1986

Dear Ernst:

I appreciate greatly your sending me a copy of your response to my essay on the history of evolutionary ideas. I am glad that you have had an opportunity to expound your views and to comment on those of Julian Huxley as well. I cannot say that you have resolved for me the paradoxes and contradictions I thought to point out in your writings and those of Huxley, but perhaps the readers of the *Revue de Synthèse* will perceive the resolution where I do not. I leave the matter to their judgment.

My only regret is that you have misunderstood my own position with respect to Darwin, to evolutionary biology, and to the relations among science, philosophy, and religion. The main corrections I would make to your presentation of my views are as follows:

1. I regard Darwin as a very great biologist, in the same class with Aristotle.

2. I agree with you that the idea of organic evolution and the Darwin-Wallace theory of natural selection had profound implications for the philosophy of nature and natural science, but I see no evidence that Darwin had much insight into these implications. As a philosopher he was, I think, on a par with Isaac Newton, his *beau idéal* of the scientist.

3. I have no quarrel with the idea that populations of organisms undergo changes in character as a result of differential survival and reproduction of those members that happen to have traits favorable to survival in local circumstances, but I do have reservations about using a teleological term like "natural selection" to designate this process (so did Wallace!), and I object strongly to describing evolutionary processes in

teleological and vitalistic figures of speech as you and Huxley and biologists generally love to do.

4. I do not ascribe, and have not ascribed, all changes in scientific theory to ideological forces, as any reader of *The Death of Adam* knows, but I am interested in the ways in which general ideas about nature, man, society, history, God, etc., influence scientific research and theory and, conversely, the ways in which scientific discoveries and theories alter those general ideas. The basic issue between you and me is the question whether this kind of interaction ceased with Darwin or whether it continues to the present day.

5. I do consider myself a Christian (though of the intellectual rather than the practicing kind), but no one except you has ever described me as devout! But if I prefer to worship the true God rather than evolution, natural selection, science, humanity, fate, or any other inferior being, what of that? It does not, as you seem to think, require that I believe (as you indicate) that "evolutionary progression…is…clear evidence of the workings of the mind of the Creator." That was Darwin's position in the *Origin*, but it is not mine. I am not privy to the thoughts of the Creator, not having been present when He laid the foundations of the Earth while the morning stars sang together and the sons of God shouted for joy.

6. I did not, and do not, ridicule Julian Huxley's idea that the fate of life on Earth depends on human choices for good or ill. I simply pointed to this patent fact (which you document with apt cases) as evidence that science, far from rendering man insignificant in the cosmos (as we are repeatedly told it has done) has tended to make us increasingly aware of man's paradoxical importance as a being who is at once a part of and *not* a part of nature. Can a being who can deliberately alter his own genetic nature be considered totally a part of nature? I do think, however, that Huxley's claim that human beings are on their way to becoming "business managers for the cosmic process of evolution" is ridiculous, preposterous anthropocentrism.

7. I do not claim, and have not claimed, that the twentieth-century developments in biology have "led to a refutation" of Darwin's theory of evolution primarily by natural selection. Since I am not a biologist, I consider myself incompetent to make any such judgement. What I have claimed is that the writings of evolutionary biologists from Darwin's time to the present display an unresolved tension between, on the one hand, conceptions of nature and science derived from the Cartesian-Newtonian period and, on the other, ideas of progress, levels of being, chance and individuality in nature, etc., that are incompatible with the mechanistic view of nature. I see no evidence that either you or Huxley have resolved that tension—quite the contrary. As for "Darwinism" as a world view, I claim only that the figures of speech biologists use to describe evolutionary processes are of a vitalistic and teleological character totally incongruous with their formal philosophy of nature and science, and I add that I suspect that the psychological function of these figures of speech is to lend meaning and value to processes and scientific studies that would otherwise, given that formal philosophy, seem destitute of meaning and value.

8. Darwin is dead (so are Aristotle, Descartes, and Newton), but Darwinism is alive and flourishing in an astonishing variety of forms (scientific and otherwise), some of which make more sense than others.

Whatever the case, I beg you to rest assured of my high personal regard for you and for your outstanding contributions to biology and to the history of biology.

Cordially,
John C. Greene

9

FROM ARISTOTLE TO DARWIN:
A CRITIQUE OF ERNST MAYR'S VIEWS

Ernst Mayr is not only a biologist and a philosopher of biology; he is also a historian of biology. It should be interesting, therefore, to see to what extent his philosophy and his religious outlook have influenced his interpretation of history. For this purpose his *The Growth of Biological Thought* (1982), an extended analysis of the development of concepts and theories in systematic natural history, in the study of inheritance, and in evolutionary research and speculation, affords an excellent case study.[1] To avoid difficulties in mastering so comprehensive a work, however, we shall confine our attention to Mayr's account of the gradual emergence of evolutionary ideas in the long transition from Aristotle to Darwin. Since Mayr has organized his treatise in tripartite fashion—systematics, inheritance, and evolution—and since evolutionary theory draws on all three of these fields of study, we shall have to compare what Mayr says about Aristotle, Linnaeus, the Count de Buffon, and other leading figures in various sections of his book in order to piece together his general view of the genesis of evolutionary ideas in biology, or "natural history," as it was known until late in the nineteenth century. Fortunately, Professor Mayr has been willing to read and criticize the present essay and to grant permission to quote from his comments, which thus present an intermittent dialogue between Mayr and the present author. The numbers in brackets in the main text refer to pages in Mayr's book. Mayr's comments on my criticisms appear in the footnotes to the present essay.

Before we examine Mayr's views about particular episodes or epochs in the history of biology, we should have some notion of his ideas about science and its relations with the rest of human culture. According to Mayr, the historian of science must pay attention to the scientist's "priorities and values" and to the "silent assumptions that influence his scientific activity."[17] The same is true in evaluating a historian of science. What, then, are Mayr's own priorities, values, and silent assumptions?

In the matter of values, the high value and broad scope Mayr assigns to science immediately strike the reader of *The Growth of Biological Thought*. The basic purpose of science, he writes, is "to increase our understanding of the world in which we live, and of ourselves."[23] Science endeavors "to understand the world", to "determine the causation of things, events, and processes," including apparently every aspect of human nature.[32] In these efforts, Mayr seems to say, science is not the handmaiden of philosophy and religion but their competitor. As to philosophy, Mayr seems to be of two minds. On the one hand, he presents science and philosophy taken together as the basic alternative to religion in mankind's effort to find "the origin and meaning of the world...and its purpose."[21] On the other, he concedes that science has been deeply involved with both religion and philosophy throughout much of its history and that only in comparatively recent times has it managed to emancipate itself not only from religion but also [13] "from philosophy and from the general zeitgeist." "The farther back we go in time," Mayr writes, "the less important becomes the store of scientific knowledge of the period and the more important the general intellectual atmosphere. As far as biology is concerned, it is not until after about 1740 that the scientific problems begin to separate themselves from the general intellectual controversies of the period."[14] Darwin's work, above all, "signaled the emancipation of science from religion and philosophy."[14] From that time on, apparently, it was the influence of "physicalism" and atomistic reductionism that impeded the emergence of an autonomous science and philosophy of biology, although the one-sidedness of philosophers of science, who continued to concentrate almost exclusively on the physical sciences, was, says Mayr, a contributing factor.

The history of biology, Mayr seems to suggest, is the history of progress in solving biological problems, a progress involving the emancipation (a) of science generally from the influence of religious dogmas and (b) of biology in particular from the equally harmful influence of physicalist ideas derived ultimately from Plato and his mathematical-physical followers in science and philosophy. In keeping with this point of view Mayr divides the causal factors affecting the development of biological science into internal and external influences. Among the external influences Mayr lays special emphasis on "universally adopted ideologies," giving as examples "the dogma of creationism and the argument from design coming from natural theology," Platonic essentialism, scholastic logic, and the extreme physicalism (including determinism and extreme reductionism) that was prevalent in Western thinking after the scientific revolution.[4] As to social factors, Mayr cites Koyré and Kuhn (in addition to his own writings) as having shown that these have been of negligible importance as influences on specific scientific advances.[6]

Among internal causes of scientific progress Mayr lists observation, comparison, experiment (chiefly for functional biology), and, above all, scientific concepts. "Observation in biology has probably produced more insights than all experiments combined," Mayr writes.[32] (Here speaks the field naturalist and systematist!) "But facts are meaningless without concepts. Those are not far wrong who insist that the progress of science consists principally in the progress of scientific concepts."[24] Despite his emphasis on scientific concepts, Mayr never explains how to distinguish between a scientific concept, a philosophical concept, and an ideology.[2] How is the historian to separate scientific from philosophic concepts in Aristotle's biological works, for example? In Mayr's view Aristotle's *eidos* is a scientific concept because one can, by ignoring the immaterial character attributed to it by Aristotle, equate it with the genetic program discovered by modern molecular biology.[4, 88] But what of Aristotle's vitalism, his static world of eternally recurring cycles, his use of the comparative method to define the essences of natural kinds? Are these philosophic or scientific concepts?

The predominantly deductive approach of the Greek philosophers, says Mayr, "helped to raise questions which no one had asked before, it led to an ever-more precise formulation of these questions, and it thereby set the stage for a purely scientific approach which ultimately replaced philosophizing."[86] At what point or period in history, one may ask, did a purely scientific approach to problems in either physics or biology replace philosophizing? When Darwin stated that "as natural selection works only by and for the good of each being, all corporeal and mental endowments will tend to progress towards perfection," was he writing as a scientist or as a philosopher or as an evolutionary theist? If a purely scientific approach to biological problems has replaced philosophizing about them, why does Mayr bother to publish a fat volume entitled *Toward A New Philosophy of Biology*?[3]

What is required, Mayr argues, is a new philosophy of science, a new philosophy of biology—in short, a new philosophical context different from that which has dominated both physical and biological science.[76] Would not Mayr be on safer ground if, instead of characterizing all contexts other than his own as unscientific ideologies, he recognized that there is no such thing as a purely scientific approach to scientific problems of general scope and that all science involves philosophical assumptions and some religious outlook? Otherwise his own philosophy of science may end by being regarded, not as one possible answer to genuine philosophical problems, but as itself an ideology. Is it safe for the pot to call the kettle black?

Beginning with the ancient Greeks, Mayr sounds the themes that are to dominate his history of biology. Plato is identified as the villain of the story, "the great antihero of evolutionism" who invented the myth of the Demiurge to explain the ordered beauty of the universe, who stressed the role of "soul" in nature, who postulated constant forms, or *eide*, of which the variable phenomena of sense experience were but poor imitations, and who consequently regarded mathematics, especially geometry, as the key to understanding nature.[304-305] By contrast, the materialists among the pre-Socratics, philosophers like Democritus and Empedocles, fell into the opposite error. They were early examples of the kind of thinkers Mayr calls "physicalists," men who, invoking chance and necessity as the architects of nature, tried to explain organic phenomena as produced by combinations of material substances.[301-303] Only Aristotle, says Mayr, had the knowledge and the patience and sagacity to construct a conceptual framework adequate for the study of living things. Against Plato he insisted on the importance of observation and comparison, rejecting the mathematical approach and the attempt to group animals by logical division. Against the materialists he stressed the need to explain the general fact of adaptation and the goal-directed character of embryological development, postulating formal and final causes for this purpose. In so doing, he created a science of natural history.

So far so good, but why should Plato, rather than Aristotle, be labeled "the great antihero of evolutionism?" Mayr himself concedes that, although Aristotle would have been "the ideal person to become the first to develop a theory of evolution," he chose instead to advocate vitalistic, teleological, and essentialistic ideas irreconcilable with evolutionary concepts.

> ...he found everywhere well-defined species, fixed and unchanging, and in spite of all his stress on continuity in nature, this fixity of species and their forms (*eide*) had to be eternal. Not only was Aristotle not an evolutionist, in fact he had great trouble imagining beginnings of any kind....He repeatedly rejected the 'evolution' theory of Empedocles. There is order in nature, and everything in nature has its purpose....The idea that the universe could have evolved from an original chaos, or that higher organisms could have evolved from lower ones, was totally alien to Aristotle's thought....This antievolutionary position of Aristotle was of decisive importance for the developments of the next two thousand years, considering Aristotle's enormous influence during that period.[306]

What better credentials could one ask for "the great antihero of evolutionism?" Would it not be best simply to say that Aristotle established a conceptual framework for biology that was not overthrown until the publication of Darwin's *Origin of Species*? That in itself should constitute a sufficient achievement for any biologist. But Mayr's antipathy to physicalism and mathematicism in biology leads him to shift onto Plato's shoulders the responsibility for ideas which Aristotle shared with Plato and to minimize Aristotle's acceptance of those ideas while praising him for rejecting other ideas associated with excessive reliance on physical causes. True, says Mayr, Aristotle postulated an immaterial *eidos* as the cause of ontogeny, but this was only a recognition of the teleonomic character of the process. True, he stressed the marvelous adaptations of living creatures and extended his teleological view of life to the whole of nature, but he did not, like Plato, attribute teleology to an "outside force." True, Aristotle made use of the comparative method to define the natures of different kinds of animals, but this did not make him a thoroughgoing essentialist. True, he was not an evolutionist, but that was because he thought the world was perfect, and there was no room for evolution in a perfect world.[50, 88-89]

What is missing in Mayr's account of Aristotle's thought is an appreciation of Aristotle's philosophy of nature and natural knowledge as it influenced his views on particular subjects. In her *Portrait of Aristotle* Marjorie Grene summarizes this influence succinctly:

> .... the core of Plato's doctrine: the Forms, recollection, the dualism of soul and body, Aristotle was at pains to refute. Yet the criteria of knowledge and of being were the same for both of them. Knowledge to be knowledge must have certainty; this it can have only if its object is permanent. That is, being, the proper object of knowledge, must contain nothing of flux, nothing indeterminate.... Aristotle's 'development'....is fettered securely to the eternity of species, the eternal round of becoming which, following forever its determinate and intelligible pattern, 'will never fail.'...Our vision of species as a concretion of history...would be for Aristotle a betrayal of the very spirit of knowledge, of mind and of the real....Only the fixity of each ontogenetic pattern through the eternity of species makes Aristotelian nature and Aristotelian knowledge possible.[4]

Aristotelian teleology, Timothy Lenoir argues, does not recognize the distinction between biological properties and the laws of physics and chemistry. "In his system of nature the laws of free fall and projectile motion were conditioned by the overarching organization of the cosmos. Each part had its proper position relative to the whole which determined its natural motion."[5] Aristotle's own vision of the harmony of nature is set forth in his *Metaphysics* in explicit terms:

> We must also consider in which sense the nature of the universe contains the good or the supreme good; whether as something separate and independent, or as the orderly arrangement of its parts. Probably in both senses, as an army does....All things, both fishes and birds and plants, are ordered together to one end; but the arrangement is like that in a household,... in which everything contributes to the good of the whole.[6]

In the light of these ideas Aristotle could describe the cycles of birth, reproduction, and death as imitations of the uniform motions of the celestial bodies and reject Anaxagoras's hypothesis that man was intelligent because he had hands. Such a view, said Aristotle, was totally incompatible with the wise economy of nature. Man was, in essence, a rational animal and hence had those organs and properties appropriate to a rational animal: "it is because he is the most intelligent animal that he has got hands. Hands are an instrument; and Nature, like a sensible human being, always assigns an organ to the animal that can use it...."[7]

Undoubtedly Aristotle's philosophy of nature was deeply influenced by his biological researches, but those researches, in turn, were dominated by his search for a solution to philosophical problems posed by Parmenides, Democritus, Plato, and other Greek philosophers. Instead of saying with Ernst Mayr that the deductive philosophical approach of the Greeks was eventually replaced by a purely scientific approach, should we not rather say that the Platonic-Aristotelian conception of science as demonstrative knowledge was replaced, at least in part, by an inductive-deductive, approximative, and experimental conception of science in the seventeenth century, a conception set forth succinctly in Newton's *Principia*? Yet, as Clifford Truesdell has shown, the deductive-mathematical model of science continued strong among mathematical physicists on the Continent from Descartes through the eighteenth century, producing some spectacular successes in the work of the Bernoullis, d'Alembert, Euler, Lagrange, and Laplace.[8]

In Mayr's view the history of biology in the Middle Ages was the sad story of religiously motivated intolerance, arid deductive disputation, and the enthronement of erroneous concepts effectively blocking the development of evolutionary ideas: creationism, cosmic teleology, Platonic essentialism, and scholastic logic.[91-94, 307-309] This seems an unduly negative view of the millenium in which the tribes of Europe were gradually civilized, universities established to transmit and reflect on the learning of antiquity and the Islamic world, and the philosophical works of Plato and Aristotle fused with Christian creationism in complex ways which resulted, first, in the triumph of Aristotle's physics and cosmology and, eventually, in its downfall and replacement by a strange but fertile mixture of creationism, Platonic mathematicism, and Democritan materialism.[9] True, there was little interest in natural history in the Middle Ages, probably because the curriculum of the medieval university had no place for it. Among the seven liberal arts the quadrivium —arithmetic, geometry, astronomy, and music—was descended from Plato's Academy, and the trivium—logic, rhetoric, and grammar—from Aristotle and various Latin writers. The three philosophies—natural, moral, and rational—had no room for natural history either. Of the three fields of professional training—law, medicine, and divinity—only medicine had a biological orientation; anatomy and physiology were dominant, but botany gradually gained a foothold in connection with materia medica.

As for creationism, it was not inherently anti-evolutionary. Darwin and Wallace were creationists of a sort when they announced their theories of evolution. (Darwin defined nature as "the laws ordained by God to govern the universe" and represented the processes of natural selection as "secondary causes" by which the Creator was bringing about adaptation and improvement in nature.[10]) Mayr himself concedes that Judaeo-Christian creationism introduced a time factor "more suitable as a base for evolutionary thought than either the constant or cyclical world of the Greeks" and opened the way to a natural theology that found evidences of God's existence and attributes in the study of nature.[91-92, 307-308] But, Mayr adds, this time scheme, synchronizing earth history with a Biblically based version of human history, was too short to allow for genuine evolution, and the essentialistic philosophy of St. Thomas Aquinas, drawing on Plato and Aristotle, dictated that species be regarded as fixed.[307-308] Actually, however, there was at this period no clear concept of plant and animal species and certainly no idea that one kind of plant or animal could not change into another.[11]

If we attempt to judge what conceptual developments were prerequisite for the emergence of evolutionary ideas not by hypothesizing about the influence of nominalism [308] but by looking at what actually happened in the post-medieval epoch, it appears that what was needed was (a) a science of systematic natural history postulating fixed species as building blocks for systems of classification and (b) a mechanistic substitute for Aristotle's cosmology, replacing his substantial forms and qualities with mathematically ordered particles of matter in motion and capable, when pushed to its speculative limits, of envisaging the mutability of the seemingly permanent structures of nature.[12] The former development we shall discuss in a moment. As to the latter, Michael Foster and Reijer Hooykaas have argued cogently that Judaeo-Christian creationism was an essential ingredient in the intellectual developments that gave rise to the mechanical world view,[13] but in Mayr's opinion this development, infused as it was with static creationism, was a totally negative factor in the history of evolutionism:

> ...the so-called scientific revolution of the sixteenth and seventeenth centuries...caused no change at all in this attitude toward creationism. All the leading physical scientists and mathematicians—Descartes, Huyghens, Boyle, and Newton—were believers in a personal god and strict creationists. The mechanization of the world picture..., the dominant conceptual revolution of the time, did not require, indeed could not even tolerate, evolution. A stable uniquely created world maintained by general laws made complete sense to one who was steeped in essentialism and who believed in a perfect universe.[309]

In the ensuing pages, however, we shall try to show that one version of the mechanistic creationist cosmology, the Cartesian, played a positive role in promoting evolutionary views in both physical and biological science.

As Mayr indicates, there was no overarching conception of a science of life embracing both natural history and the medical sciences in the centuries after Aristotle. Natural history, conceived as the study of the earth and its productions, drew inspiration from Aristotle and Theophrastus but without an accepted conceptual framework until the seventeenth century, when the rapid growth of collections gave rise to systematic natural history focussed on naming, classifying, and describing plants and animals and on the search for the natural method of classification. So conceived, systematic natural history was a science of nature in the full sense, possessing a definite subject matter, methodological rules and techniques, institutions and publications, and its own concept of nature and natural science.

But, instead of recognizing systematic natural history as a full-blown science, Mayr treats it as an offshoot of natural theology: '.... science and theology had been synthesized as natural theology (physico-theology), the science of the day. The natural theologian studied the works of the creator for the sake of theology."[103] This is a very misleading way of looking at the science of the time. John Ray certainly knew the difference between a scientific work like his *Historia Plantarum* and a work in natural theology like his *The Wisdom of God Manifested in the Works of the Creation*. And, Mayr to the contrary notwithstanding,[14] Newton's *Principia* was a treatise on physics and astronomy (natural philosophy), not one on natural theology despite the religious sentiments expressed in some of its scholia. If Mayr's way of thinking were adopted for twentieth-century science, we should have to label Julian Huxley's *Evolution. The Modern Synthesis* and Mayr's own *Animal Species and Evolution* works in moral philosophy because of the moral sentiments expressed in the final chapters. Jacques Roger makes the point cogently in his review of Mayr's *Growth*:

> A scientist inherently believes that ideologies always stand outside of science, generally as obstacles to its 'normal' development. It is hard for him to accept the idea that ideologies act within scientific thought and may temporarily direct its development, which is never 'normal,' even in modern science. Thus we willingly recognize the role of ideologies in old

science only. Ernst Mayr is fully aware of their importance in the special-creationist world view of the seventeenth century, but he does not seem to realize their role in modern theories of evolution.[15]

This is an important point. If we cannot find some way of distinguishing analytically between religion, science, philosophy, and ideology, we shall end in utter confusion, as in Mayr's statement [504] that: "The battle about evolution (and particularly natural selection) was not a purely scientific controversy; rather it was a struggle between two ideologies, natural theology and objective science." "Objective science," which was, earlier in Mayr's book, said to have replaced philosophy and the general zeitgeist, is now represented as an ideology!

For my part, I would argue that the systematic natural history of Tournefort, Ray, Linnaeus, and others was in many respects simply a Christianized Aristotelianism, although much narrower in scope than Aristotle's biology. True, Ray's world was created, Aristotle's eternal, but in either case the species were fixed and given. Aristotle postulated final causes in nature to explain the adaptations of plants and animals, Ray a transcendent Creator; in either case nature did nothing in vain. Aristotle distinguished between essential and accidental characters in defining kinds of animals; Ray employed the same distinctions in arriving at species and constructing his systems of classification, adding, however, the novel idea that the members of each species were related by common descent.

The static character of Ray's natural history was no more dictated by the doctrine of creation than was Aristotle's equally static view by his metaphysics. If Ray mistook the relative stability of species for an absolute stability, his mistake sprang partly from common sense observation, partly from a strongly felt scientific need for a stable building block on which to erect systems of classification, partly from the philosophical tradition (going back to Plato and Aristotle) that regarded form as immaterial and eternal, partly from the traditional interpretation of Genesis (which, Ray said, could be adduced if further arguments were needed), and partly from the general belief, grounded in experience, that all of the basic structures of nature are fundamentally unchanging. Natural theology was one way of making religious and philosophical sense of the apparent facts; Aristotle's cycles of eternal recurrence motivated by aspiration after the perfection of the Prime Mover were another.[16]

As Mayr himself concedes, systematic natural history was a necessary prerequisite for the emergence of evolutionary biology, and this not only because it called attention to the diversity and marvelous adaptations of organisms (Mayr's point) but even more because clear notions about the nature of species and their relations to each other were prerequisite to any sound discussion of the origin of species and because the intense search for the natural method of classification raised problems that could not be solved within a static framework.

The main obstacle to the rise of evolutionary ideas, whether in the biological or in the physical sciences, was not Platonic essentialism (Linnaeus accepted the reality of hybrid species, "daughters of time") but rather the widespread assumption that all of the basic structures of nature were permanent, an idea grounded less in Scripture than in common observation. Physico-theology, a static, truncated version of St. Thomas Aquinas's fifth demonstration of the existence of God, simply combined patent evidences of adaptation and structural stability with traditional interpretations of the Bible to produce a world view which, as Mayr notes, gave a powerful impetus to the study of nature conceived as God's works. Not only Christians but deists as well, used the design argument to prove the existence of God.[17]

What, then, brought about the gradual erosion of belief in the absolute stability of the basic structures of nature, species included? Scientific observations—Tycho Brahe's new star, the discovery of extinct volcanoes in the Auvergne region of France, the growing awareness of fossil remains of organisms apparently no longer extant—played their part, but they were not sufficient in and of themselves to overthrow the dominant belief in stability. The scientists themselves found ways of explaining away or sweeping under the rug these inconvenient evidences of universal mutability. Something more was needed to accomplish the overthrow of established belief. What was needed was an alternative conception of nature, which, if pushed to its speculative limits, could make sense of these anomalous facts.

That alternative view, it turned out, was the Cartesian conception of nature as a lawbound system of matter in motion, every state of the system being derivable in principle from previous states of the system. In vain did Newton and Boyle protest against Descartes' speculative extrapolation of this idea to embrace the evolution of stars and planets from a primeval mass of moving matter, insisting that "it became Him who created them" (the ultimate particles of matter) so to arrange their properties and motions as to produce from the beginning the harmonious world we now behold. The speculative cat had been let out of the bag, and bold minds began to derive basic structures of nature—stars, solar systems, mountain ranges, and species—from the operations of the lawbound system of matter in motion.

If the foregoing analysis is correct, Descartes, whom Mayr depicts as an arch-villain, second only to Plato in his malign influence on the development of biological science, was the grandfather of evolutionary conceptions in the Western world. It was he who launched the enterprise of deriving the apparently stable structures of nature from some previous, more homogeneous state of the system of matter in motion by the operation of natural laws. True, he was also the grandfather of mechanistic explanations in functional biology, but that fact in no way diminishes his claim as a pioneer in evolutionary thinking. And, since Mayr accepts "constitutive reductionism" in the realm of functional biology, he grants much to the Cartesian tradition in this field of research also. The only alternative historically to mechanistic reductionism seems to have been some version of Aristotelian vitalism, and Mayr will have nothing to do with vitalism.[18]

The introduction of a dynamic and causal point of view into natural history, Mayr writes (and I agree completely), was the work of the Count de Buffon. Buffon, says Mayr, painted vivid pictures of different kinds of animals, "thereby foreshadowing the modern age of ethology and ecology." He proposed a "rather 'biological' way of looking at species" and focussed attention on the problem of establishing reproductive isolation between two incipient species. He founded biogeography, grouping animals according to their country of origin and suggesting that the fauna of North America was derived from that of Europe, thus raising the question whether closely related species might be related by common descent. He developed the idea of the unity of plan in the structure of animals and propounded the first rational and internally consistent concept of Earth history envisaging a greatly extended time scheme. In short, says Mayr, he "brought the idea of evolution into the realm of science" and transformed natural history from a hobby to "the status of a science." No evolutionist himself, he was nevertheless "the father of evolutionism."[329-337, 260-263]

Yet, despite this high praise of Buffon, Mayr does not regard him as the instigator of a major conceptual revolution in natural history. Unfortunately, says Mayr, Buffon's thinking was corrupted by essentialism and by the influence of the physical sciences. His concept of a species-specific *moule intérieur* "shared many attributes with Plato's eidos." His species were "essentialistically conceived."[261] "Species, for Buffon, are types and not populations [334], hence he could not concede an evolutionary derivation of one species from another one." Moreover, Buffon remained "a physical scientist" in discussing variation and its causes [335], attributing variation to factors such as climate and nutrition. Thus, Mayr's criticism of Buffon attributes his shortcomings to the two erroneous concepts, essentialism and physicalism, which Mayr regards as the chief stumbling blocks on the road toward the modern synthesis in evolutionary biology.

In arguing thus, Mayr fails to perceive the source of Buffon's revolutionary views, namely, his importation into natural history from natural philosophy of the conception of primary nature as a lawbound system of material particles in motion and of the accompanying idea, advanced by John Locke, of the secondary world of sense experience as a kaleidoscope of sensations produced in the human mind by the impact of these particles on the human sense organs. Buffon's organic molecules and his *moule intérieur* were modeled explicitly on Newton's atoms and his law of gravitation.[19] From this general view of nature and sense experience flowed also Buffon's rejection of final causes and of taxonomic systems based on Aristotelian logic. In his view, observations and comparisons were aimed, not at discovering the essential natures of different kinds of organisms or at classifying them in categories of ascending generality, but at uncovering uniformities in the ways natural phenomena present themselves in sense experience, thereby setting the stage for forming hypotheses designed to exhibit these uniformities as necessary consequences of the operations of the hidden system of matter in motion.

Mayr seems not to have grasped Buffon's distinction between primary nature and the secondary world of sense experience. Thus, after stating that Buffon believed in an eternal order and in laws of nature, Mayr asserts: "In this concept Buffon is remarkably close to Aristotle who, on the basis of the same concept of an eternal order of the universe, also came to reject evolution."[332] But Aristotle's eternal order was the order of the visible world, Buffon's the order of the hidden system of laws, elements, and forces, a system capable of producing a solar system from the collision of a comet with the sun, of molding and remolding the surface of the Earth by the daily action of material processes, of altering the forms of animals exposed to new climates and types of food by migration, thereby giving rise to "families conceived by Nature and produced by time."

To describe Buffon's thinking about species as "essentialistic," as Mayr does, is misleading. Buffon had no use for essences or for emanations of ideas in nature. True, he postulated a fixed number of *moules intérieurs* operative in nature, probably because he thought of the *moule* as a force analogous to the force of gravity and hence an essential component of primary nature. But each *moule* was capable of giving rise to a considerable variety of animal forms, both by artificial selection and by changing environmental influences.[20] There was, in principle, no limit to the variability of nature. "How many others [besides the mammoth]," asks Buffon, "have undergone such changes, whether from degeneration or improvement, occasioned by the great vicissitudes of the earth and waters, the neglect or cultivation of nature, the continued influence of favorable or hostile climates, that they are no longer the same creatures. Yet the quadrupeds, next to man, are beings whose nature and form are most permanent. Birds and fishes are subject to greater variations: the insect tribes are liable to still greater vicissitudes: and, if we descend to vegetables...our wonder will be excited by the quickness and facility with which they assume new forms."[21] These are not the words of an essentialist!

What was missing in Buffon's thought so far as evolutionism is concerned was the idea of progress. Looking back at Buffon from the closing years of the twentieth century, we naturally focus attention on those aspects or his writings that seem to anticipate Darwinian evolution: his naturalism, his theory of pangenesis, his emphasis on the unity of plan in animals, his experiments in hybridization, his interest in artificial selection, his acceptance of the extinction of species, his study of geographic distribution, his notion of "families conceived by nature and produced by time." But, as Jacques Roger has shown us, Buffon's general view of nature, however much it owed to seventeenth-century confidence in science and in the idea of nature as a lawbound system of matter in motion, was deeply tinged with the older idea of decline from original perfection and vigor. Not evolution, but devolution, was the central concept; not competitive struggle eventuating in gradual improvement in all corporeal and mental endowments, as Darwin was to believe, but the slow refrigeration of the earth ending in the extinction of all life. In this respect Buffon was more the forerunner of modern thermodynamicists than of Darwin. The idea of progress had not yet taken firm hold on the Western mind, nor was the fossil record yet sufficiently well known to give credence to that idea. It was Buffon's *protégé*, Jean Baptiste de Lamarck, who would reverse the course of the history of nature and make man the endpoint, rather than the center of nature's operations. On that point Ernst Mayr and I are in perfect agreement.

When Mayr turns in his capsule history of biology [83-132] to the period from the death of Buffon to the publication of Darwin's *Origin of Species*, he seems at a loss to find any conceptual framework other than "natural theology" in terms of which to interpret developments in natural history. Even natural theology, he maintains, lost its hold in France and Germany, although not in Britain. Instead, Mayr turns to a discussion of the rise of research centers and the differences in national mood in various countries, saying that "each country had its own intellectual and spiritual milieu."[110]

Actually, however, there seem to have been several distinct conceptual frameworks vying for favor in this period. The first was the Christianized Aristotelianism already described, which reached its climax in the brilliant work of Georges Cuvier, "the Aristotle of the nineteenth century," as he was known. The second was the dynamic, time-oriented, causal approach to natural history inaugurated by the Count de Buffon and carried farther by Erasmus Darwin, Lamarck, and others. The third was the search for a science of pure form, manifested especially in the work of the Naturphilosophen—Goethe, Oken, Carus, etc.—and also, independently, in the work of Étienne Geoffroy St. Hilaire. The fourth was the teleo-mechanical approach to the study of organisms outlined by Blumenbach and Immanuel Kant and developed further by Meckel, Mueller, von Baer, and other German biologists. Unfortunately, Mayr's *Growth of Biological Thought* was published just before the appearance of Pietro Corsi's *Oltre Il Mito* (translated as *The Age of Lamarck*) and Timothy Lenoir's *The Strategy of Life*, hence Mayr was unaware of the continuation of the Buffonian tradition in France after 1788 and less aware than he might have been of the Kantian tradition in Germany described by Lenoir.[22] It may be well, therefore, to say something of the influence of these various approaches in natural history in the post-Buffonian, pre-Darwinian period.

In France, Corsi shows, there was a spirited debate about basic concepts, aims, and methods in natural history, and although the battle was won by the traditionalists favoring specialization within a static, creationist framework, led by Georges Cuvier, nevertheless there was persistent opposition from dedicated Buffonians like Delamétherie, Sonnini de Manoncourt, Virey, and Lamarck. Moreover, Corsi shows that some of the central ideas in Lamarck's position after 1800—spontaneous generation, evolution from simple to complex forms, and the geological basis of organic mutability—were advanced by some of Lamarck's associates in the Buffonian party before he himself adopted them. Next, Corsi makes it clear that, however much Lamarck may have been influenced to evolutionary conceptions by his work on fossil mollusks, as Mayr and Burkhardt have argued, his ultimate aim was the elucidation of meteorological, mineralogical, geological, and biological phenomena as effects of the general movement of terrestrial and atmospheric fluids operating throughout vast periods of time. Lamarck eventually abandoned this grandiose ambition, truly Buffonian in character, placing greater emphasis in his later works on the taxonomic "proofs" of the organic movement from simple to complex organisms, yet without ever giving up his outmoded ideas in chemistry, mineralogy, and geology. Lamarck was no essentialist, but he certainly was a "physicalist."

As for Cuvier, Mayr leans over backward to exonerate him from the charge of permitting his religious beliefs to influence his science. Cuvier, says Mayr, "never used the marvels of the world to demonstrate the existence and benevolence of the creator....His theism never intrudes...except perhaps in the Academy debate of April 5, 1832."[364] Yet two pages later Mayr writes: "...a concept of evolution was quite incompatible with Cuvier's concept of the harmonious construction of each organism. Each species had been created by divine will, and each was assigned from the beginning its special place in the economy of nature from which it could not depart."[366] Cuvier, says Mayr, was a brilliant comparative anatomist, taxonomist, and paleontologist who, for reasons Mayr cannot fathom, failed to ask the "right questions." For myself, I see Cuvier as the Tycho Brahe of natural history, a man who made brilliant discoveries within a static, Christian-Aristotelian framework but who, appalled by the implications of those discoveries for that framework, proposed an explanation that would concede what had to be conceded about earth history but at the same time would continue to define natural history as *nommer, classer, et décrire*.

Turning now to Naturphilosophie, Mayr gives its advocates credit for proposing a science of morphology, for developing the concepts of affinity and analogy, for inventing the erroneous but stimulating vertebral theory of the skull, and for envisaging static parallels between the stages of embryonic development and the degrees of structural complexity revealed by comparative anatomy, but he fails to appreciate fully the underlying conceptions of science, nature, and natural history.[387-390] Describing Naturphilosophie as "a special branch of Romanticism, "an optimistic movement, seeing development and improvement everywhere, a striving toward higher levels of perfection," Mayr praises the Naturphilosophen for rejecting the mechanistic approach of the Newtonians but finds "no constructive new paradigm" but only "fantasies" and "silly constructions" emerging in the writings of Schelling, Oken, and Carus.[130]

Constructive or not, was there not a new paradigm here, a paradigm closely related to the emergence of a distinctive philosophical tradition in the German universities? As Mayr himself concedes in his work with William Provine entitled *The Evolutionary Synthesis*, philosophical idealism continued to exert a powerful influence on German science, and on some non-German biologists as well, right into the twentieth century. Again, the recent emphasis by Stephen Gould and others on the constraining influence of the Ur-form, or Bau-plan, on evolutionary options during natural selection is reminiscent in some respects of the Naturphilosophische idea that form determines function. Instead of treating Naturphilosophie as an aberration of biological thought that happened to produce a few good ideas, would it not be better to view it as one historical incarnation of a general view of nature as old as biological inquiry itself, namely, the idea that nature is a manifestation of idea? Edward S. Russell suggests as much.

Seen in this way, Naturphilosophie appears to flow naturally, although not inevitably, from Immanuel Kant's revolutionary declaration that the human mind imposes its categories on experience and that experience is therefore essentially mental, the general character of the world of phenomena being dictated by the structure of the mind. From that point of view it was but a step to Schelling's notion that the whole of nature is a manifestation of Idea, or Spirit, and that science is an esthetic activity directed toward grasping the living forms of things. So Goethe argued:

If we once recognize that the creative spirit brings into being and shapes the evolution of the more perfect organic creatures according to a general scheme, is it altogether impossible to represent this original plan, if not to the senses at least to the mind...?[23]

Thus, in the thought of the Naturphilosophen the leaf becomes the unit idea on which the plant is constructed, the intermaxillary bone helps reveal the archetype of the vertebrate skeleton, and the pattern of human ontogeny mirrors the degrees of complexity of the entire animal kingdom as revealed by comparative anatomy. Indeed, embryology assumes a new importance, revealing the unity of anatomical plan in those cases where the adult organisms fail to show it.

Finally, what of the fourth tradition in early nineteenth century biology, a tradition stemming more directly from Kant's writings than Naturphilosophie, namely, the tradition of teleo-mechanism described in Timothy Lenoir's *The Strategy of Life?* According to Lenoir, who approaches the history of biology with a philosophy of biology rather different from Mayr's, the German biologists of this period worked out "a very coherent body of theory based on a teleological approach," which provided "a constantly fertile source for the advance of biological science on a number of different research fronts." This body of theory, first adumbrated by Johann Friedrich Blumenbach and his colleagues at the University of Goettingen, was given a sharper focus by Immanuel Kant in his effort to adapt the methods and conceptual framework of Newtonian science to the special requirements of the life sciences. The teleo-mechanist approach, says Lenoir, underwent further development and modification in the writings of Treviranus, Kielmeyer, Meckel, von Baer, Mueller, Bergmann, Leuckart, and others, reaching (in von Baer's work) "a limited form of evolutionism confined to major organizational types."[24]

Thus, whereas Mayr depicts early and mid-nineteenth century biology as wandering about in search of a theory of common descent, struggling vainly to throw off the fetters of creationism, essentialism, and teleology, Lenoir presents German biology as forging ahead victoriously within a teleo-mechanist research tradition that held its own against the reductionism of Helmholtz, Dubois-Reymond, and others and made room, in von Baer's writings, for organic evolution, although not for a theory of natural selection.[25]

Given this diversity in conceptions of nature and natural history, how did it happen that in Britain, where (as Mayr says) natural theology retained its grip on the scientific mind more firmly than elsewhere in Europe, evolutionary ideas took root and flowered in forms as diverse as those proposed by Erasmus Darwin, Robert Grant, Patrick Matthew, Robert Chambers, Herbert Spencer, Alfred Russel Wallace, and Charles Darwin? Why should Great Britain, where science and religion were closely interpenetrating, have been a seed-ground not only for evolutionary ideas in general but also, in particular, for that most revolutionary conception the theory of natural selection? Mayr never succeeds in resolving this paradox. On the one hand he concedes that natural theology and providentialism stimulated detailed study of organic adaptations [371] and the rapid development of stratigraphical geology and palaeontology. On the other he concludes that the rejection of Lamarck's evolutionism by Lyell, Sedgwick, Murchison, and others sprang from "natural theology and a very literal creationism together with essentialism." [381] After Lyell's refutation of Lamarck, says Mayr, "evolutionism seemed quite absent from the thinking of British scientists. The rejection was universal, ranging from philosophers like Whewell and Herschel to geologists, anatomists, and botanists."[381] "What was needed for the victory of the new ideas was a cataclysmic event that would sweep the boards clean. This event was the publication...of the *Origin of Species* by Charles Darwin."[393]

Mayr's apocalyptic view of Darwin's role in the triumph of evolutionary ideas appeals to our sense of drama, but it overlooks several developments that help to explain why Britain became the scene of a revolution in biological thinking. It was no accident that British naturalists took a strong interest in the geographic distribution of plants and animals and the theoretical problems connected therewith. Botanical and zoological exploration of Britain's far-flung empire proceeded steadily from early colonial times; the voyage of the *Beagle* was but one of several naval expeditions accompanied by a ship's naturalist. Nor was it an accident that theories emphasizing competitive struggle as an engine of improvement in society and nature flourished in Britain, whether in the sunny, optimistic guise of Adam Smith's *Wealth of Nations*, in the darker tones of Malthus and Ricardo, in Herbert Spencer's transmutation of British political economy into a full-blown social evolutionism, or in the Darwin-Wallace theory of natural selection. Nor, given the tradition of physico-theology stemming from Derham, Ray, and Paley and the empiricist-utilitarian tradition dating from the age of Bacon and Locke, was it surprising that an evolutionized natural theology and an empirico-utilitarian view of nature should have gone hand in hand with evolutionary speculation from the time of Erasmus Darwin to that of Herbert Spencer, Charles Darwin, and Alfred Russel Wallace. (Mayr seems to believe that deists abandoned natural theology. On the contrary, static deists like Paine and Jefferson carried it over lock, stock, and barrel, and evolutionary deists like Erasmus Darwin, Robert Chambers, A. R. Wallace, and Charles Darwin simply evolutionized it, as can be seen in the last two paragraphs of Darwin's *Origin of Species*.)

Finally, Mayr's statement that evolutionism effectively died in British scientific circles after Lyell's rejection of Lamarck's hypothesis [381] needs to be qualified by the recent researches of British historians of science showing conclusively that Geoffroy St. Hilaire's transcendental morphology, and to some extent the evolutionism of Lamarck and the post-1820 Geoffroy St. Hilaire, were taken up by medical reformers bent on breaking upper-class monopolization of places of power and profit in the British medical world and that evolutionary progress by natural law was becoming the ideological slogan of middleclass reformers like Robert Chambers and of proletarian revolutionaries as well. As for Charles Darwin, Adrian Desmond places him politically "on the ideological perimeter of the Broughamite-manufacturing camp."

Darwin made the competitive social views of the utilitarians central to his science of human progress. 'There should be open competition for all men,' he pleaded in the *Descent of Man*, 'and the most able should not be prevented by laws or customs from succeeding best.'...he was far from alone in this view. In the 1830s such calls were rampant among the reformers attacking aristocratic Anglican privilege, and social evolutionists such as [Patrick] Matthew and Southwood Smith saw nature sanction their utilitarian rallying cry in just the same way. The language was absolutely *de rigueur* among the free traders crying to open up society when Darwin was devising his theory.[26]

The developments in Britain just described help to explain how Darwin, "a born naturalist" as Mayr says, happened to be in a position to survey at first hand and compare the plants and animals of the world, why the idea of competitive struggle took on for him the aspect of a providential mechanism for generating improvement in nature and society,[27] and why his mind ran to material utility in the competition of the marketplace rather than to transcendental Ur-types and mysterious tendencies toward organic complication in his theoretical speculations. But they do not explain his remarkable powers of observation and scientific reasoning, his grand vision of a science of evolutionary biology embracing, clarifying, and rejuvenating the work of field naturalists, systematists, paleontologists, morphologists, embryologists, anthropologists—in short, the whole of the life sciences—or, finally, the determination, resourcefulness, and zest with which he pursued this vision for twenty years despite constant ill health and the fear of social opprobrium. The example of Alfred Russel Wallace, an Englishman with field experience rivaling Darwin's, shows that another mind could draw the same general conclusions in the same cultural and political environment, but only Darwin had the mental power and imagination to convert his grand vision into a research program and publications that would convert the scientific world to an evolutionary point of view and, eventually, to his own way of conceiving how the living world evolves. And only Ernst Mayr, it should be added, has had the knowledge, training, and insight to analyze the problems Darwin faced in constructing his various theories and to evaluate from the viewpoint of current evolutionary theory his successes and failures in attacking those problems.

Turning, finally, from Mayr's brilliant performance as an appreciator and analyzer of Darwin's intellectual achievement to his general account of the rise of evolutionary ideas in the Western world, I cannot help thinking that his view of the history of biology, like Georges Cuvier's one hundred fifty years earlier, is shaped by his polemical position with respect to the major issues confronting biologists in his own day. But whereas Cuvier was defending a Christianized Aristotelianism against Naturphilosophie and the practitioners of Buffon's dynamic and causal approach to natural history, Mayr is defending his version of the modern synthesis in evolutionary biology against old-fashioned creationists, vitalists, and teleologists on the one hand and mechanistic or mathematical reductionists on the other. Hence his ambivalent attitude toward Aristotle and toward Naturphilosophie, his detestation of Plato and Descartes, his reduction of John Ray's and Carl Linnaeus's natural history to natural theology and all this within a positivistic view of intellectual history which conceives science as gradually freeing itself from religion and philosophy.[28]

To a non-scientist less deeply involved than Mayr in current controversies in biology and the philosophy of biology the historical picture presents itself in a different light. The interaction of science, philosophy, and world view (including religious attitudes) appears, not as something which came to an end with Charles Darwin, but as a perennial feature of Western intellectual history, past, present, and future. As with many scientists, there is a strong holdover in Mayr's thinking of Auguste Comte's view that Western thought has moved slowly but inevitably from a theological to a metaphysical to a positive, or scientific, view of the world. Hence the widespread belief among scientists that, however much science may have been entangled with philosophy, religion, and ideology in the past, it is now free from entanglements of this kind. But, as Mayr's own writings attest, such is not the case. With all due admiration for Mayr's erudite and spirited defense of his central convictions in *The Growth of Biological Thought* one must question the philosophy of history underlying that defense and, with it, some of his interpretations of key developments in the transition from Aristotle to Darwin.

NOTES

1. Ernst Mayr, *The Growth of Biological Thought* (Cambridge, Massachusetts and London: Belknap Press of Harvard University, 1982).

2. Ernst Mayr writes me (May 20, 1991) concerning this passage: "...you are quite correct that nowhere I explain how to distinguish between a scientific concept, a philosophical concept, and an ideology. Actually they run into each other, and I presume that every basic biological concept is also a philosophical concept. In fact that is one of the themes of my recent essay volume...." This statement is hard to reconcile with Mayr's statement in his *Growth* that the Greeks "set the stage for a purely scientific approach which ultimately replaced philosophizing."[86]

3. In a letter to me April 8, 1991, Mayr writes: "I am not in the slightest replacing philosophical concepts by a purely scientific approach. What I have been trying to show for many years is that many of the traditional concepts are invalid, and must be replaced by new concepts which, admittedly, were developed on the basis of scientific studies. Hence creation was replaced by the concept evolution, typological thinking by population thinking, cosmic teleology by programmed developments and activities, etc. etc. All these new concepts are...philosophical concepts just as much as the replaced concepts were....In other words, the modern history of ideas does not consist in a rejection of philosophical concepts but rather in a replacement of refuted philosophical concepts by a new set of concepts which up to now have not yet been refuted." To this explanation I replied (April 12, 1991): "This is quite a different position from that implied in your published statements that only in recent times has science managed to emancipate itself not only from religion but also " from philosophy and the general zeitgeist"; or, again, that Darwin's *Origin* signaled the emancipation of science from religion and philosophy." My main reservation with respect to your newly stated position...is that, in my view, broad philosophic concepts are seldom, if ever, refuted. They may go out of fashion for long periods...but they have a way of cropping up again in changed situations. I don't know of any major philosophical view of the world that can be said to have been "refuted." As to religious views, static creationism was discredited with the rise of geology, evolutionary biology, etc., but the central concept of creationism—that everything in the universe depends absolutely on God for its existence, whereas God does not depend on the universe for his existence—does not seem capable of either scientific refutation or scientific proof. In my opinion Mayr does not seem sufficiently aware of the distinction Jean Piaget made between scientific problems, which "have been successfully isolated in such a way that their solution does not question everything," and philosophical problems, which "stand as bound up with an indefinite sequence of preliminary questions which require the adoption of a position on the totality of reality." (Jean Piaget, *Introduction* à *l'épistémologie génétique*, 2nd ed., vol. 1 Presses Universitaires de France, Paris, 1973, p. 14, as translated in Jean Gayon, "Critics and Criticisms of the Modern Synthesis. The Viewpoint of a Philosopher," *Evolutionary Biology* 26 (1989), p. 2)

4. Marjorie Grene, A *Portrait of Aristotle* (Chicago: University of Chicago Press, 1963), pp. 65, 136-137. Mayr comments here: "There has been a great change in the

Aristotle literature. It would seem to me that Balme and Gotthelf have in many respects made Marjorie Grene's writings obsolete." See Alan Gotthelf and James G. Lennox, eds., *Philosophical Issues in Aristotle's Biology* (Cambridge: Cambridge University Press, 1987), chaps. 1, 7, 8, 10, 11, especially Chapter 11, "Aristotle's Biology Was Not Essentialist" by D. M. Balme. Balme says (p. 301) concerning Aristotle's view as to why animals differ: "...each animal form is the best possible: that is, the form which brings it the most functional advantage....And no further premise is needed to show that this principle will produce species. For in given circumstances, animals that have the most useful form will all have the same functions and lifestyle, served by the same organs grown in the same field conditions, and will therefore be the same in all essential details in Aristotle's sense of essential: therefore they will fall under one kind, one universal....What mechanism might Aristotle have in mind to explain why animals have the 'best possible' forms? He does not offer a physical explanation, no doubt because he was unable to....For our purposes...it is enough to know that a naturalistic basis was available to Aristotle's teleology, and that there is no call for vaster speculations." Balme does suggest, however, that Aristotle may have been presuming a vague 'survival of the fittest' explanation. This seems highly unlikely in view of Aristotle's emphatic rejection of Empedocles' ideas on this subject; and how would Balme square his non-essentialist, "naturalistic" version of Aristotle's views with the following passage from Aristotle's pen: "Man is the only animal that stands upright, and that is because his nature and essence is divine. Now the business of that which is most divine is to think and to be intelligent; and this would not be easy if there were a great deal of the body at the top weighing it down...."? (*Parts of Animals With an English Translation by A. L. Peck*....(Loeb Classical Library, London: William Heinemann Ltd, 1937), Iv. x. 686a, 25 ff., pp. 371-373.

5. Timothy Lenoir, The *Strategy of Life. Teleology and Mechanics in Nineteenth Century German Biology* (Dordrecht, Boston, and London: D. Reidel Publishing Co., 1982), p. 10.

6. Aristotle, *Metaphysics*, XII, X., 2-4, translated by Hugh Tredennick (Loeb Classical Library, London: William Heinemann Ltd, 1936), pp. 167-169.

7. Aristotle, *Parts of Animals*, I. v. 645a, 24 ff., p. 101.

8. Clifford Truesdell, "A Program Toward Rediscovering the Rational Mechanics of the Age of Reason," *Archive for History of Exact Sciences* 1 (1960-1962), pp. 1-36.

9. This interpretation is developed more fully in John C. Greene, "The History of Ideas Revisited," *Revue de Synthèse*, IVᵉ Série 107 (juillet-septembre 1986). pp. 203-205.

10. Charles Darwin, *Charles Darwin's Natural Selection. Being the Second Part of His Big Species Book Written from 1856 to 1858*, Robert C. Stauffer, ed. (Cambridge: Cambridge University Press, 1975), p. 224. On the following page Darwin says: "If we admit, as we must admit, that some few organic beings were originally created, which were endowed with a high power of generation, and with the capacity for some slight inheritable variability, then I can see no limit to the wondrous and harmonious results which in the course of time can be perfected through natural selection." See also Charles Darwin, *On the Origin of Species. A Facsimile of the First Edition with an Introduction by Ernst Mayr* (New York: Atheneum, 1967), pp. 488-490.

11. Conway Zirkle, "Species Before Darwin," *Proc. Amer. Philos. Soc.* 103 (1959), pp. 640-641. Zirkle quotes St. Thomas's *Summa*, Pt. I, quaest. 73, art. 1, ad. 3 as saying: "...new kinds arise occasionally from the connection of individuals belonging to different species." Also, that new species arise "by putrefaction by the powers which stars and elements received at the beginning."

12. See Jacques Roger, "La Théorie de la Terre au XVIIᵉ siècle," *Revue d'Histoire des Sciences* 26 (1973), pp. 23-48 for an exposition of the view that the geocentric cosmology of Aristotle and the Bible had to be overthrown before there could be an historical theory of the earth.

13. Michael B. Foster, "The Christian Doctrine of Creation and the Rise of Modern Science," *Mind* 43 (1934), pp. 446-468; Reijer Hooykaas, *Religion and the Rise of Modern Science*, rev. ed. (Edinburgh: Scottish Academic Press, 1973).

14. In his letter to me May 20, 1991 Mayr argues that Newton's *Principia* was indeed a work in natural theology. "Several authors have referred to Newton's works as works of natural theology."

15. Roger, essay review cited in Footnote 1, p. 408.

16. Mayr writes me (May 20): "The 'first approach' constancy of all phenomena is taken as obvious by the naive mind. It has nothing to do with the Bible but is equally found among primitive natives, etc. Furthermore, it is encapsulated in our language, which uses words like tree, mountain, river, storm, etc, for highly variable phenomena 'as if' there was a constant essence underlying these phenomena." Jacques Roger, in his review of Mayr's book, makes the additional important point about typology (p. 407): "Typological thinking is an answer to a basic need of rationality. It prevails not only because of the success of physical science, as Ernst Mayr rightly points out, but because without typology it is extremely difficult to introduce any rational order into the formidable disorder of natural things." It may be, then, that a typological approach to natural history was an essential first step on the way to evolutionary views.

17. Mayr seems to believe that deists did not argue from the design of the structures of nature to the existence of an omnipotent, omniscient, and benevolent God. On the contrary, their writings are full of arguments of this kind, as when Thomas Paine argued that God had so constructed the solar system that the inhabitants of each planet would be able to discover the laws of motion by studying the movements of the other planets. The deists (other than evolutionary deists like Erasmus Darwin) retained Christian natural theology in full force, divorcing it from revealed theology.

18. Mayr disagrees strongly here: "At the particular place where you invoke him I doubt that Descartes had any influence in biology whatsoever." In my opinion, Mayr is looking for too direct an influence. Before the idea of the mutability of species could take hold something had to undermine confidence in the stability of the physical environment, and, as Jacques Roger shows in his essay on the rise of theories of the earth (see Footnote 12), there is a direct link between Descartes' speculations about Earth history in his *Principia* and the subsequent publication of Thomas Burnet's *Telluris Theoria Sacra* in London in 1681. Roger doubts that Descartes himself had any *historical* intention in his speculations in Part IV of the *Principia*, but there is no doubt that Burnet applied Cartesian principles to developing a theory of earth history. He delighted, as he said, "to take in Pieces this Frame of Nature, and melt it down into its first Principles; and then to observe how

the Divine Wisdom wrought all These Things out of Confusion into Order, and out of Simplicity into that beautiful Composition we now see them in." (*The Sacred Theory of the Earth*, 7th ed., London, 1759), 66-67. Newtonian principles were used to the same effect by William Whiston. One must not confine his attention to biology in looking for the origins of evolutionary ideas but must enlarge the view to embrace all the developments that were shaking confidence in the absolute stability of the structures of nature. In the Appendix to his *Discours D'Ouverture de L'An X* Lamarck says of the origin of his doubts about the fixity of species: "I thought for a long time that there were constant species in nature....Now I am convinced that I was in error....The origin of this error, which I shared with many naturalists who still hold to it, is found in the *long duration* with respect to us of the same state of things in each place which each living body inhabits; but that duration of the same state of things for each place has a limit, and with plenty of time it undergoes mutations at each point of the surface of the globe which change the circumstances for all the living bodies inhabiting it." (my translation) Descartes' vortex theory, whatever his own intentions, set in motion a mode of reconstituting the history of nature from the operations of the lawbound system of matter in motion that was ultimately to undermine fixity everywhere in nature.

19. Georges Louis Leclerc, Count de Buffon, *Natural History, General and Particular*, William Smellie, tr. 3rd. ed. (London, 1791), II, p. 48: "In my theory...I first admit the mechanical principle, then the penetrating force of gravity, and, from analogy and experience, I have concluded the existence of other penetrating forces peculiar to organic bodies. I have proved by facts, that matter has a strong tendency towards organization; and that there are in Nature an infinite number of organic particles. I have, therefore, only generalized particular observations, without advancing any thing contrary to mechanical principles, when that term is used in its proper sense, as denoting the general effects of Nature." For a perceptive discussion of Buffon's views on the ontolological and epistemological issues raised by Descartes, Newton, Locke, and Leibniz in connection with the seventeenth-century revolution in science and cosmology see the "Introduction" to *From Natural History to the History of Nature: Readings from Buffon and His Critics. Edited, translated, and with introductions by John Lyon and Phillip R Sloan* (Notre Dame, Ind. and London: University of Notre Dame Press, 1981), pp. 1-32. Sloan's various articles on Buffon are listed in the bibliography accompanying Jacques Roger's *Buffon*, cited immediately below.

20. See, for example, Jacques Roger, *Buffon: un philosophe au Jardin du Roi* (Paris: Fayard, 1989), pp. 389, 400-404, 440. Roger quotes Buffon's *Histoire Naturelle*, essay entitled "Le Cheval" (IV, pp. 215-216) as follows: "Le premier animal, le premier cheval, par exemple, a été le modèle extérieur et le moule intérieur sur lequel tous les chevaux qui son nés, tous ceux qui existent et tous ceux qui naîtront ont été formés; mais ce modèle, dont nous ne connaissons que des copies, a pu s'altérer ou se perfectionner en communiquant sa forme et se multipliant." In consequence, Roger notes, "...Si, dans chaque espèce, 'l'empreinte originaire subsiste en entier dans chaque individu,' 'aucun de ces individus,n'est cependant semblable en tout à un autre individu, ni par conséquent au modèle dont il porte l'empreinte.' Affirmation importante, car elle ruine toute définition de l'espèce comme collection d'êtres absolument semblables. Il serait donc tentant d'y voir l'origine d'une pensée 'populationelle' au sens d'Ernst Mayr." Again (p. 440): "...parti du simple

renouvellement des forme, Buffon est passé à leur dégénération, à leur diversification, à leur multiplication."

21. Buffon, *Natural History*, V, 150; IX, 45 ff.

22. Lenoir, *Strategy of Life*; Pietro Corsi, *The Age of Lamarck.Evolutionary Theories in France 1790-1830*, Jonathan Mandelbaum, tr. (Berkeley, Los Angeles, London: University of California Press, 1988). The Italian edition of Corsi's work (Bologna: Il Mulino, 1983) bore the title *Oltre Il Mito. Lamarck e le scienze naturali del suo tempo*.

23. Quoted in Edward S. Russell, *Form and Function. A Contribution to the History of Animal Morphology* (Chicago and London: University of Chicago Press, 1982), p. 51, citing J. W. Goethe, *Werke*, J. G. Cotta, ed. 20 v. (Stuttgart and Tuebingen: 1806-1819), IX, p. 490.

24. Lenoir, *Strategy of Life*, chaps. 1, 2, 4, 6.

25. Lenoir (p. 270) quotes von Baer's praise of Darwin for having discovered and stressed the importance of variability in plants and animals, adding: "But variability was not the only biological phenomenon one could focus upon for the purposes of constructing a model of evolutionary change, and indeed von Baer did not think it was even the most natural candidate. Rather, first consideration seemed more appropriately to belong to embryogenesis and development processes in general." In Mayr's view this latter approach involved a misguided effort to transfer the teleological aspect of ontogeny to the cosmos as a whole: "Because the development of the chick embryo...was so clearly goal-directed, therefore the universe as a whole and all historical processes in it...had to have some unknown goal-directed manner." One should not overlook the influence of Naturphilosophie on von Baer's thinking, however. S. J. Holmes quotes von Baer's discourse in 1834 entitled "The Most General Law of Nature in All Development" as follows: "Now we manifest only the evidences of the inadequacy of our notions of creation if we believe it would be easier to transform an ape into a man than to form man anew [i.e., by spontaneous generation]. Just as little can we explain the apes as being transformations of other creatures, and if once an ape or any other mammal is produced in whatever way it would not be more difficult, by a hair's breadth, to consider man to arise *de novo* without the form of reproduction. It all depends on whether the production of man does or does not belong as a necessary consequence in the series of thoughts whose presentation we see in the creation. If it belongs in this series man certainly so arose; if it does not belong—never." See Samuel J. Holmes, "K. E. von Baer's Perplexities Over Evolution," *Isis* 37 (1947), p. 10. Later in life, Lenoir observes, von Baer tried to conceive an evolutionary mechanism based on the phenomena of alternating generations as providing a model for discontinuous evolution, but with limited success because these phenomena were limited to invertebrates.

26. Adrian Desmond, *The Politics of Evolution. Morphology, Medicine, and Reform in Radical London* (Chicago and London: University of Chicago Press, 1989), pp. 405-406. See also the essays in James R. Moore, ed., *History, Humanity and Evolution. Essays for John C. Greene* (Cambridge: Cambridge University Press, 1989).

27. In his letter of May 20, Mayr points out that awareness of the struggle for existence in the organic world was not confined to Great Britain. This is true, but I am arguing that only in Britain did it take on "the aspect of a providential mechanism for generating improvement in nature and society."

28. In his criticisms of my essay Mayr is insistent that, whatever he may have said in his *Growth of Biological Thought*, it is not philosophy as such which he regards as being displaced by evolutionary science but rather physicalist philosophy of science. He writes (May 20, 1991): Reading journals like the *Philosophy of Science* is a depressing experience. The authors deal almost exclusively with how to explain things, whether a semantic or syntactic approach is more fruitful, whether refutation is the only way to approach truth, etc. etc. They simply no longer deal with the actual contents of what used to be the major preoccupation of the philosophers. And when I say that science has emancipated itself from philosophy, this is what I have in mind....What I have criticized, indeed attacked, is the philosophical establish-ment....And why do seven or eight philosophers (including Nagel, Hempel, Carnap, even Popper up to 1976) refer to philosophy of science when they dealt only with logic, mathematics, and physics? You lump all philosophy together. I hope that there will be a good philosophy of biology in due time, and to bring us to this end has been the major objective of my recent writings." For a good summary of his main contentions as a philosopher of science Mayr refers me to David L. Hull's "Ernst Mayr on the Philosophy of Biology: A Review Essay" in *Historical Methods* 23 (1990), pp. 42-45. The present essay is not a critique of Mayr's philosophy of science but only of the historical generalizations he makes in his *Growth of Biological Thought*, including those about science and "philosophy".

10

SCIENCE, PHILOSOPHY, AND METAPHOR IN ERNST MAYR'S WRITINGS

Like Sir Julian Huxley, Ernst Mayr ranks as a founding father of the neo-Darwinian synthesis in evolutionary biology. Now in his nineties and still very active, Mayr upholds a world view similar in many ways to Huxley's, but different in important respects.[1] Like Huxley, he looks to science, and especially to evolutionary biology, to loosen the grip of traditional religions and idealistic philosophies on modern thought and to provide a scientific basis for a new ethics, a new secular faith, and a new image of humankind.[2] But whereas for Huxley this ethical-religious motive dominated nearly everything he wrote, in Mayr's case the scientific impulse toward discovering and expounding a new version of the theory of evolution by natural selection, giving pride of place to the naturalist-systematist, has been the driving force. Whereas Huxley gave up a secure position in a great university in order to write books and essays designed to propagate a new faith based on Darwinian biology, Mayr turned to the history and philosophy of biology only in his later years. Nevertheless, as we shall see, Mayr and Huxley have much in common both as evolutionary biologists and as advocates of a neo-Darwinian view of man and nature.

Like Huxley, Mayr is anti-reductionist and anti-determinist and at the same time anti-vitalist, anti-teleologist, anti-theist, and anti-creationist. Like Huxley, he looks to Charles Darwin as the thinker who developed a scientific world view fatal to both mechanistic reductionism and creationist finalism and who laid the groundwork for a historico-organicist conception of evolutionary development. Like Huxley, he believes that science has become increasingly

independent of religion and philosophy: "Nothing signaled the
emancipation of science from religion and philosophy more
definitely than the Darwinian revolution."[3] Like Huxley, Mayr
believes that science can supply a description of reality capable of
providing an adequate basis for ethics. It should be interesting,
therefore, to analyze Mayr's writings, especially his volume of
essays entitled *Evolution and the Diversity of Life*, his explicitly
philosophical work *Toward a New Philosophy of Biology*, his *The
Growth of Biological Thought*, and the concluding chapter of
Animal Species and Evolution, to see whether he succeeds in
maintaining these positions or whether, like Huxley, he encounters
difficulties in the undertaking. First we shall examine his attack on
teleology, then his refutation of mechanism and of atomistic
reductionism, then his exposition of the organicist-historical
alternative to these with respect both to functional and to
evolutionary biology, and, finally, his conception of neo-Darwinian
biology as providing a new image of humans, a new idea of science,
and a new guide to ethics.

PART I—THE ATTACK ON TELEOLOGY

Traditional teleological interpretations of biological phenomena
Mayr regards as discredited holdovers from an age when theology
and idealistic philosophies dominated biological thinking. In
contending against them he appeals to concepts of reality, science,
nature, causation, mechanism, and materialism characteristic of
positivistic philosophies of science. Ontologically he holds that
"only individual phenomena have reality," "only the variation is
real"; "the ideal type does not exist." (Mayr makes no distinction
between being real and existing.) Rejecting "any mixing of
philosophy and science" in favor of "truly objective and
uncommitted science," he dismisses vitalism and finalism as non-
scientific ideologies involving "unverifiable theological and
metaphysical doctrines." Scientific explanations, he declares, must
be "mechanistic and causal." Teleological explanations are "noncausal"; causes must be "material" and "not in the future," whether

in functional biology (embryology, anatomy, and physiology) or in evolutionary biology.[4]

Thus, in molecular biology, the seemingly goal-directed character of embryological development, to explain which Aristotle postulated an immaterial *eidos*, or form, is explained "mechanistically" by the controlling action of the genetic program "represented by" the nucleic acids in the DNA. This program, says Mayr, is translated into growth processes through "appropriate signals" to each cell lineage in the organism "in order to provide it with the mixture of molecules, which it needs to carry out its assigned tasks."[5] This is rather teleological language, Mayr concedes, but it is "objective and free of metaphysical content" because the DNA is "something material and [existing] prior to the initiation of the process" and hence "consistent with a causal explanation." Likewise, the marvelous adaptations of plants and animals, which led Aristotle to imagine final causes, have been explained "mechanistically" by Darwin's theory of natural selection.[6]

Turning to evolutionary biology, Mayr again sets out to discredit teleology in all its traditional forms, classifying these as cosmic teleology, belief in final causes, and natural theology. By "natural theology" Mayr seems to mean primarily, if not exclusively, the static design argument advanced by John Ray, William Paley, and others to explain what Mayr calls "the beautiful adaptation of organisms, their adjustment to each other, their well-organized interdependence, and indeed the whole harmony of nature." Darwin's *Origin of Species*, writes Mayr, "amounted to the proposal to replace the hand of the Creator by a purely material and mechanical process," a proposal Mayr heartily endorses.[7] The exquisite adaptations of organisms are now seen to be the "automatic" result of genetic variation, struggle for existence, and differential survival and reproduction. They are to be explained, not by invoking final causes or divine wisdom, but by an historical analysis of the selective pressures exerted by the changing environment in relation to the varying forms thrown up in biopopulations by genetic mutation and recombination.

"Cosmic teleology" Mayr defines variously as "the belief that there is a force immanent in the world which guides it toward a final goal or at least to ever greater perfection" and "the belief that the world was established toward an end or was still moving toward an objective either by the guiding hand of a Creator or by secondary causes."[8] These beliefs he rejects on the ground that science has been unable to discover any natural law or any "proper program" which could make such a cause scientifically meaningful and believable. Apparently he has in mind discovering something analogous to the apparent teleology, rooted in the chemical properties of DNA, which science finds in the phenomena studied by functional biologists, or, possibly, something analogous to the gravitational law which seems to control the motions of the planets. By these same analogies, however, such a program or law, if actually discovered, would not, in Mayr's view, be teleological but only "teleonomic" (apparent teleology) or "teleomatic" (like physical laws).

In the *Origin of Species* Darwin represented the system of processes he called "natural selection" as a system of secondary causes" by which the Creator was bringing about adaptation and improvement in nature, insuring that "all corporeal and mental endowments will tend to progress towards perfection," but Mayr will have none of this. A final cause, he writes, must be "a cause responsible for the orderly reaching of a preconceived ultimate goal."[10] But the process of natural selection, described variously by Mayr as "a purely material and mechanical process," a "probabilistic process," "capricious," "haphazard," and "opportunistic," gives no evidence of guiding organisms toward a preconceived ultimate goal. It has indeed produced "enormous evolutionary progress in...many phyletic lines, whether that leading to the highest mammals and birds, to the social insects, to orchids, or to giant trees, but it has not done so in the orderly, straight-line manner one would expect if a final cause were at work. In that case, Mayr argues, "one should find far more perfection in nature than one actually encounters." "There is not even a trace of...any final cause because perfection is simply the product of the *a posteriori* process of natural selection."[11] This process, Mayr adds (quoting Darwin in support), is analogous to the slow perfecting of human technology by the uncoordinated activities of isolated inventors and the competition of their devices in the market place.

Mayr's strategy in the foregoing arguments seems clear. He begins by insisting that teleology requires orderly movement toward a preconceived goal, just as in "teleonomic" processes there is "some endpoint, goal, or terminus which is foreseen in the program that regulates the behavior." He then argues that, since the evolution of plants and animals shows no sign of being directed toward a specific end, and since ninety-nine percent of species become extinct, evolution cannot be teleological in character. "A discussion of legitimately teleological phenomena would be futile," Mayr concludes, "unless evolutionary processes are eliminated from consideration."[12]

In consequence, Darwin's view of natural selection as a system of secondary causes designed to produce adaptation and improvement must be rejected, Mayr argues, because natural selection does not involve "the orderly reaching of a preconceived ultimate goal." Likewise F. J. Ayala's contention that evolution is teleological "in the sense of being directed toward the reproduction of DNA codes of information which improve the reproductive fitness of a population in the environments where it lives" and C. R. Waddington's argument that natural selection insures "an increase in the efficiency of the biosystem as a whole in finding ways of reproducing itself" are rejected because they invoke broadly generalized ends like survival and reproductive success rather than "definite and specified goals."[13] Mayr concedes that the "end" of end-directed activity may sometimes be the maintenance of the *status quo*, but he is not willing to regard the maintenance of adaptation amid changing circumstances as a definite and specified goal of evolution. Even the progressive adaptation evident to Mayr in evolutionary progress toward "ever greater perfection" does not qualify as teleological in his terms because it is the unintended result of material processes devoid of any goal-directed program or controlling law; moreover, this result is less perfect than would be expected from a teleological process.

By "perfection" Mayr, like Darwin, usually means perfect adaptation to circumstances, perfect fitness for survival, although sometimes he defines it as optimal efficiency of the biosystem in utilizing ecological resources: "...in a perfectly designed world all resources ought to be utilized with optimal efficiency."[14] In either case, writes Mayr, evolution fails to achieve perfection. There are unutilized woodpecker niches in the forests of New Guinea, and the wholesale extinction of species in the course of evolution shows how limited is the power of natural selection to maintain or improve the adaptability of species or lineages indefinitely.[15] Unlike a truly teleological force or cause, natural selection, the blind *deus-in-machina*, waits for variation to occur and then "rewards" the organisms that survive, certifying their momentary excellence *a posteriori* without guaranteeing the survival of their kind at any future date. The reward of survival is the opportunity to struggle for continued survival, a reward that goes to the offspring, not to the original survivors. "Natural selection rewards past events, that is the production of successful recombinations of genes, but does not plan for the future."[16] Yet it produces "ever greater perfection."

Mayr's term "perfection" is ambiguous. If it means nothing more than perfect adaptation to local circumstances, humans are no more perfect than the amoebae—probably less so in terms of their chances of survival and reproduction for millions of years. As for the biosystem as a whole, the species *Homo sapiens* is rapidly increasing the number of unoccupied niches in the world by its progressive extermination of other species. When Aristotle spoke of more and less perfect animals, he had in mind something more than capacity for survival and reproduction. Man was pre-eminent by virtue of his reason, and human reason was pre-eminent by virtue of its likeness to divine reason. Neo-Darwinian biologists have no such philosophical justification for assigning degrees of perfection. Like Aristotle, they sense the qualitative difference between humans and other animals, but their philosophy of nature precludes their finding any basis for human superiority other than likelihood of survival and reproduction—a very dubious basis in the present state of the world.

As in the case of "perfection," Mayr's discussion of evolutionary "advance," or "progress," displays a marked ambivalence. He is determined to vindicate the idea of evolutionary progress, but not in such a way as to make room for the operation of final causes. To those biologists who reject the concept of progress as being incompatible with "a strictly opportunistic competitive struggle" and the continued existence of "lower" forms of life, Mayr answers:

> ...who can deny that overall there is an advance from the prokaryotes that dominated the living world more than three billion years ago to the eukaryotes with their well organized nucleus and chromosomes as well as cytoplasmic organelles; from the single-celled eukaryotes to metaphytes and metazoans...; within the metazoans from ectotherms that are at the mercy of the climate to the warm-blooded endotherms, and within the endotherms from types with a small brain and low social organization to those with a very large central nervous system, highly developed parental care, and capacity to transmit information from generation to generation?[17]

But when it comes to defining the nature and criteria of evolutionary progress and determining how it occurs, Mayr encounters difficulties. Movement toward a hominid status will not do as a criterion, he concludes, since diversification is the predominant characteristic of evolution and most phyletic lines have shown no tendency to diverge toward the hominid type. Nor will Huxley's conception of a succession of dominant groups leading to man suffice; insects and vascular plants are as dominant as man, if not more so. As for structural complexity, trilobites and placoderms were more complex and specialized than modern man. The only objective criteria of progress, Mayr concludes, are (1) parental care, which makes possible the transmission of learned behavior and information, and (2) an enlarged central nervous system, which makes possible speech and culture, "setting man quite aside from all other living organisms." And why are these criteria "objective?" Because these traits are "of considerable value in the struggle for existence."[18]

Thus "progress," like "perfection," boils down to capacity to survive and reproduce. The theory of evolution by natural selection knows no other criterion. Survival-with-reproduction is the *summum bonum* of neo-Darwinian biology. The plants and animals that are "better than," "improved upon," other plants and animals are better, more improved, because they have a better chance of surviving and reproducing. Judged by this criterion, it is by no means clear that human beings, with their large central nervous systems and their need for parental care in infancy, are more likely to survive and reproduce during the next million years than bacteria, fungi, or insects. The truth is, of course, that neo-Darwinian biologists, like other men and women, consider human beings higher that bacteria and insects for reasons that have nothing to do with likelihood of survival and reproduction. But their philosophy of science has no room for value judgements except the implicit judgment that it is better for an organism to live and reproduce than to die, a judgment which is not always true for human beings. As scientists, evolutionary biologists can say of the idea of progress what Pierre Simon de Laplace said of the idea of God: "I have no need of that hypothesis." But, as human beings who seek some structure of meaning capable of guiding and inspiring action and who at the same time reject traditional structures of meaning, they stand in urgent need of that hypothesis. How else are they to make sense of human life and their own activity as scientists?

In the end, Mayr's discussion of evolutionary progress remains incomplete and inconclusive. Like Darwin, he rejects any idea of "necessary progression" in evolution. "Seeming progress," he declares, is a long-term, overall result of competition within and between species, especially the latter.

> An individual organism competes not only with the members of its own species but 'struggles for existence' also against members of other species. And this process [the latter] is probably the greatest source of evolutionary progress....Each newly formed species, if it is evolutionarily successful, must represent, in some way, evolutionary progress.[19]

But if every new species that manages to survive and reproduce represents progress, there *is* necessary progression in evolution by natural selection: "Any successful new species is thus...an advance over previously existing ones."[20]

Mayr's idea of progress through "evolutionary inventions" is extremely vague. An evolutionary invention may be "an improvement in its [the organism's] digestive physiology or its nervous system or its lifestyle or any other of the countless ways by which the so-called 'higher' organisms differ from the lower ones"—in short, anything that, in retrospect, is seen to characterize the "higher" organisms. But what makes the "higher" organisms higher? Mayr does not say. He argues only that evolutionary progress, however defined, does not require any "finalistic agent."

> Progressive changes in the history of life are neither predictable nor goal-directed. The observed advances are haphazard and highly diverse....Evolutionary trends are rarely rectilinear...each evolutionary line goes its own way, and evolutionary progress can be defined only in terms of that particular lineage....On the other hand, many evolutionary lines have displayed no evidence of progress in hundreds of thousands or millions of years, and yet they have survived to the present day, as the archaebacteria and other prokaryotes. Progress thus is not at all a universal aspect of evolution, as it ought to be if evolution were generated by final causes.[21]

Thus, the argument reduces to Mayr's preconceived ideas as to what would constitute evidence of teleology in evolution: not the maintenance of adaptation in the biosystem as a whole; not the emergence of teleonomic systems in which "the existence of some endpoint...is foreseen in the program that regulates the behavior;" not the "executive structures" which "facilitate" goal-directed behavior; not the "ever greater perfection" displayed in the evolution of phyletic lines; not the emergence of human beings capable of searching out the history of the cosmos. None of these things. And why not? Because, Mayr argues, science can discover no program or law which controls or directs these developments; because, if what has evolved was intended to evolve, those results (and much better ones) could have been achieved more efficiently by a truly intelligent agent; because scientific theories about why things happened the way they did eliminate the need for any other explanation.

To which the teleologists might reply that scientific explanations are not total explanations; that, since finite minds cannot know what purposes an infinite mind might have, they are not in a position to judge the appropriateness of the apparent means to the supposed ends; and, finally, that since Darwinian biology offers no vision of "perfection" other than fitness to survive and reproduce, it is poorly equipped to say whether, in any general sense, the perfection observed in the living world is sufficient or not. Darwin was well aware of the imperfections of natural selection as a *deus-in-machina*, but he could not help admiring the "endless forms most beautiful and most wonderful" which it had produced in accordance with laws established by the Creator.

Oddly enough, although Mayr is hostile to any suggestion of teleology in evolutionary science, he continually uses highly teleological language in describing evolution by natural selection. The "real function" of mutation, he writes, is the replenishment of the gene pool. The "function" of isolating mechanisms is "to prevent interspecific courtship." Reproductive isolation is a "method of guaranteeing evolutionary success." Biological species were "invented" in the course of evolution as a "method" of preventing unsuccessful gene combinations from occurring. Natural selection, although a "purely statistical phenomenon" without any aim, can nevertheless improve adaptation continually until it seems "as perfect as if it were the product of design." It can "remodel proteins in order to improve interactions." It does its best to favor the production of genetic programs "guaranteeing behavior that increases fitness." But it can "fail" when the "right genes" are not available for selection.[22] Apparently, Mayr is torn between his admiration for the wonderful accomplishments of natural selection in producing ever increasing adaptation, efficiency, and improvement and his concern lest these results be taken as proofs of the designing intent of some "outside agency."

PART II—MAYR CONTRA THE REDUCTIONISTS

When Mayr turns from his creationist-teleologist foes to confront his reductionist opponents, a rather different picture emerges. Reductionists, it appears, are of two kinds: (1) "physicalists" who attempt to reduce biology to physics and chemistry, and (2) mathematical population geneticists who reduce evolution to changes in gene frequencies brought about by the action of natural selection on individual genes and the traits they control. Against the physicalists Mayr adduces (1) the peculiar nature of individual organisms and species and (2) the peculiar character of the processes by which biopopulations evolve new forms and properties. Evolution, writes Mayr, involves the emergence of constellations of matter organized in such a way as to display properties not found in the inorganic world, and these organisms have the capacity to evolve ever new properties and abilities through a process of multiplication, variation, and differential reproduction that has no counterpart in the inorganic world. The same genetic codes which control the development of the visible organism and thereby give the lie to vitalism and finalism also give the lie to theoretical reductionism. For these genetic programs have powers and properties unknown to inorganic matter, which knows nothing of information storage and genotype-phenotype distinctions. Moreover, they give rise to organisms exhibiting goal-directed activity, qualitative differences, and individuality, properties unlike anything in inanimate nature. Biopopulations composed of unique individuals are themselves like individuals. They differ from classes of inanimate objects "not only in their propensity for variation but also in their internal cohesion and their spatio-temporal restriction." "There is nothing in inanimate nature that corresponds to biopopulations."[23] Finally, the gene pools of these biopopulations undergo slow change by processes of variational evolution entirely different from the transformations known to physics and chemistry. The processes producing these changes, Mayr adds, are the ultimate causes of biological evolution. They can be studied and comprehended, not by searching for causal laws of the kind known to physical scientists, but only by historical analysis of the complex interplay of chance and anti-chance factors in the interactions of organisms and their environments, an interplay so complicated as to preclude prediction of its outcome. "There is nothing in the physical sciences that corresponds to the biology of ultimate causations," Mayr concludes.[24]

Strange to say, the genetic code plays a dual role in Mayr's double warfare against mechanistic reductionists on the one hand and vitalists and finalists on the other. Against the vitalist-finalist camp the genetic code conceived as having originated mechanistically by ordinary chemical processes, serves as a mechanistic explanation of embryological development in terms of chemical properties and reactions that leave no room for entelechies, vital forces, or final causes. Against the physicalists, however, the genetic code serves to distinguish organic from inorganic phenomena both by its capacity for self-replication and for initiating and controlling goal-directed development and behavior and also by its peculiar mode of undergoing slow transformation through variational and selective processes of a kind unknown in inanimate nature.

In the evolutionary process, says Mayr, "new properties and capacities *emerge* at higher hierarchical levels and can be explained only in terms of the constituents at those levels."[25] The scientific understanding of this process, Mayr insists, requires a new kind of science, a science comparable in scope, explanatory power, and factual support to physical science but demanding "a broader recognition of stochastic processes, a pluralism of causes and effects, the hierarchical organization of much of nature, the emergence of unanticipated properties at higher hierarchical levels, the internal cohesion of complex systems," and the like.[26]

Thus, in his struggle against the physicalists Mayr becomes committed to a philosophy of nature and of biological science involving ideas of creativity, emergent properties, levels of being, hierarchical organization, and the internal cohesiveness of genotypes and phenotypes—ideas frequently invoked by writers who describe themselves as vitalists or teleologists. How, then, is Mayr to dissociate himself from these writers? How can he adduce the goal-directed activities of animals as an argument against the mechanists without committing himself to some kind of teleology in nature? If he concedes goal-directed activity in functional biology, how can he exclude it from evolutionary biology?

To resolve the dilemma with respect to functional biology Mayr invokes concepts and terminology borrowed from cybernetics and information theory. Like a computerized robot, organisms are said to be programmed in the DNA to develop and behave in certain ways, hence their development and behavior are not teleological but "teleonomic." There is an apparent purposiveness in these activities, but it is a "mechanistic purposiveness."[27] Thus, Mayr adopts the mechanist position with respect to functional biology. But this resolution of the dilemma is not without its difficulties. The mechanist may be somewhat mollified by Mayr's acknowledgement of "constitutive reductionism" in the realm of functional biology, but at the same time be perplexed as to why the materialistic mechanism of the genetic program should then be adduced as evidence of the incommensurability of organic and inorganic phenomena. As for the finalists and vitalists, they may be inclined to question the analogy between an organism and a computerized robot. The information in the "blueprint" of the computer is put into the computer by an intelligent being for a definite purpose. Where is the analogous intelligence in the case of the organism? Has Mayr really solved Aristotle's problem of the teleological aspect of living beings or has he only rephrased it in computer jargon? In any case, it is clear that Mayr chooses to base his argument against mechanistic reductionism on the nature and processes of evolutionary rather than functional biology, yet without relinquishing entirely his argument from the peculiar goal-directed, holistic, and hierarchical character of organic development and activity.

Moving, to the seemingly safer ground afforded by evolutionary biology, Mayr sets out to show that, however mechanistic the controlling action of genetic codes may be, the processes by which they undergo slow change (with consequent changes in the corresponding phenotypes) are totally different from those known to physicists and chemists and hence irreducible to physical and chemical laws and models of explanation. In developing this line of argument Mayr resorts to a strategy he has found useful in combating the teleologists; he calls attention to the unpredictability of organic evolution, an unpredictability arising from the important role played by chance factors, which "interfere with the superficially so deterministic process of selection."[28] These factors, he insists, operate not only in the genetic lottery which takes place during sexual reproduction but also in the development of the fertilized egg in interaction with its internal and external environment, as well as in the stochastic processes characteristic of populations of finite size, including genetic drift and the effects of linkage. "It is thus evident that a considerable percentage of differential survival and reproduction is not the result of ad hoc selection but rather of chance."[29]

Looking at the whole course of evolution on the planet Earth, Mayr is struck by its inherent unpredictability and improbability. To support life, he writes, a planet "must be just the right distance from the sun, have the right temperature, a sufficient amount of water, a sufficient density to be able to hold an atmosphere, a protection against damaging ultraviolet radiation, and so forth. Furthermore, every planet changes in the course of its history, and the sequence of changes has to be just right."[30] Presumably, on Mayr's view, the existence of such a planet as we inhabit was a cosmic accident, but even supposing the occurrence of myriad other accidents of the same kind, the evolution of intelligent life on those planets could not be predicted, Mayr argues. Indeed, it would be highly improbable.

> ...the origin of a new taxon is largely a chance event. Ninety-nine of 100 newly arising species probably become extinct without giving rise to descendant taxa. And the characteristic of any new taxon is to a large extent determined by such chance factors as the genetic composition of the founding population, the special internal structure of its genotype, and the physical as well as biotic environment that supplies the selection forces of the new species population....There were probably more than a billion species of animals on earth, belonging to many millions of separate phyletic lines, all living on this planet earth which is hospitable to intelligence, and yet only one of them succeeded in producing intelligence.[31]

A similar argument is then turned against those mathematical population geneticists, typified by Sir Ronald Fisher, who reduce natural selection to changes in gene frequencies, the fitness of any gene being given by its rate of increase in successive generations, and who represent the process of natural selection as "a strictly deterministic optimization process." Like the physicalists, Mayr argues, these biologists overlook the important role that chance plays in the process.

> In a group of sibs it is by no means necessarily only those with the most superior genotypes that will reproduce. Predators mostly take weak or sick prey individuals, but not exclusively, nor do localized natural catastrophes...kill only inferior individuals. Every founder population is largely a chance aggregate of individuals, and the outcome of genetic revolutions, initiating new evolutionary departures, may depend on chance constellations of genetic factors. There is a large element of chance in every successful colonization. When multiple pathways toward the acquisition of a new adaptive trait are possible, it is often a matter of a momentary constellation of chance factors as to which one will be taken....[32]

But although Mayr finds "chance" a convenient means of fending off mechanistic determinists and Fisherian optimizers, he is not prepared to adopt Jacques Monod's view that evolution is a product of chance and necessity. Rejecting Monod's "Epicureanism," Mayr seeks to define an alternative to the ancient dichotomy chance-or-necessity without conceding anything to the finalists and vitalists. The theory of natural selection, he argues, provides just such a *tertium quid*.[33] Natural selection broadly conceived, says Mayr, is a two-stage process involving (1) the production of genotypic and phenotypic variants and (2) the differential survival and reproduction of phenotypes and their associated genotypes. In the first stage, chance (defined as "the incidental byproduct of stochastic processes,"[34]) prevails, but in the second stage (described by Mayr as "natural selection proper") selective "forces," or "pressures," come into play, introducing an "anti-chance" factor into evolution. The organisms which survive and reproduce do so, not by happenstance, but because they are better adapted to environing circumstances than other members of the same population and competing individuals of rival populations. The possession of the features which make them "better adapted" is chance in the sense that the genetic lottery which produces these genotypes and corresponding phenotypes takes place without reference to the terms of survival dictated by the environment, but the survival and reproduction of certain ones of these organisms is anti-chance because it is related probabilistically to the possession of traits satisfying those terms. The overall result of these interactions between organisms and their environments, Mayr concludes, is a "creative process" unlike anything observable in the inanimate world, a process which generates not only novelty but, in the long run, something worthy to be called "progress."[35]

Despite his rejection of the dichotomy chance-or-necessity Mayr seems at times reduced to these alternatives. There are, he states, "only two evolutionary mechanisms as possible causes of evolutionary change including adaptation: chance and selection forces."[36]

> Almost any change in the course of evolution might have resulted by chance. Can one ever prove this? Probably never. By contrast, can one deduce the probability of causation by selection? Yes, by showing that the possession of the respective feature would be favored by selection. It is this consideration which determines the approach of the evolutionist. He must first attempt to explain biological phenomena and processes as the product of natural selection. Only after all attempts to do so have failed is he justified in designating the unexplained residue tentatively as a product of chance.[37]

The terms "selection forces" and "selection pressures" bring to mind the idea of physical necessity. But what are these "forces" and "pressures?" They are certainly not forces and pressures in any sense known to physicists. They are metaphors indicating certain aspects of the ecological situations in which populations of organisms find themselves. Some of these organisms survive to reproductive age; others do not. Among those that survive to reproductive age, some are more successful in leaving progeny than others. The next generation of a given population will thus have a gene pool and corresponding phenotypic features different in some respects from those characterizing the parental population. There has been no selection, but only differential reproduction. The concept of "selection" is introduced by the evolutionary biologist to indicate the putative reason for the observed differential, namely the possession by the surviving, reproducing organisms of certain traits which are known, or assumed, to have conferred a competitive advantage in the struggle for life. The successful organisms are then said to have survived because they were "better adapted" to the ecological situation than rival organisms. They survived because they had the traits in question, and their offspring had similar traits conferring similar advantages. And since, through mutation and genetic recombination, new traits continue to appear amid changing circumstances, some of which confer advantages on their possessors, still further but unpredictable changes in the descendant populations can be expected.

The physicalists cannot understand this process, says Mayr, because it cannot be reduced to a controlling law or proper program. Nor can the mathematical population geneticists explain it (1) because chance factors preclude conceiving it as a strictly deterministic optimization process, and (2) because natural selection acts on phenotypes, not genes, and both the organism and its underlying genotype are integrated wholes in which the genes interact and maintain genetic homeostasis. Why should all insects have three pairs of extremities and all spiders four pairs? Atomistic genetics cannot explain the stability of these master plans, Mayr declares. "There are evidently internal structures of the genotype which account for the conservation of the basic structure."[38] Reductionism, whether of the physicalist or the geneticist variety, is as impotent as teleology to explain the phenomena of evolution.

PART III—ORGANICIST-HISTORICAL BIOLOGY

What, then, is the true mode of explanation in evolutionary biology? In Mayr's view, the evolutionary biologist is essentially a historian seeking to explain evolutionary changes by constructing an historical scenario in which a wide variety of interacting factors play indeterminate roles. Mayr's scenario, in contrast to that of the Fisherian optimizers, places little emphasis on gradual phyletic evolution as a consequence of changes in gene frequencies, "the slow piling up of gene differences."[39] These processes, Mayr argues, can produce intra-specific variation (microevolution), but they cannot account for the emergence of new species, for the stability of structural plans, or for the evolutionary novelties that initiate macroevolutionary developments. To explain these, the biologist must take account of the cohesion of the genotype and the consequent necessity of its major restructuring in the genetic revolutions which occasionally occur in isolated founder populations accidentally separated from larger populations.

> The production of such peripherally isolated new species seems to proceed at a high rate, but most of these experiments of nature are unsuccessful....
> Occasionally, however, the genetic revolution in the founder population may lead to such a loosening up of constraints that the neospecies can enter a new adaptive zone or make some other kind of evolutionary innovation....
> Any new conquest of a major adaptive zone produces such a rapid chain-effect of improvements and extinctions that the new 'type' will soon be drastically discontinuous with its ancestors. Since the connecting links are of very short duration, and of limited geographic range, they are not likely ever to be found in the fossil record.[40]

Mayr regards this theory of genetic revolutions in founder populations followed by breakthroughs into new adaptive zones and widespread extinctions consequent on interspecific competition as a sufficient answer to those critics who doubt that macroevolution can be explained by selection and gradual evolution. In the past, he explains:

> It was generally recognized that regular variational evolution in the Darwinian sense takes place at the level of individual and population. However, that a similar variational evolution occurs at the level of species was generally ignored. Transformational evolution of species (phyletic gradualism) is not nearly as important in evolution as the production of a rich diversity of species and the establishment of evolutionary advance by selection among these species. In other words, speciational evolution is Darwinian evolution at a higher hierarchical level.[41]

All that was needed to bring about this conceptual revolution in evolutionary biology, Mayr adds, was "a less atomistic, less reductionist concept of the genotype" and a shift of emphasis from the purely genetic component…to the phenomena of natural history such as population, isolation, geographic location of populations, competition, and behavioral shifts."[42]

As yet, Mayr concedes, science cannot explain the supposed cohesion of the genotype or the nature of the supposed genetic revolutions. Moreover, the localized and geologically ephemeral character of the supposed macroevolutionary events renders highly unlikely any paleontological confirmation of their actual occurrence. Yet biologists should not despair, even though their science does not conform to the prototype established by Galileo, Newton, and their contemporaries. That prototype is inapplicable to evolutionary biology, Mayr insists:

> Although evolutionary phenomena are subject to universal laws…, the explanation of the history of a particular evolutionary phenomenon can be given only as a 'historical narrative.' This can be done only by inference. The most helpful procedure…is to ask…what is or might have been the selective advantage that is responsible for the presence of a particular feature.[43]

In the last analysis, then, Mayr's science of evolutionary change boils down to what has been called "the adaptationist program," namely, "to determine for a given trait whether it is the result of natural selection or of chance." This, in turn, reduces to showing that the trait in question did or did not confer greater fitness or adaptedness on the organisms possessing it. "If there is heritable variation in fitness in a population, evolution ensues automatically." Evolution, Mayr explains, is "a change in the adaptation and in the diversity of organisms," including both adaptive "vertical" change from generation to generation in a given population and, simultaneously, the "horizontal" splitting off of populations to form new species and, eventually, new higher taxa. Thus, "fitness" is an essential component of Mayr's theory of evolution by natural selection.

The fittest, or fitter, members of a given population are said to be "selected," but what qualities rendered them fitter can only be determined or guessed at after the fact. Selection, far from involving any element of choice, is "simply the fact that in every generation a few individuals...survive and are able to reproduce because these individuals happened to have a combination of characteristics that favored them under the constellation of environmental conditions they encountered during their lifetime."[44] The quality of "fitness" is imputed to the survivors as the cause of their survival and their consequent disproportionate contribution to the gene pool of the next generation, without which evolution would not take place.

But, in Mayr's view, making a disproportionate contribution to the gene pool of the next generation is not necessarily a proof of fitness, as mathematical population geneticists suppose. By reducing evolution to changes in gene frequencies these biologists make it impossible to distinguish between natural selection, in which *truly* fitter, better adapted individuals and species survive, and sexual selection, in which some individuals make a larger contribution to the gene pool not because they possess traits valuable for survival in the local circumstances but because they have characteristics that enable them to secure a disproportionate number of mates.[45] Survival-with-reproduction, says Mayr, is not a proof of fitness unless the traits responsible for it increase the capacity of the species to survive in a given environment. "A purely egotistical selection for reproductive success might favor the evolution of traits that do not add to fitness (as traditionally understood) but might actually make the species more vulnerable," as in the case of the gorgeous plumes of birds of paradise, the beautiful tail of the peacock, and the gigantic size of elephant seal bulls.[46] On the other hand: "A behavior program that guarantees instantaneous correct reaction to a potential food source...potential enemy,...or potential mate will certainly give greater fitness than a program that lacks these properties."[47] Depending on circumstances, the greater fitness of certain members of a population may be due to a single feature of the phenotype dependent on a single gene or to the "integrated selective value" of the phenotype and its underlying genotype as a whole. A species becomes adapted to its environment owing to the reproductive success of some of its members only insofar as that success results from their possessing traits useful for survival in particular circumstances and not from traits that give them an advantage in the mating game, unless these traits also have survival value for the species.

What, then, is "natural selection"? In Mayr's essays it is characterized variously as a principle, a fact, a theory, and a process. As to the principle, or concept, Mayr quotes Darwin: "The preservation of favorable variations and the rejection of injurious variations, I call Natural Selection."[48] The fact, presumably, is the fact of differential survival and reproduction. The theory is the hypothesis that certain members of a population survived and reproduced because they possessed characteristics favorable to survival in the existing circumstances. The process envisaged by the theory is called "selection," but there is no selection whatsoever. There is only the fact of differential survival-and-reproduction, which, in turn, is imputed to be the cause of "evolution," i.e., the gradual alteration of the character and diversity of populations and of their adaptation to changing circumstances.

This process is *a posteriori* (Mayr's term) in the sense that the biologist cannot predict which individuals will survive and reproduce, but also in the sense that "natural selection proper" is but the second stage of the more general process of evolution. According to Mayr:

> ...natural selection proper is only the second stage of a two-step process. The first step consists of the production of variation in every generation, that is, of suitable genetic or phenotypic variants that can serve as the material of selection, and this will then be exposed to the process of selection. This first step of variation is completely independent of the actual selection process, and yet selection would not be possible without the continuous restoration of variability...the second step, selection *sensu stricto*,...deals with the previously produced variation (*a posteriori*) and is not a process which itself produces variation.[49]

A very curious situation indeed, in which it is difficult to disentangle scientific fact and reasoning from the teleological language in which it is enmeshed. The process of sexual reproduction is said to produce "suitable" genetic or phenotypic variants which then "serve" as "material" to be "exposed" to the process of "selection." The first step is completely independent of the second, yet it produces suitable materials on which the process of the second step can operate to produce organisms suited to environmental circumstances. In actual fact, of course, organisms reproduce in greater numbers than the environment can sustain; their offspring survive and reproduce with varying success and thus contribute differentially to the make-up of the next generation, which as a result differs in some respects from that of the parental generation. As this process is repeated, changes of character take place in the population. It is the biologist who conceives the process by analogy to a manufacturing process which turns raw materials into products suited to the demands of the marketplace, with ever escalating improvements in the finished product as a consequence of unrelenting competition. Evolution, writes Mayr, limits in every generation the genetic endowment of the few survivors during sexual reproduction and thus creates abundant new genotypes, which are then tested in the next generation. Each individual is, so to speak, a new experiment that is tested for its fitness in the struggle for existence." [50]

The analogy between technological improvement in the competition of the marketplace and biological improvement in the struggle for existence has been a favorite one from Darwin onward, for it seems to suggest that evolution by natural selection must produce better, more efficient products *ad infinitum* in the long course of time. As Darwin put it in a letter to Charles Lyell in 1859:

No modification can be selected without it be an improvement or advantage. Improvement implies, I suppose, each form obtaining many parts or organs, all excellently adapted for their functions. As each species is improved, and as the number of forms will have increased, if we look to the whole course of time, the organic condition of life for other forms will become more complex, and there will be a necessity for other forms to become improved, or they will be exterminated; and I can see no limit to this process of improvement. [51]

Mayr seems to agree completely:

As I stated previously, each newly formed species, if it is evolutionarily successful, must represent, in some way, evolutionary progress: 'Each species is a biological experiment....And speciation, the production of new gene complexes capable of ecological shifts, is the method by which evolution advances. Without speciation there would be no diversification of the organic world, no adaptive radiation, and very little evolutionary progress. Any successful new species is thus, in a way, an advance over previously existing ones.' Darwin explains this as follows: 'But in one particular sense the more recent forms must, on my theory, be higher than the more ancient; for each new species is formed...by having some advantage in the struggle for life over other and preceding forms.'[52]

But how convincing is this argument and the accompanying analogy to technological improvement through economic competition? In the Darwin-Mayr version of evolutionary progress both the production of variants and the changes in the environment are random with respect to the needs of the organism in its struggle to survive and reproduce. In technological progress, however, the invented variants are not random with respect to the demands of the market place; indeed they are purposefully directed toward meeting those demands by increasing the efficiency with which a machine performs its assigned task. But what is the task or end of a biological improvement? "Improvement" consists in enlarged capacity to survive and reproduce in particular circumstances, not in some kind of generalized fitness to survive and reproduce in other unspecified environments, as Darwin seemed to imagine in the case of the replacement of Australian marsupials by European mammals. The theory of natural selection implies nothing with respect to relative fitness in competition with other organisms in other circumstances, past, present, or future. Its "improvements" are not additive, as Darwin and Mayr seem to suggest. That this is so is shown by the fact that relatively simple organisms like bacteria have a much longer record of survival and reproduction than mammals and will undoubtedly continue to flourish when human beings have disappeared from the face of the earth. Increased complexity of organization is no proof of higher status in the Darwinian world unless it confers increased likelihood of survival, and it would be a brave biologist who would maintain that complex forms have a better chance of this kind than simpler forms.

We conclude, then, that Mayr's organicist-historical revolution in evolutionary biology is not without its difficulties. Its organicism seems to consist largely in Mayr's insistence on the cohesive unity of the genotype and gene pool, a theoretical position directed against Fisherian optimizers and designed to elevate the role of field naturalists in evolutionary theory at the expense of geneticists. "Constitutive reductionism" is still conceded by Mayr with respect to embryological development, and there is nothing noticeably "organicist" about the processes, such as geographic isolation, inbreeding, and natural selection, Mayr envisages as bringing about genetic revolutions and consequent macroevolution.

As for historicalism, any science of past events, whether cosmological, biological, or cultural, is bound to be historical and based on inferences from present evidence. It can, at best, devise an historical scenario consistent with known facts and accepted theoretical principles. Cosmological history depends upon reasoning from the known laws of physics, Mayr's evolutionary history on reasoning based on the theory of natural selection and the current facts and principles of functional biology. As a science which includes human beings both as scientists and as objects of science, however, evolutionary biology suffers from an inevitable anthropocentricity despite its best efforts to the contrary.

PART IV–SCIENCE, VALUE, AND THE IMAGE OF MAN

From the foregoing discussion it appears that words like "progress," "improvement," "advance," "higher," "lower," "perfection," "fitness," and the like have a double meaning in the writings of evolutionary biologists. Scientifically, in Darwinian terms, they reduce to the likelihood of survival and reproduction in particular circumstances. Psychologically, at least with respect to animals, they are shot through with the presumption that human beings are the highest beings on earth, that animals rank in the scale of being in proportion as they approximate to human nature and that consequently evolution has involved progress toward higher forms of life, however haphazard that progress may seem from a human point of view. When challenged with the value-laden character of the normative terms they use, most biologists reply that these words can be reduced to their scientific meaning and hence are harmless.

Others, however, sensing a certain truth in the idea of biological progress, attempt to give it scientific status without admitting value judgments into science, but value judgments creep unacknowledged into their definitions of "progress," "higher," "lower," and the like.[53] It never seems to occur to Mayr or to anyone else to conclude that, whatever may be true in the philosophy of physics and chemistry, the philosophy of biology requires some kind of value premises, especially in the case of evolutionary biology, which claims to include the scientist him-or-herself within the scope of its generalizations and explanations.

In reality, however, the idea that science can in principle explain the scientists themselves in every aspect of their being is nonsensical because scientists, as scientists, stand outside the phenomena they seek to explain, and if those phenomena include knowing, self-conscious, valuing beings like themselves, they cannot avoid placing a high value on their existence. The knower is higher than the known unless the known is also a knower. In that sense all science is anthropocentric.

The main obstacle to constructing a set of value premises for biological science is the lack of a metaphysics capable of taking into account the value aspect of reality. Aristotle had a metaphysics of this kind and hence could make sense of concepts like "perfection." Alfred North Whitehead attempted to build such a metaphysics for our own time; Father Teilhard de Chardin did likewise. For Darwinians like Mayr, however, human beings and their values constitute an anomaly in the system of nature. Purposeful, self-conscious, value-oriented beings, they are nevertheless accidental products of processes devoid of aim or purpose. In a Darwinian world, reason is of no importance except as an instrument of survival and reproduction, an instrument by means of which the human species has multiplied and achieved dominion over other living beings, only to find its dominion menaced by the very faculty that made it possible.

But do scientists really believe that science is valuable only as a means of survival? They do not. The ethos which has guided and inspired science from the Greeks onward is grounded in the conviction that knowledge is valuable for its own sake, that truth ought to be pursued and proclaimed, come what may. The heroes of science are persons like Copernicus and Galileo and Darwin who clung to their vision of truth despite the opposition of popular opinion and the powers that be. But these value judgments make no sense in a world where survival and reproduction are the only criteria of value. Darwin was deeply moved by Victorian ideas of beauty, truth, and goodness. He recoiled from regarding the universe, and especially the nature of man, as products of chance and struggle for survival and reproduction. But science gave him no insight into a deeper reality. Instead, it assailed him with the "horrid doubt" whether the mind of man, so recently evolved from that of lower animals, could be trusted to know any reality other than that provided by science.[54]

The basic difficulty for Darwin and for many after him seems to have been the notion that scientific explanations are total explanations, that nature as known to science exhausts reality, whereas in truth science is only one way of grasping reality, and a limited way at that. Among evolutionary biologists Sewall Wright understood this truth. In his view, the primary reality for human beings was "the kind of knowledge provided to each person in his own stream of consciousness."

> Nothing [he wrote] could contrast more than the precise determinism of our knowledge of the external world when pains are taken to control conditions, and the fitful character and apparent freedom of choice of the stream of consciousness.

> The latter, nevertheless, is obviously the primary reality. The former is wholly derived from bits of the streams of consciousness of many observers and is restricted to those aspects, which can be communicated....Its restriction to the so-called primary properties of matter...contrasts with the richness of the stream of consciousness. Colors and sounds are reduced to wavelengths; sensations of heat and cold are reduced to readings on a thermometer; taste, smell, feel are ignored in precise formulations....

> Moreover, all of this common knowledge of the so-called primary properties is based on measurements in terms of units: centimeter, gram,

second, with operational definitions which are recipes for *voluntary* actions. Reality clearly consists primarily of streams of consciousness. This fact must take precedence over the laws of nature of physical science, even though it must be largely ignored in science itself.[55]

A similar argument applies to the abstractions of neo-Darwinian biology, summarized aptly by George C. Williams as "a cybernetic abstraction, the gene, and a statistical abstraction, mean phenotypic fitness."[56] The theory of natural selection does not purport to explain the existence of living beings. It presupposes their existence as going concerns and seeks to discover the processes by which they undergo changes of form and behavior and to construct as plausible a history of those changes as the available data and abstract theory permit. It makes no attempt to enter into the inner states of organisms, to see the world as they see it, to experience value as they experience it. As a human being the scientist appreciates the realization of value in the history of life; as a scientist he or she ignores this aspect of the historical reality because science provides no way of dealing with it.

From the Darwinian point of view, human beings are simply animals possessing a high degree of intelligence, which enables them to compete successfully with other organisms and proliferate at will. Biological science places no value on the human species as such. If one variety of the human species should out-propagate, out-fight, and exterminate other varieties, that would simply be a fact of natural history from a Darwinian point of view. The same would be true if human beings should bring about the destruction of their own species as a result of overpopulation, intraspecific warfare, and impoverishment of the biotic and physical environment. If, on the other hand, human beings should learn to live together peacefully and preserve a favorable environment for human and other life, that, too, would have no moral or esthetic significance from a strictly scientific point of view.

But that does not mean that the *philosophy* of biology cannot take account of the value aspect of reality by placing biology within the context of a general view of the world that relates the scientific way of grasping reality to other ways—the artist's way, the philosopher's way, the poet's way, the mystic's way, the common man or woman's way—and by recognizing that historically the pursuit of science has been grounded in a love of knowledge for its own sake, in a passion for truth which biological science can neither explain nor validate. But this cannot be done within a mechanistic context, nor is it possible within Mayr's "organicist" context, in which the development, functioning, and behavior of every organism are reduced to the chemical "translation" of a mechanistic "program," while the history of life is reduced to the interaction of the mechanistic genetic lottery with the equally mechanistic lottery of environmental change. What is "organicist" about either of these processes or about their presumed result? Organisms are said to "struggle" for existence, but the theory of natural selection takes no account of their struggles, it is interested only in the result, which is said to be the survival and reproduction of the fit, or fitter, or fittest. But, as we have seen, the theory says nothing about any substantive excellence in what survives and reproduces. All ideas of substantive excellence—"fitness," "improvement," "advance," "progress," and the like—are grafted on to the result by the scientist in his non-scientific role as an appreciator of value. Concerning the emergence of that role in the history of life the theory of natural selection has nothing to say. Indeed, it cannot even account for the existence of the scientist as a seeker after truth.

It was considerations of this kind that presumably led Julian Huxley, Sewall Wright, and other biologists to adopt a panpsychist view of the world, a view which led Wright to acknowledge the necessity of "dealing with the Universe as the world of mind, within which all subordinate minds must be included in some sense."

> The question is whether, at one extreme, the mind of the Universe is all-knowing and omnipotent, or at the other, it is merely that which is superimposed on the point-to-point interactions of the minds of the components as the integrating factor, in much the same relation as that of my mind to the minds of my cells and lower entities in the hierarchy of existence. As one concerned with the philosophy of science rather than philosophy in general, I must take the latter view, recognizing that there is a great deal that science does not and probably never can know.[57]

Thus, Wright found in panpsychism a general point of view which enabled him to recognize "that the only reality directly experienced is that of mind, including choice [and hence, presumably, value]; that mechanism is merely a term for regular behavior, and that there can be no ultimate explanation in terms of mechanism—merely analytic description," and at the same time to insist that analytic description of this kind be pushed as far as possible, but with the realization "that failure to accept the reality of choice, a fatalistic acceptance of absolute determinism, may lead to such slackening of individual and social effort as to bring about the end of civilization."[58] Wright found "real satisfaction" in discovering a philosophic point of view which could reconcile "the vast body of secondary but verifiable knowledge of the external world which constitutes science, with its necessarily deterministic and probabilistic interpretations," with "the primary but private knowledge which each of us has of his own stream of consciousness, more or less continually directed toward the finding of an acceptable course through the difficulties of the external world by means of voluntary actions."[59]

For Ernst Mayr, however, panpsychism is not a viable option. As has been seen, he inclines instead toward a philosophy of emergence: "…new properties and capacities *emerge* at higher hierarchical levels and can be explained only in terms of the constituents of those levels."[60] Among these emergent properties and capacities are those of the nucleic acids in the DNA molecules of living creatures, in which "the existence of some endpoint…is foreseen in the program that regulates the behavior" but which requires "translation" into growth processes through "appropriate signals" to each cell lineage "in order to provide it with the mixture of molecules which it needs to carry out its assigned tasks." At a higher hierarchical level mental properties and capacities emerge from combinations of material elements heretofore lacking these properties and capacities. At a still higher level emerge those capacities of language, rational thought, esthetic judgment, and moral deliberation which have the effect of "setting man quite aside from all other living organisms" and making possible the emergence of the scientist himself or herself.

What the underlying nature of reality must be to give rise to emergences like these, Mayr does not say. Somehow or other all these properties and capacities of the "substrate" of the world are perpetually there in potency, waiting for the lawbound transformations of valueless, purposeless, non-mental matter-energy to actualize them in its random combinations.[61] But, strange to say, if Mayr is right, they have been actualized only on one insignificant planet in a minor galaxy among millions of galaxies. The vast, unthinking, value-blind complex of matter-energy euphemistically called a "universe" by the only beings capable of conceiving it as such has become aware of itself, so to speak, in that peculiar form of human consciousness known as science, and it has done so by what Mayr calls "a sequence of improbabilities." It is, he declares, "a miracle that man ever happened."[62]

But what could be more implausible than this emergentist scenario? In one breath Mayr dismisses the Biblical miracles and tells his readers that Darwin, Ernst Haeckel, and T. H. Huxley exploded "the traditional anthropocentrism of the Bible and of the philosophers."[63] In the next, he pictures the evolution of mankind as unique, unrepeatable, and unpredictable and warns that the future of mankind is not something controlled by the laws of nature; rather "it is we humans ourselves who hold the fate of our species in our hands."[64] What a paradoxical situation for the chance product of a sequence of improbabilities!

Like Sir Julian Huxley, Mayr believes that neo-Darwinian biology has given us a new image of man, a new idea of science, and a new system of values.[65] Man, he declares, "is no longer a static being created within an equally static nature that is subservient to him." Instead, he is an evolved and evolving organism whose dominance over the rest of evolving life, established by competitive struggle, now threatens his own and their existence and, for some unexplained reason, imposes on him a moral responsibility to prevent this eventuality. Man, says Mayr, no longer has a soul, "something animals did not have," but he has a "spiritual life,"[66] which, so far as anyone knows, is also something animals do not have. Just when and how human beings acquired a spiritual life is never made clear. Was it when they acquired a large brain, or self-consciousness, or speech, or a knowledge of their own mortality, or the enjoyment of the beauty of nature, or "ethics based on decision making," or some combination of these attributes? Mayr does not say, but he offers some suggestions as to the origin of "human ethics" during the gradual evolution of *Homo sapiens* from his primate ancestors.[67]

Biologically speaking, Mayr explains, altruistic behavior is behavior which "benefits another organism, not closely related, while being apparently detrimental to the organism performing the behavior." Detrimental in what sense? In the sense that the altruistic individual's behavior lessens his or her chances of contributing to the gene pool of the next generation. But why must the recipient of the altruistic behavior be "not closely related" to the benefactor? Because, if the recipient shares the genotype of the benefactor, the beneficial sacrifice would be "egotistical" in the sense of increasing the "inclusive fitness" of the genotype in the struggle for existence [68] The theory of natural selection imputes no altruistic merit to any behavior which even indirectly promotes the spread of the benefactor's genotype. Mother-love and in-group versus out-group norms are strictly egotistical from a Darwinian point of view. Likewise, says Mayr, the moral norms and injunctions laid down in the Old Testament are "remnants of inclusive fitness altruism."[69] For his own part, however, Mayr concludes: "...I do not believe that inclusive fitness is all there is to human ethics."[70]

What, then, is the origin of "genuine ethics," "uniquely human ethics," as contrasted to "instinct altruism" or "inclusive fitness altruism?"[71] The rise of genuine ethics based on decision making ("perhaps the most important step in humanization") probably occurred, Mayr speculates, when some hominid group discovered that a group enlarged to include members not closely related to the main body "had a better chance of being victorious in a fight" than a group whose membership was confined to blood relatives. Those groups would be most successful which developed genetic mechanisms, analogous to the imprinting mechanisms observed by Konrad Lorenz in ducks, which insured that children would accept and internalize ethical norms and reinforcing religious dogmas conducive to group solidarity.[72] Thus the ethical system of each social group or tribe would be modified continuously by trial and error, success and failure, as well as by "the occasional modifying influence of certain leaders."[73] History shows, says Mayr, that "those behaviors will be preserved and those norms will have the longest survival that contribute most to the well-being of a cultural group as a whole." Without attempting to support this dubious historical generalization with evidence, Mayr concludes that moral norms are the result of cultural, not biological, evolution.[74]

At this point in an argument remarkably similar to Darwin's speculations in The *Descent of Man*, Mayr, like Darwin, comes face to face with the problem of the relativity of moral norms, each tribe or nation developing its own set of norms haphazardly. This must have been true of primitive tribes, Mayr concedes, but the striking similarity of the ethical maxims enjoined by the great religions of the world suggests that these norms must have been the product of "reason," not of random, separate cultural evolutions: "The norms announced by Moses or by Jesus in the Sermon on the Mount were surely to a large extent the product of reason"; "...the philosophers, prophets, or lawgivers responsible for these codes must have carefully studied their societies and...decided which norms were beneficial and which others were not."[75] With respect to the Ten Commandments, Mayr does not specify which ones were the product of reason and which were remnants of inclusive fitness altruism, nor does he explain what reasoning process might have led Jesus to conclude that the meek shall inherit the earth or that the pure in heart shall see God. Instead, he turns from the "inadaptive," "individualistic" ethics of the Judeao-Christian tradition to the new value system and the new age of man and science prescribed by reason reflecting on the lessons of neo-Darwinian biology.[76]

What are these lessons? First, we learn that "behavioral tendencies that are ultimately selfish vastly preponderate in the inherited component of our behavioral attitudes; selfish behavior was strongly favored by natural selection in pre-human days."[77] It follows that the "principal function" of cultural ethics is "to restrain the selfish impulses of the individual and to further the well-being of the community by the application of laws and customs." To this end the "excessive egocentricity and exclusive attention to the rights of the individual so characteristic of modern culture must be corrected by moral education stressing the individual's duties toward society, toward mankind, toward all living things and the environment that sustains them."[78]

> The dilemma we are facing is the conflict between traditional values and newly discovered values. Let me remind you of the conflict between man's right to unlimited reproduction and to the unlimited exploitation of the natural world, as against the needs of human posterity as well as the right to existence of the millions of species of wild animals and plants...if mankind and the world as a whole are to have a future, it will be necessary that we reduce the selfish tendencies in our ethics in favor of a higher regard for the community and for the *whole* of Creation.[79]

The basis of these newly discovered values, Mayr contends, is evolutionary biology as expounded by Darwin and revised in the neo-Darwinian synthesis.

> The individualistic admonition, "Love thy neighbor" is no longer sufficient; the new ethic must include also a concern for the community as a whole, it must include a concern for posterity....

> The theory of common descent places man squarely into the stream of life from the lowest bacteria and amoebas up to the most advanced plants and animals. Man no longer stands outside nature, no, man is part of nature. The evolutionist no longer holds the anthropocentric belief that the whole world was created for the benefit of man, and that man has a complete license to do anything with nature he pleases....Every creature is a unique and irreplaceable product of evolution, and man has no right whatsoever, to exterminate even the least of them.[80]

Thus Mayr, like Julian Huxley, winds up preaching a gospel of evolutionary humanism.

> Evolutionary humanism is a demanding ethics, because it tells every individual that somehow he has a responsibility toward mankind, and that this responsibility is or should be just as much part of his ethics as individual ethics. Every generation of mankind is the current caretaker not only of the human gene pool but indeed of all nature on our fragile globe.

> Evolution does not give us a complete codified set of ethical norms such as the Ten Commandments, yet an understanding of evolution gives us a

world view that can serve as a sound basis for the development of an ethical system that is appropriate for the maintenance of a healthy human society, and that also provides for the future of mankind in a world preserved by the guardianship of man.[81]

One cannot help admiring the humanistic values espoused by Mayr and Huxley, but at the same time one cannot suppress astonishment at the idea that the wellspring of these values is evolutionary biology, whether of the Darwinian or any other variety. Darwin himself, despite his obvious desire to reconcile evolution by natural selection with Victorian ideals and his own humanitarian feelings, drew rather a different social moral from his evolutionary theory than that drawn by Mayr and Huxley. Man, Darwin wrote, has risen to his present high estate through a severe competitive struggle, and if he is to continue to advance, must continue to remain subject to the same struggle:

> ...our natural rate of increase, though leading to many and obvious evils, must not be greatly diminished by any means. There should be open competition for all men; and the most able should not be prevented by laws or customs from succeeding best and rearing the largest number of offspring.[82]

As to the competition between the races of man in the struggle for existence, Darwin was prepared to "show fight on natural selection having done and doing more for the progress of civilization" than his correspondent William Graham was ready to admit.

> The more civilized so-called Caucasian races [Darwin wrote] have beaten the Turkish hollow in the struggle for existence. Looking to the world at no very distant date, what an endless number of the lower races will have been eliminated by the higher civilized races throughout the world.[83]

Despite his admiration for Darwin as a biologist and as a human being, Mayr cannot countenance the idea that the progress of civilization takes place by the progressive extermination of the "lower races." On the contrary, he insists that the ethics of the future must be based on "the unrestricted principle of equality between members of one's own group and outsiders."[84] Most people nowadays would agree with Mayr's views, not Darwin's, even though the theory of evolution by natural selection is more consistent with the latter. Mayr's egalitarianism obviously has sources other than evolutionary biology.

On the question of population increase Mayr shares Darwin's concern that the tendency of the less gifted members of society to multiply more rapidly than the gifted may retard or halt the improvement of the human stock (he suggests that the leveling off in the increase of human brain size and intelligence may have resulted from this cause), and he recommends that laws and customs be modified to encourage achievers to multiply their numbers. But he flatly rejects Darwin's injunction in favor of unrestricted population increase. He does so, moreover, not on the ground that human technology could never manage to provide food and other necessities for the multiplying hordes, but rather because the press of population in urban centers would impoverish the spiritual life of mankind. In a world crowded with billions of people, he writes:

> ...man's struggle and preoccupation with social, economic, and engineering problems would become so great, and the undesirable by-products of crowded cities so deleterious, that little opportunity would be left for the cultivation of man's highest and most specifically human attributes. Nor do I see where natural selection could enter the picture to halt this trend. Man may continue to prosper physically under these circumstances, but will he still be anywhere near the ideal of man?[85]

But if, as Mayr suggests, man does not live by bread alone, by what "ideal of man" shall he live? To suggest that evolutionary biology can answer this question is folly. As we have seen, Mayr's own values are not derived from science, but rather from the traditional sources of Western values: the philosophy and literature of Greece and Rome, the Judaeo-Christian tradition, and the Enlightenment, itself a compound of the first two sources. Evolutionary humanism bids us to be loyal to mankind, but what does neo-Darwinian biology tell us about mankind? It tells us that the biological species *Homo sapiens* is an accidental result of material processes having no aim or purpose; an intelligent animal whose intelligence is the accidental outcome of a series of competitive struggles among non-human and proto-human animals;

an ethical animal whose ethical norms are, except when modified by "reason," the product of group selection in the rivalry of groups, tribes, and nations; a species as vulnerable to extinction as any other species, and, indeed, tending to extinction as a result of its destructive impact on the global environment. Darwinian biology knows nothing of "reason", of an "ideal of man," of the "spiritual life" of mankind. It does, indeed, tell us that we are organically related to a long succession of other animals, but it says nothing of loyalty to the species or responsibility for the preservation of other species, or their "right to existence." On the contrary, it envisages intraspecific and interspecific competition and differential survival and reproduction within and between species as a necessary component of evolutionary "progress".

Undoubtedly ecological studies from Darwin onward have given mankind increased awareness of the interrelatedness of all living things and their environing circumstances, but the recent concern for the survival of the human species and the preservation of plant and animal species generally is not the result of evolutionary science. Nor is the "new image of science" as being "no longer conducted merely for its own sake" but rather "to build a better world" a product of Darwinian or any other biology. One does not need to be an evolutionary biologist to appreciate the devastating impact of science-based technology on the biosphere, or to lament the extinction of myriad creatures by the hand of man, or to proclaim the need to "reduce...selfish tendencies...in favor of a higher regard for the community and for the whole of Creation." The Christian doctrine of creation is an adequate basis for ethical commitments of this kind. Indeed, it is probably the ultimate source historically of Mayr's own commitment to altruism and the preservation of "the whole of Creation." Gerard Manley Hopkins put the matter succinctly in a poem that Darwin himself would probably have liked:

All things original, spare, strange,
Whatever is fickle, freckled, (who knows how?)
With swift, slow, sweet, sour, adazzle, dim;
He fathers-forth whose beauty is past change:
Praise him.[86]

We conclude, then, by admiring both Julian Huxley and Ernst Mayr for their outstanding contributions to biology and for the sincerity and elevated quality of their humanistic outlook on life, but at the same time questioning whether their deeply felt commitment to a humanistic ideal of man either originates in or finds rational justification in neo-Darwinian evolutionary biology. The sources of their resolute rejection of teleology and of all philosophies and religions that presuppose it are clear enough. In their view, teleology and creationism have impeded the progress of science, given moral and intellectual support to outmoded or unjust social programs and institutions, and erected obstacles to the rational solution of pressing problems. Like Auguste Comte, they look to science to provide a new moral basis for society, not realizing that science as currently understood and practiced ignores the value aspect of reality and hence is in no position to provide a moral basis for anything.

The pursuit of science presupposes many kinds of metaphysical, moral, and esthetic commitments, but the conceptual framework of modern science, established in the seventeenth century, strips nature of aim, purpose, and value, and hence of any meaning other than purely scientific intelligibility. Caught in this dilemma, the advocates of evolutionary humanism are reduced to claiming the sanction of evolutionary biology for values that originated elsewhere and to introducing the forbidden elements of teleology and value into their science in figures of speech. Whether this disingenuous mode of procedure is likely to produce social results of the kind envisaged in their ideal of man and society remains to be seen. That it can only be detrimental to science itself seems abundantly clear.

All praise, then, to Ernst Mayr for his humanistic values and for his clear demonstration that biological science requires concepts and methods unfamiliar in the physical sciences. Having repudiated reductionism in biology, let him go on to repudiate it in science generally, recognizing that human beings, whatever their biological heritage, have a dual nature, spiritual as well as animal, that makes science possible and at the same time transcends the set of abstractions known as "nature" which science postulates for its limited but important purposes.

NOTES

1.　For purposes of comparison see the preceding essay in the present volume.

2.　Ernst Mayr disclaims any attempt to criticize other people's religious views. As will be seen, however, he does believe that Darwinian biology has rendered theistic creationism untenable and has provided the basis for a new image of man and a new social ethics.

3.　Ernst Mayr, *The Growth of Biological Thought. Diversity, Evolution and Inheritance* (Cambridge, Mass. and London: The Belknap Press of Harvard University Press, 1982), p. 14.

4.　Ibid., pp. 4, 75-76; Mayr, *Toward a New Philosophy of Biology. Observations of an Evolutionist* (Cambridge, Mass. and London: The Belknap Press of Harvard University Press, 1988, pp. 40-41; Mayr, *Evolution and the Diversity of Life. Selected Essays* (Cambridge, Mass. and London: The Belknap Press of Harvard University Press, 1976), pp. 12, 380-384.

5.　Mayr, Toward a New Philosophy of Biology, pp. 50-57.

6.　Ibid., pp. 38-60, especially 38, 48.

7.　Ibid., pp. 178-179.

8.　Ibid., p. 58, 178.

9.　Ibid., pp. 58, 248.

10.　Ibid., p. 29.

11.　Ibid., pp. 233-255, especially 240-241, 250-251.

12.　Ibid., p. 44.

13.　Ibid., pp. 42-.143.

14.　Ibid., 1-36.

15.　Ibid.

16.　Ibid., p. 43.

17.　Ibid., pp. 251-252.

18.　Ibid., pp. 252-253.

19.　Ibid., p. 253.

20.　Ibid.

21.　Ibid., pp. 254-255

22.　Mayr, *Evolution and the Diversity of Life*, Part I, pp. 17, 19, 34, 39, 42, 66, 70, 89, 93, 95, 104-106.

23.　Ibid., p. 15.

24.　Ibid., p. 17.

25.　Ibid., p. 11.

26.　Ibid., p. 21.

27.　Ibid., p. 31.

28.　Ibid., p. 108.

29. Ibid., p. 111.

30. Ibid., p. 68.

31. Ibid., pp. 71-72.

32. Ibid., p. 150.

33. Ibid., p. 211, citing Sewall Wright, "Comments," in P. S. Moorhead and M. M. Kaplan, eds. *Mathematical Challenges to the Neo-Darwinian Interpretation of Evolution* (Philadelphia: Wistar Institute Press, 1967), p. 117.

34. Ibid., p. 150.

35. Ibid., pp. 251-253, 259.

36. Ibid., p. 150.

37. Ibid., pp. 150-151.

38. Ibid., p. 40.

39. Ibid., p. 445.

40. Ibid., p. 145.

41. Ibid., pp. 483-484.

42. Ibid., pp. 145-146, 452.

43. Ibid., p. 149.

44. Ibid., pp. 96, 163.

45. Ibid., p. 128.

46. Ibid., p. 104.

47. Ibid., pp. 30-31.

48. Ibid., p. 95.

49. Ibid., p. 98.

50. Ibid., p. 99.

51. Charles Darwin to Charles Lyell, Ilkley, Yorkshire. October 25, 1859, in Francis Darwin, ed., *The Life and Letters of Charles Darwin....* 3 v (New York, 1898), I, 531.

52. Mayr, *Toward a New Philosophy of Biology*, p. 253. The quotation within the quotation is from Mayr's *Animal Species and Evolution* (1965), p. 621.

53. See John C. Greene, "Progress, Science, and Value: A Biological Dilemma," *Biology and Philosophy* 6 (1991), pp. 99-106.

54. Charles Darwin to William Graham, Down, July 3, 1881, in Francis Darwin, ed., *Life and Letters*, I, 285.

55. Sewall Wright, "Panpsychism and Science," in *Mind in Nature: Essays on the Interface of Science and Philosophy*, John B. Cobb, Jr. and David R. Griffin, eds. (Washington, D. C.: University Press of America, 1977), pp. 79-80.

56. George C. Williams, *Adaptation and Natural Selection. A Critique of Some Current Evolutionary Thought* (Princeton, New Jersey: Princeton University Press, 1966), pp. 33, 254-255.

57. Wright, "Panpsychism and Science," p. 85.

58. Ibid., p. 87.

59. Ibid.

60. Mayr, Toward a New Philosophy of Biology, pp. 15-16.

61. Ibid., p. 12.

62. Ibid., p. 5.

63. Ibid., p. 176.

64. Ibid., pp. 293-294.

65. Ibid.

66. Ernst Mayr, *Animal Species and Evolution* (Cambridge, Mass.: The Belknap Press of Harvard University Press, 1965), p. 662.

67. Mayr, Toward a New Philosophy of Biology, p. 75.

68. Ibid., pp. 75-76.

69. Ibid.

70. Ibid.

71. Ibid., p. 77.

72. Ibid., pp. 75-85.

73. Ibid., pp. 80-81.

74. Ibid., p. 81.

75. Ibid., pp. 85-89.

76. Ibid., p. 82.

77. Ibid., pp. 86-87.

78. Ibid., pp. 87-88.

79. Ernst Mayr, "The World View of an Evolutionist," MS of Commencement Address at the University of Guelph, Guelph, Ontario, June 3, 1982, p. 5. See also Mayr, "Evolution and Ethics," in *Darwin, Marx, and Freud*, Arthur L. Caplan and Bruce Jennings, ed. (New York: Plenum, 1984), pp. 35-46.

80. Mayr, *Toward a New Philosophy of Biology* (above, n. 1), p. 89.

81. Charles Darwin, *The Descent of Man and Selection in Relation to Sex* (New York: D. Appleton, 1896), p. 618.

82. Darwin to Graham (above, n. 52).

83. Mayr, Toward a New Philosophy of Biology, p. 86.

84. Mayr, *Animal Species and Evolution* (above n. 53), p. 662.

85. Gerard Manley Hopkins, "Pied Beauty," in *The Poetical Works of Gerard Manley Hopkins*, ed. Norman H. Mackenzie (Oxford: Clarendon Press, 1990), p. 144. Quoted with the permission of the publisher.

11

THE MAYR-GREENE CORRESPONDENCE: SOME PASSAGES AT ARMS

NOTE: From my extensive correspondence with Ernst Mayr, beginning in September 1979, I have selected passages, which illustrate main themes in our continuing dialogue. Passages dealing with the difficult problem of defining the term "Darwinism" have already been published in the notes to Chapter 6, "Darwinism as a World View," of my book *Science, Ideology, and World View. Essays in the History of Evolutionary Ideas* (University of California Press, 1981), pp. 151-155.

March 31, 1980

Dear Ernst:

I appreciate greatly your willingness to let me quote from our correspondence about Darwinism and to read the new final essay of the collection,* which I enclose herewith. I quite agree with you in prizing our ability to take issue strongly on Darwinian themes without any personal rancor. You have no idea how helpful it is to me to receive criticisms from one of the leading evolutionary biologists of the 20th century, even when I decide to reject or qualify some of the criticisms. I am well aware of how much I owe you....

In reading my final essay, please understand that my objection is not to the values Huxley and Simpson espouse (they are pretty much

---

* Published under the title "From Huxley to Huxley: Transformations in the Darwinian Credo," in *Science, Ideology, and World View*, pp. 158-193.

my own) or to science itself properly conceived, but rather to their notion that these values can and should be derived from evolutionary biology. These are the hard-earned values of Western civilization, derived from Greek and Roman culture, the Judaeo-Christian tradition, and the Enlightenment. There is nothing to gain and very much to lose by rejecting these sources of our values in favor of an illusory and self-defeating derivation of them from science of any kind. The authors of the Bridgewater treatises should have taught us that, if nothing else.

Cordially,

John Greene

April 8, 1980

Dear John:

Here is the next installment in our mutual education correspondence. No harm is done in presenting excerpts from the writings of the Huxleys, Simpson, Darlington, and Wilson. They are valiantly trying to arrive at a non-supernatural basis of human ethics and beliefs. I regret that your critique is so exclusively negative. One continuously reads between the lines "let us go back, let us go back to God, then we will be comfortable, and then we can refer all objections to all viewpoints to Him." You try to undermine the claims of these evolutionists but I fail to see that you propose anything else instead. Simpson perhaps makes the point most clearly by saying that as modern scientists we must reject escape into non-material causations and if we look for the science that can serve as the basis for our interpretations we find that the only one that is suitable for this purpose is evolutionary biology (broadly defined to include psychology and sociology, as far as they are evolutionary).

I find two basic weaknesses in your argumentation. The first one is you still have the 19th century concept of science as something absolute, something that provides ironclad proofs and totally logical conclusions. But this is no longer the concept of science and even Popper is now hedging on his falsifiability criterion. All conclusions of science are tentative, they are what at this moment is most probable and consistent with the greatest amount of evidence. Hence the alternatives which you offer on p. 33 [the "positivistic dilemma"] are a parody.

Your second weakness is that you obviously take little stock in natural selection. This is alright, for someone who always has God to fall back on when he encounters something puzzling, but if you are obliged, on the basis of looking at all aspects of this world, to deny the existence of a supreme being, and if one then looks at all the phenomena of living nature, one has no choice but saying that natural selection is by all odds the most probable cause of observed phenomena. This does not deny a considerable stochastic element, but it is certainly the only possible causation of consistent changes. I for one, just like Simpson, find nothing improbable about the selection for "open programs" that permit ethical systems. I think Waddington in his *The Ethical Animal* has worked this out very nicely. You really ought to quote him....All a modern evolutionist claims is that ethical principles are indispensable for the harmonious functioning of society and that any society that lacks such principles will soon go under. I think H. J. Muller and others have gone too far in believing in definite genes for charity, compassion, love, unselfishness, etc. But I believe with Waddington in the social human animal there has been definite selection for brain mechanisms (open programs) that would permit the development of a constructive ethic....

Cordially yours,
Ernst Mayr

April 11, 1980

Dear Ernst:

As I suspected, there are fundamental conflicts in point of view and basic premises that make it difficult for us to understand each other. Let me try to make my own point of view clearer. You are wrong in thinking that my objections to the Simpson-Huxley-Darlington-Wilson line of argument are essentially religious. They are philosophical. My basic method is to take what these writers say at face value, juxtapose what they say at different times and places in their writings, and show that they become involved in contradictions and paradoxes. To me this suggests some error or omission in the premises of their argument.

Now this is a perfectly valid type of criticism....And you do not answer the criticism effectively by accusing me of being religious, of having wrong ideas about science, etc. Either these writers wind up in contradictions, or they don't. To answer my criticism you must show that the alleged paradoxes and contradictions are not there or that they can be resolved. Your only move in that direction, so far as I can see, is your statement that "I for one, just like Simpson, find nothing improbable about the selection for 'open programs' that permit ethical systems....For an evolutionist... Simpson's conclusion...is by no means paradoxical." In this case, however, the paradox I pointed to was not the emergence of choice-making animals in an amoral universe but rather the contradiction between Simpson's rejection of "progress" as a characteristic of the evolutionary process and his subsequent assertion that man "is the most progressive product of evolution," not to mention his further assertion that man, being "highly endowed," has a responsibility to "rise still farther." This is all of a piece with Julian Huxley's assertion that man has an obligation to the blind, amoral cosmic process to carry it farther in a direction it does not know it is going. If you can make sense of this kind of reasoning, please do so. I can't. Neither can I make any sense of [E.0.] Wilson's "epiphe-nomenon of the neuronal machinery of the brain" that has reason as "one of its techniques."

Instead of resolving these paradoxes, you resort to a line of argument that seems to me to have little logical force. You say that these writers, whatever the paradoxes and contradictions in their writings, are to be excused because "they are valiantly trying to arrive at a non-supernatural basis of human ethics and beliefs." But this is a poor excuse. In the first place, it assumes without proof that a supernatural basis for ethics is to be avoided at all costs and that any amount of illogicality may be excused if it rests on some other basis. In the second place, it assumes that all non-scientific systems of ethics rest on a supernatural basis. But this is obviously not true—witness the ethics of Plato, Aristotle, Epicurus, Epictetus, the Confucians, Kant, and a host of ethical systems proposed by modern philosophers. Does anyone excuse whatever illogicalities can be found in their systems on the ground that they valiantly seek a non-supernatural basis of human ethics and beliefs?

One suspects that Simpson and Huxley regard all philosophical systems that postulate some principle of reason or order in the universe as having a "supernatural" basis. But this attitude, in turn, presupposes that nature is devoid of reason or any ordering principle. So the Atomists argued, but there are strong philosophical arguments against this position (e.g., the relevance of mathematics to the understanding of nature), and, in any case, there is no justification for asserting this position dogmatically as self-evident. That would be to beg the question at issue: What is nature? How can we best conceive it so as to make sense not only of what we see, feel, etc. "out there" but also of our inner experience as rational, moral, beauty-loving beings?

I come next to your argument that "as modern scientists we must reject escape into non-material causations, and if we look for the science that can serve as the basis for our interpretations, we find that the only one that is suitable for this purpose is evolutionary biology (broadly defined to include psychology and sociology, as far as they are evolutionary)." What a host of philosophical assumptions and attitudes lie embedded in that statement! Let us begin with the first: that scientists must reject non-material causations. But first I must ask for clarification. Do you mean that scientists *as scientists* must reject non-material causations or that scientists *as philosophers* must also reject non-material causations. The first proposition would seem easier to defend though I am not even sure about that. I would first have to know what the words "material" and "causation" mean. Simpson (*This View of Life*, p. 291) says: "By 'material' I mean existent as phenomena in the universe accessible to our (aided or unaided) perception as opposed to the spiritual, the supernatural, or the ineffable." Thus, "material" seems to mean "capable of being perceived by our senses, directly or indirectly." "Causation," as you know, is a very difficult concept, but I won't go into that. I suppose that what you and Simpson mean is that science deals with relationships (causal and otherwise) among phenomena and excludes *a priori* all reference to things that do not appear. Perhaps this is so (though I am not entirely sure about that), but in any case it does not settle the question of what the scientist *as philosopher* is bound to exclude, unless you take the position that science and philosophy are the same thing, and I think that this is the nub of the issue between me and your camp.

You accuse me of believing that science is "something that provides ironclad proofs and totally logical conclusions." I have no such concept of science, though I hope that scientists will continue to be strictly logical in their reasoning....I recognize that scientists work by hypotheses and reach only probable conclusions. But that is not the issue. The issue is: what is the relation between scientific representations of reality and reality itself? As Whitehead pointed out long ago, science succeeds by constructing highly abstract pictures of reality, eliminating all the aspects it cannot deal with successfully. It talks about ideal gases and frictionless planes and perfectly competitive market systems in which all buyers and sellers are perfectly informed and perfectly rational in their decisions. This kind of abstraction is justified by its practical results. But if the scientist then assumes that his scientific representation of reality is a true description of the reality in all its complexity and concreteness, he commits the "fallacy of misplaced concreteness" and leads himself and his fellow men into grievous error with possibly disastrous consequences. *Laissez-faire* political economy and social Darwinism are good examples of this kind of thing.

You say that I "take little stock in natural selection." That is not true. Though I am no biologist, I can see that natural selection, as a scientific theory, sheds a great deal of light on events in the biological world, both past and present. But many of the claims made for the efficacy of natural selection in the biological and human worlds go far beyond anything capable of scientific verification. Some of them are patently absurd, as in Darlington's book [*The Evolution of Man and Society*, 1971]. But we are asked to swallow these "explanations" without question on the ground that natural selection might *conceivably* be the cause of the phenomena and that the evolutionary biologists who propose these explanations cannot conceive of any other explanation, or that the other explanations they can conceive involve a resort to "non-material causation," which is a no-no.

Moreover, these supposedly scientific explanations in terms of natural selection are embedded in a matrix of philosophical interpretation of physical science. We are told that evolution is a "mechanistic process." But what does "mechanistic" mean? To me it means either "exemplifying the principles of mechanics" or "like a machine," but it is doubtful whether evolution is mechanistic in either of these senses except insofar as all bodies in the universe exemplify the principles of mechanics. Again, we are told that the evolutionary process is "materialistic," but this turns out to mean that the process involves nothing spiritual or "supernatural" or "ineffable." But this is a philosophical assertion based on the maxim that nothing can be attributed to nature that is not manageable within the frame of reference of scientific investigation. In short, scientific investigation exhausts the field of rational inquiry.

But there is more to it than that. There is also a deep-seated fear that to admit the validity of metaphysics and theology as intellectual disciplines would be to undermine the security of the scientific enterprise by opening the door to non-material causation. It is this fear that underlies your belief that I must be motivated by religious considerations: "One continuously reads between the lines 'let us go back, let us go back to God, then we will be comfortable, and then we can refer all objections to all viewpoints to Him." You sense a threat to the autonomy of science in any suggestion that the positivistic world view associated with much (though not all) of modern evolutionary biology is open to question. Your mind conjures up fanatical creationists crusading to force creationist biology on school children. The threat is a real one, but it is generated in considerable measure by the insistence of Huxley, Simpson, Darlington, Wilson, and others on palming off evolutionary biology as the only safe guide to human duty and destiny. The claim is preposterous. It is one thing to argue, as you do, that natural selection might select for "open programs" that *permit* ethical systems. It is quite another to claim that evolutionary biology (and only it) can discover human duty and destiny. If evolutionary biologists go around making claims of this kind, they should not be surprised if parents decide to take a hand in determining what kind of biology their children will be exposed to. Take a look at Simpson's nine "firm evolutionary generalizations and principles" which he would inculcate in the schools (*This View of Life*, p. 38). Would you favor palming off that hodgepodge of science, amateur philosophy, and ideology as the "findings" of evolutionary biology? I think not.

The same goes for [Edward O.] Wilson's "evolutionary epic." I am interested that you concede that faith in science can be no less a religion than faith in God. But who would pretend that the world views promulgated by Julian Huxley, Simpson, and Wilson in the name of science are "science" in any proper sense of the word? They preach faith in science and make use of scientific discoveries in building their picture of the world, but it is essentially a philosophical interpretation of the results of scientific investigation with strong religious overtones. Huxley is quite explicit on this point: "I find myself driven to use the language of religion." Simpson is more restrained, but it is plain that he thinks his world view should be taught in the schools and guide mankind in its onward course. Wilson concedes without argument that the world view associated with this kind of evolutionary biology is a myth, the myth of the heroic epiphenomenon "mind" driven on by blind hope and by faith in science. Well, if we are thus reduced to faith and hope, perhaps I may be permitted to have faith and hope in something besides these idols.

You assert that I am a "cosmic teleologist" and ask that I state what I think is "the force or agent or person who directs the cosmic teleology." Actually, I have no systematically elaborated view of cosmology in relation to metaphysics. It seems obvious to me, however, that *if* one attempts to envisage reality as an evolutionary process that has produced and is producing higher and higher levels of order and value, one must presuppose some creative ground of the process capable of envisaging its possibilities. Otherwise the conception makes no sense, and we wind up in Julian Huxley's absurdities.

On the ethical side, I think that history shows that profound ethical systems can be and have been elaborated by philosophical reflection on human experience without reference to evolutionary biology. Ultimately one's ideas about ethics are grounded in one's concept of the nature of reality and man's place therein. If ultimate reality is truly as Simpson, Huxley, and Wilson represent it, the rational man will be more likely to take [Thomas] Hobbes' ethical advice than to pretend with Huxley, et al., that biology confirms the Biblical injunction to do justly, love mercy, and walk humbly with one's God. But if, on the other hand, God exists and has revealed himself to us in his son, then we know beyond a shadow of a doubt that we ought also to love one another.

Cordially,

John Greene

April 21, 1980

Dear John:

Thank you for your detailed reply to my comments....As far as I am concerned, it does not properly answer my objections, but it will of course be up to the reader to make that decision. What your postscript makes much clearer than your other discussions is that you see a contrast between scientist and philosopher, a contrast I do not see. You also seem to think that all science is positivistic science, and I would like you to define this somewhere more clearly....In fact, as I think I implied already in my previous letter, you are concentrating too much on criticizing others without making sufficient of an effort to replace it with positive statements of your own....This you have side-stepped far too much. Somewhere the reader will want to know, if ethics cannot be based on the findings of evolutionary biology, what should it be based on?....It is always easier to criticize than to be constructive.

Cordially,

Ernst Mayr

May 15, 1980

Dear Ernst:

....In answer to your latest queries, my objections to positivism apply to positivistic world views claiming validation by "science," not to science itself. History shows plainly that excellent scientific work can be and has been done within a great many kinds of world view—e.g. Aristotle, Kepler, al-Battani, Einstein, G. G. Simpson, Mendel, etc. But most scientists have sense enough to recognize that science *per se* does not dictate any particular world view (theistic, non-theistic, idealistic, materialistic, etc.) simply because science excludes *a priori* all those aspects of experience that are not amenable to its techniques and presuppositions, i.e. value judgments, reference to non-empirical entities, etc. Only when a scientific theory is extrapolated into a general view of what is real does it become "positivistic" (as a philosophical outlook). Freud's theory of neurotic behavior may be called a scientific theory; "Freudianism," as in *Civilization and Its Discontents* or *Totem and Taboo*, is a positivistic world view.

You are wrong in thinking that I do not distinguish between an ethics (supposedly) derived from science and an ethics that takes into account the findings of science. Obviously any adequate ethics must take into account all relevant knowledge of what is. But that is quite a different thing from saying that scientific knowledge of those aspects of reality that are amenable to scientific inquiry can yield an adequate ethics derived from that knowledge. Simpson et al. have the illusion that this is possible only because they come to the study of science with their values already derived from the philosophical and religious traditions of Western civilization, just as the authors of the Bridgewater treatises [in the early nineteenth century] found in nature and natural science what their Christian upbringing had taught them to expect to find.

Cordially,

John Greene

NOTE: The Mayr-Greene correspondence in the autumn of 1985 concerned the views I expressed in my essay "The History of Ideas

Revisited" in the *Revue de Synthèse* and Mayr's strong objections thereto (see Chapters 6, 7, and 8 of the present work). Fortunately our disagreements in print and in correspondence did not erode the foundation of mutual respect undergirding our friendship, but instead led us to open up to each other more fully.

May 1, 1989

Dear John:

    .... At this time I will answer only the marginal question of your letter of April 5 where you ask about upbringing. I have described in other autobiographical notes how nature-loving my parents were and how almost every Sunday they would take us on hikes showing us birds, flowers, mushrooms, and fossils. Indeed I had a most fortunate childhood that way. You also ask about my religious upbringing. I presume both of my parents were agnostics, but they were quite anxious to give us a good religious upbringing. As small children we said a prayer when going to bed, and we had religious instruction in school and went to church occasionally, not regularly. When I was about 14 I decided that the Bible was quite ridiculous, and that what was going on in the world could not be reconciled with the concept of a just God. By that time my father had died, but my mother insisted that I was confirmed, and for the better part of a year I took confirmation classes. The minister was an extreme liberal, and managed to make Christianity palatable to me. I came back to Christianity for a while, but this did not last very long. I have been an atheist all my adult life. The Protestant ethics, however, had been preached so strongly by my parents that they have lasted all my life. On the whole I have always avoided controversies about religion, being afraid that I might destroy somebody else's faith if my arguments were too convincing. In my student days my closest friend was a Protestant divinity student. Now, 60 years later, I am still corresponding with this Protestant minister. My wife is the daughter of a Protestant minister, and one of her two brothers is a Protestant minister likewise. However, my wife lost her faith before we met. Religion was never an argument in our marriage....I might finally add that when I read [Julian]

Huxley's *Religion Without Revelation*, I found it on the whole quite congenial. I have always insisted that I have religion, perhaps a stronger religion than most church-going people, but it does not fall under the word religion in the vocabulary of most of those who belong to a particular congregation.

Cordially yours,
Ernst Mayr

May 5, 1989

Dear Ernst:

I am much indebted to you for your prompt response to my query about your religious upbringing....My own parents were church-going Congregationalists in Vermillion, South Dakota, and I attended a liberal, non-doctrinal Sunday school and sang in the choir. On going to Harvard for graduate school, I sampled Christian services in several denominations and eventually settled on the Episcopal service as most to my liking. Unlike you, I found parts of the Bible, mainly the New Testament, deeply moving and appealing and the Christian conception of human nature highly realistic and I still do. The problem of evil you allude to is a difficult one, but it is not confined to the Christian faith. Darwin was troubled by it too, and T. H. Huxley's attempt to find an answer to it in our animal inheritance ("men's inheritance from the ancestors who fought a good fight in the state of nature, their dose of original sin") will not wash. The "instinct of unlimited self-assertion" (Huxley) is not of animal origin; it is more reminiscent of the cardinal sin of pride, or the Greek *hubris*. I freely admit that there are enormous difficulties in Christian faith and doctrine (so many that I sometimes call myself a "Christian agnostic"), but I find greater difficulties in Julian Huxley's faith and doctrine. I quite agree with you that religious belief and religious attitudes are not confined to "organized" religions; indeed that is the underlying point of view in *The Death of Adam* and *Science, Ideology, and World View*. I like your (and Darwin's) reluctance to impose one's own religious beliefs and attitudes on others, and I try to practice that myself....

Meanwhile I continue to study your attempt to find an organicist *tertium quid* somewhere between the teleologists-vitalists and the atomistic reductionists. It would take a very long letter indeed to explain my difficulties in defining (to say nothing of accepting) your resolution of this problem. Instead, when I have managed to put together an intelligible critique thereof, I shall solicit your reactions to what I have written. In any case, whatever I write will be along my usual line as exemplified in *The Death of Adam*. I am not equipped scientifically to do justice to your stellar accomplishments as a systematist....

Cordially,

John Greene

August 11, 1989

Dear John:

I am delighted you had such a good time on the Galapagos Tour. I once served as one of the guides on such a tour, which forced me to do a lot of preparatory reading from which I learned a lot. Yet, seeing everything "in the flesh," so to speak, was a memorable experience. Did you have a chance to observe the differences among the three "kinds" of mocking birds? Remarkable, how different they are in behavior.

Now as to my *tertium quid* view, let me tip you off on the importance of *emergence*. It is a concept neither the reductionists nor the vitalists like. Yet, it is something one encounters everywhere. Niels Bohr, more than 30 years ago (after a lecture of mine), pointed out to me, that it had nothing to do with living but was quite as prominent in the inanimate realm....

The stem of a hammer and the head of a hammer do not have the functional properties of a hammer until they are fitted together. My friend [Bernhard] Rensch could never accept emergence, which forced him—as far as *mind* is concerned—into panpsychism.

Emergence, of course, was an alien concept to classical physicalism, but many modern physicists (like Bohr) have accepted it. It solves many problems to accept it. The hammer example shows that no special metaphysical forces are involved. It is simply that a more complex system often can perform certain functions which a simpler system can not....

Cordially,
Ernst

August 29, 1989

Dear Ernst:

Enclosed herewith are Parts I-III of a four part essay[*] I have written in provisional form. I will send Part IV ("Science, Values, and the Image of Man") along later when it is in better shape. I have tried to expound your views as accurately as I can, keeping close to your texts and citing page numbers. Unless otherwise indicated, the page numbers in brackets refer to your latest book *Toward a New Philosophy of Biology*....

As you will see, I have formulated your views in a way that makes sense to me and here and there have added some critical comments. I am especially concerned to have you note any misrepresentation of your views or statements that are inaccurate or nonsensical biologically on my part. As to my own commentary on your views (or supposed views), I shall, of course, be interested in your reactions thereto....I look forward eagerly to hearing from you.

Cordially,
John Greene

September 4, 1989

Dear John,

....On the whole, I think you have done a remarkable job of representing my ideas fairly. But every once in a while you have slipped. For instance, science has never for me been something "to loosen the grip of traditional religion." Such an intent has been far

---

[*]Republished in the present work from the *Journal of the History of Biology* 27 (Summer 1994), pp. 311-347.

from my mind, indeed I have been quite careful to avoid anything that might be offensive to my orthodox friends. However, I can't help it if the findings of science make the claims of some organized religions rather ridiculous. And, the conflict is not between religion and science, but between "revealed" religion and science. And every scientist I know, no matter how much of an atheist he may be, has religion.

By far the most serious weakness of your account is that you do not seem to be able to shake the typological aspects of certain concepts, as teleology and reduction. With your "physical" eye you have read that there are 4 very different phenomena that have been designated teleological. Each should have (and now has) a different name, because they really have nothing in common. With your "intellectual" and "spiritual" eye you still consider them all branches (or parts) of teleology. Hence you are puzzled (or seem to be) that I reject cosmic teleology (the only genuine teleology) and yet accept teleonomy. If you fully accepted that the two have nothing in common, you would see nothing paradoxical in the rejection of one and the acceptance of the other....The minute you postulate an "infinite mind," you are way outside the scholarly ball park. Also you get on rather thin ice: why didn't the infinite mind prevent the holocaust and Stalin's massacre of 20 million Russians? etc. etc....

If you claim that my account is anthropocentric (which Huxley's clearly was), then you have to explain this in more detail. I deny it flatly!

Cordially,
Ernst Mayr

September 14, 1989

Dear Ernst:

I was enormously heartened and relieved to receive your letter saying that I had succeeded fairly well in representing your views as expressed in the publications I drew upon. In those cases where I have not done so, I will make every effort to get things right.... Now that you have read Parts I-III without disowning me forever, I take courage to send you Part IV, which should give you a better idea of my argument about the anthropocentricity of evolutionary science. With respect to many of the issues raised in Part IV I suppose we shall have to agree to disagree, but I should like very much to have your comments both as to my representation of your views and, as to my criticisms of these views. We should never give up hope of converting each other! Now to some remarks about your comments on Parts I-III.

1. I will certainly rewrite the passage on the opening page to make it clear that you, like Darwin, and unlike J. Huxley, have never been a crusader against religion. I do think that some passages in *The Growth of Biological Thought* give that impression (certainly some reviewers have thought so), but your point in these passages seems to be that science through Darwin has become emancipated from the baneful influence (on science) of the Judaeo-Christian tradition and philosophical idealism. As you will see in Part IV, I think you owe a good deal to these traditions, especially the former, in your own value-attitudes.

2. As to teleology, you mention four types of phenomena that have been called "teleological," whereas I found only three in your essays. I suppose that the fourth consists of the phenomena you call teleonomical, but these are the same phenomena Aristotle called teleological. Correct me if I am wrong about this. I cannot agree with you that the three types derived from your essays (in my essay) have nothing in common. Paley's design argument is itself an example of cosmic teleology. It is also a Christianized version of Aristotle's argument for final causes. The common element in all three is the idea that the order of the universe (in this case the adaptation of structure to function and the character of directed development) requires some intelligent agent or principle as one ingredient in their coming to be. Darwin (in the *Origin*) simply transferred the element of intelligent purpose from the creation of the organism to the process by which the organisms came to be, as his grandfather did before him (evolutionary deism). You object to my assuming an infinite mind, but Darwin assumed it when he defined the laws of nature (*C. D.'s Natural Selection*) as "the laws ordained by God for governing the universe." Newton, Galileo, Clerk Maxwell, and many other scientists have made a similar assumption.

"Mechanistic purposiveness" is a contradiction in terms, unless it means that some machine has been constructed with some purpose in mind. Are there purposes apart from minds?

Nor can I understand your argument, repeated copiously by myriad biologists, that teleological language in biology is simply a device for saying things more economically than would be possible in honest-to-God scientific language. Do you save any words by saying that the replenishment of the gene pool is the *function* of sexual reproduction instead of saying that that is its *effect*? And you yourself say that some "information" is lost when non-teleological language is used. But is this not a way of saying that the purposive element in embryological development and the process of adaptation is lost when non-teleological language is used?....

Finally (for now), what do you mean by saying that evolution is not teleological because science cannot discover any "proper program" or "law" governing evolutionary development? By your argument, if such a program or law were discovered, it would not constitute teleology but only teleonomy. Also, how can you at one and the same time adduce DNA programs as evidence against physicalist reductionism and against teleology? By admitting "constitutive reductionism" in embryological development you blunt the force of your anti-reductionist argument.

Time for lunch
John Greene

NOTE: Mayr's strongly negative reaction to the draft of Part IV of my essay "Science, Philosophy, and Metaphor in Ernst Mayr's Writings" [see pp. 210-213] was sent to me on tape and answered by me in a letter dated November 30, 1989. In April 1990, Mayr sent me a typescript of his earlier tape-recorded letter, which I had already answered. As a result, the following two letters seem in reverse chronological order but are really in the order in which they were received and answered.

April 19, 1990

Dear John,

My secretary is ill, and under the circumstances the simplest way to give you my comments on your Part IV is to dictate them into a tape. My impression is that you talk mainly about Julian Huxley. Which other modern Darwinian has said that, "human beings are the highest, noblest beings on earth, that animals rank in the scale of being in proportion as they approximate to human condition, etc. etc."? Have you not read my recent refutation of extraterrestrial intelligence, where I point out that in the millions of evolutionary lineages only one led to intelligence? There are about 70 phyla of animals, they all have specialized in something or other, but only one phylum shows the steps toward mankind. Hence, what you claim to be the view of the Darwinian is, I am afraid, your invention. You criticize that value judgment creeps into evolutionary biology. If you have natural selection, in which only some of the offspring survive, or, as Campbell says, are retained, you cannot escape a value judgment. There is no such thing in physics or chemistry, as natural selection, and therefore they have it easy to do without value judgments. Simpson, myself, and many other Darwinians have pointed out that there is no way to decide whether a bee, a squid, or a penguin is higher. The idea that there is a scala naturae, which worries you so much, is mostly in your own mind. When an animal or a plant switches into a new adaptive zone, it is at first very poorly adapted. As it speciates and as numerous similar species originate, some are better adapted than others, some even make new "inventions," and they prevail, while the others die out. Therefore we have a long list of fossil bats, but none of the very first steps from the insectivore to the bat. Exactly the same is true for avian evolution and in fact for almost all major evolutionary shifts. It is not a value judgment but simply a statement of fact to say that those who were better adapted to the new adaptive zone survived and those that were not, succumbed. Of course Aristotle would have a metaphysics of higher and lower, because he believed in the *scala naturae*. The Darwinian who does not believe in it and who quite contrary to what you say does not have a definite ranking of higher or lower except within certain lineages, naturally can have no special metaphysics. Don't forget that Darwin himself wrote the words "never say higher or lower" on the margin of his copy of the *Vestiges.*[*]

On p. 35 you claim that I consider man a miraculous anomaly. Well, for that matter, give me any special creature that is not a miraculous anomaly by your definition. Man is simply unique. Yes, man has extraordinary characteristics. But in their particular way, so have many other organisms. You say that humans are "purposeful, self-conscious, value oriented beings in a purposeless, valueless, unreasoning universe." Of course each of your statements is incorrect. If you see a predator stalking his prey, he is exceedingly purposeful; and so are many organisms in their daily life. Whether or not they are self-conscious, we don't know, but anyone who has watched a dog who had done a misdeed, realizes his obvious guilt feelings are an expression of self-consciousness. And when it comes to value-orientation, every animal is value-oriented in its food and habitat references and most of them in their mating drive. You say that in the Darwinian world reason is of no importance. However, much of the behavior of organisms at least of those with a higher developed central nervous system, shows that reason is indeed of importance to them. When it comes to your sentence "but do scientists really believe that science is valuable only as a means of survival," I would like to see you quote at least five authors who have made such a statement. If you have read my chapter on the origin of ethics, you will know that I point out that ethical values can be also of survival value, particularly for cultural groups such as exist in man. I shall make no comments on Sewall Wright's views. For me, consciousness is obviously not the primary reality. By the way, when quoting from people's writings please always add the year of original publication. Almost all scientists have modified their views throughout their life, and it is quite unfair to extract a sentence from one of their earlier writings as if this had been their viewpoint all through their life. The bottom paragraph on your p. 37 ignores that nearly all Darwinians have expanded at great length on the

---

[*] Robert Chambers' *Vestiges of the Natural History of Creation*, published anonymously in 1844.

importance of culture. And when it comes to values, I would like to point out that nearly all the leaders in the conservation movement were convinced Darwinians. I simply cannot understand your insinuation that Darwinians are as in the last century they were described in the period of social Darwinism. And I can not see any possible conflict between having a feeling for esthetics and moral values, and yet believing in Darwinian evolution. But this is the way you seem to present the case. At the bottom of p. 38 you omit the open part of the program. Not only I but many others, beginning with Konrad Lorenz's following reaction, have written about the open program. I am surprised you are not aware of it. And if you are aware of it, I would be even more surprised at your suppressing its existence. If, on p. 39, you attack organicists, you must at least in a footnote give a definition of organicist based on the writings of Ritter, Bertalanffy or others who have claimed to be organicists.

I am afraid I am not as impressed with Sewall Wright's enthusiasm for mind; to say that the world is full of mind is for me nothing but words. And reading these claims of Wright's, I have to think of Haeckel's crystal souls. My very good friend Bernhard Rensch is also a pan-psychist, and I have never been able to come to any agreement with him. For me it is simply a dodge to say that even every atom and elementary particle has soul or mind. It is pushing the problem under the rug. It corresponds to the attempt of some astronomers to say life did not originate on earth, but was brought to earth from other planets. They thought they had solved the problem of the origin of life. You think you have solved the problem of the origin of mind.

Your discussion…indicates that you don't understand what a program is. It is not a single DNA molecule or a base pair or a couple of base pairs. Perhaps some computer person can tell you a little of what a program is…. On p. 42 I did not "scoff" at miracles, nor did I "explode" the traditional anthropocentrism….At the bottom of this page…you overlook the fact that man is a cultural animal. I have never written in detail about this because others have done so, and have done so very well. However, in my discussion of groups I have recognized for man and perhaps for some kinds of animals the existence of cultural groups. As far as my ideas on ethics are concerned, I have not yet finished my thinking. The paper in the recent essay volume was my first major endeavor, and I am not entirely happy with it. Furthermore, I did not come to grips in that paper, except marginally, with the problem of what actually good ethics are. I was discussing only how a human being acquires his moral values.

It is precisely because cultural values are acquired they do not have a genetic basis, but any generation can develop new cultural values, good ones or bad ones. There is no reason whatsoever why it should not be possible to develop a new kind of ethics in this day and age without this fact being in any conflict whatsoever with the Darwinian theory. You seem to be particularly astonished that the ideas of evolutionary humanism should be attributed to evolutionary thinking, because in your mind evolutionary thinking equals social Darwinism. If you would carefully read and try to understand the reasoning of people like myself or Huxley…, you will find that they are not in any conflict with Darwinism. You may say that these ideas are at least in part influenced by Christian thinking, and I would be the last one to deny it. When one tries to develop a superior ethical system one may go to Buddhism, Christianity, or just plain common sense. Darwin's particular views on the so-called lower races are not a necessary consequence of Darwinian theory. Neither is mine, but it is compatible with it. I would only wish that you would get out of your mind the thought that Darwinism must be social Darwinism. You will of course vigorously deny this accusation, but this is the way you phrase almost all of your arguments.

….The species *Homo sapiens* may not have any purpose, but there is no reason why a cultural group should not adopt certain value systems, and in fact the whole history of mankind shows that that is what human cultural groups have always done. Many of the adopted value systems were not viable in the long run. But there is no reason why modern man could not develop a better system. There are numerous statements in the Bible, which I think are opposed to your claim…that the Christian doctrine of creation is an adequate basis for ethical commitments of this kind. For me there is basically nothing wrong with occasional value judgments. Even if I should be attacked for this belief I do believe that man is somehow "higher" than the chimpanzee. The minute one goes further away and compares man with bees or marine organisms, one is doing something impossible. This is not a time in which one is particularly proud of being a human being—but there is no reason why we could not and should not develop an ethical system that would bring us back again to a situation where we could again be proud of being humans. This may not be the direct outcome of neo-Darwinism, but it is totally compatible with it.

Best regards,

Ernst

November 30, 1989

Dear Ernst:

After a month of work...I managed to get my tape recorder repaired and to play the tapes you sent me in response to receiving Part IV of my essay. In reply, let me begin by assuring you that I have no intention of publishing anything about you and your work which you think misrepresents your ideas and attitudes or which you consider hostile or disrespectful toward you personally. The whole point of sending you the tentative draft of my essay was to guard against any such eventuality....Let me try to clarify several points.

As to science and ethics, my position is that science generally and neo-Darwinian evolutionary biology in particular cannot legitimately yield any ethical system whatsoever. Science ignores the value aspect of reality because, it has no way of dealing with it (cf. [Francisco] Ayala's statements to this effect in *Evolutionary Progress*), and hence it is in no position to derive ethical systems from scientific research and theory. In your taped letter (though not in your published essays) you seem to concede this point when you say that Darwin's ethical views and your own, are "not a necessary consequence of Darwinian theory," but that yours, at least, are "compatible with neo-Darwinism." From my point of view almost *any* ethical system is *compatible* with Darwinian scientific theory because that theory has nothing legitimate to say about ethics one way or another. I quite agree with you that ethical reflection must take into account what science appears to tell us about the world, but that is very different from saying, as J. Huxley, G. G. Simpson, E. O. Wilson, etc. say, that evolutionary biology can and does inform us about human duty and destiny. If you and they would tell your readers that, *as philosophers*, you hold a general view of reality in terms of which certain ethical maxims make sense, no one could legitimately object. But to present these philosophical reflections based upon a general philosophy of nature, man, and reality generally as the findings of science is pure scientism. Moreover, as Balfour pointed out in 1895 (*Foundations of Belief*), when the value systems of those claiming to speak for science are examined carefully, they turn out to be parasitic on the traditional sources of Western values: the literature and philosophy of Greece and Rome, the Judaeo-Christian tradition, and the Enlightenment. Darwin's values, for example, had nothing to do with his theory of natural selection. Julian Huxley's values, yours, and mine are substantially alike because they are derived from the sources I have mentioned and not from evolutionary science.

In this connection, I did *not*, as you allege, say that scientists believe that science is valuable only as a means of survival. On the contrary I said that they did not believe this, even though the theory of natural selection as a *scientific theory* has no room for valuing *anything* except as it contributes or fails to contribute to survival and reproduction. The point of this paradox is that the scientist's values are *not* derived from his scientific theories. Hence your criticism that scientists have played leading roles in the conservation movement, have well developed esthetic sensibilities, etc. is beside the point. I have stated explicitly that I admire the values and humanistic outlook of Huxley and you; I only deny that these values are derived from evolutionary biology.

This brings me to the subject of value judgments in science. My position here has always been that biologists, especially evolutionary biologists, should *either* frame a philosophy of biology that includes a value framework based on a general philosophy of man and nature *or* frame a philosophy of biology that excludes value judgments but at the same time places biological science in a general philosophical framework that takes account of the value aspect and the volitional aspect of reality. I cite Sewall Wright's ideas here, not because I accept them as a valid solution of the problem, but rather because he seems aware of the problem and tries to deal with it, whereas you (so far as I can see) largely ignore the problem or try to deal with it by talking about "emergence" with no clear metaphysic which could make sense of this concept. Your concept of "organicism" seems to me to be infected with a similar vagueness. Since you have introduced the concept in your essays, it is *your* job, not mine, to define it adequately.

Finally, as to the position of man in nature, I did not intend to say that evolutionary biologists generally explicitly *believe* and *say* that man is the highest organism on Earth, but rather that their use of the terms "higher" and "lower", etc. seem to imply some notion of this kind. (Darwin wrote to [Joseph Dalton] Hooker that man was the involuntary standard of comparison in discussions of "higher" and "lower," and although Darwin warned himself 'Never say higher or lower,' he seems never to have been able to follow his own advice.) It is precisely this discrepancy between profession and action, between rejecting teleology in nature and using teleological language to describe natural processes, which convinces me that there are unresolved tensions in Darwinian and neo-Darwinian thought, tensions which can only be resolved by re-examining the philosophical foundations of biological science. Likewise with respect to the idea of man. It is no sufficient answer to the problem of man's place in nature to say that man is "somehow" higher than the chimpanzee, especially when the theory of natural selection gives one no other criterion of value than the implicit one of survival-with-reproduction. One must define this "somehow" in terms of some general view of reality that makes the judgment intelligible—for example I think Whitehead would say that man is "higher" because he prehends (takes account of) the universe more fully than the "lower" animals, or plants, or sticks and stones. The knower is higher than the known unless the known is also a knower. That is why I think all science is anthropocentric. We may not be *physically* at the center of the universe, but *mentally* we grasp the galaxies, the dinosaurs, and the like into our own being, and that being transcends the objects thus known in the act of knowing them. You hope for an ethical system "that would bring us back again to a situation where we could again be proud of being human." Can any other organism have such a wish? To have it is to know at one and the same time the majesty and the misery of being human, and it is to this condition of mankind that the great religions address themselves. "What is man that thou regardest him, and the son of man that thou visitest him?"

With high regard –

John Greene

December 18, 1989

Dear John,

Thank you for the return of the tapes [recording Mayr's reactions to Part IV of Greene's "Science, Philosophy, and Metaphor in Ernst Mayr's Writings"—see pp. 242ff], and your comments. But, before I forget it, you might be interested to know that the card which you wrote me on July 6 from the Galapagos Islands was received by me on September 18. I think delivery would have been a good deal faster in Darwin's days.

Now to your comments. Frankly, it is not, as you believe, so much the aggressive tone of your writing that disturbed me, but the fact that you seem to have developed certain ideas 30 or 40 years ago and you still argue against their opposites. In part this is due to the fact that although you refer to the writings of your contemporaries, your discussions clearly indicate that you did not read them carefully….For instance, where have I ever said that our ethical values are derived from evolutionary theory? If you read my essay on ethics carefully you will see how much I have avoided making any such statement. Furthermore, you use the word ethics in a very broad sense (as do other historians and philosophers). One must make a distinction between definite value systems, and the way they are acquired. One must also leave open the possibility of pluralism, that is that certain values, let us say the love of a mother for her child, were acquired through natural selection, while others are purely culturally conditioned. Your discussion on these subjects is, in my opinion, distinctly inferior to some of those you criticize. Nowhere is your inconsistency better expressed than in your accusation that I "reject, teleology in nature" and "use teleological language to describe natural processes." If you had only taken the trouble to study the application of the word teleological as carefully as I have done, you would have seen that I use teleological language only in connection with teleonomic processes, where this is quite legitimate, and in describing adaptedness, which the result of natural selection. However, since...you and other historians and philosophers make little effort to dissect equivocal terms and concepts into their components, you are naturally unable to see where the modern argument is.

One other point you seem to have great trouble in understanding is that there is quite a difference between deriving ethical systems from evolution (which I have never done) and accepting ethical systems that do not violate our knowledge of evolution. This is what I tried to do in my chapter on ethics, which you ignore so consistently. An ethical system must have some foundation and except for the Bible I cannot find in any of your descriptions what foundation for an ethical system *you* propose.

Somewhere in your letter you imply that I base my ethical system on "emergence." Please tell me where I made such a claim. Furthermore, for me emergence is not a metaphysical principle but simply an empirical fact. When I put the stem of a hammer and its head together, I have something new, a functional tool called hammer. There is no metaphysics involved. The same is true for combinations of molecules or organic structures.

The real crux of the conflict of our philosophical systems is that you want to derive ethical values directly from scientific theories, which is of course nonsense. You yourself can derive yours apparently...directly from statements in the Bible. However, a scientist can derive his value systems from a general world picture, which he has acquired as a scientist, and through his scientific understanding. Such a value system is, although indirectly, derived from science, just like yours is from the Bible. I fail to see any arguments in your letters that would discredit this interpretation of mine....

To realize this is important for your admonition that one should not confuse the philosophy of biology and biological science. There you are of course completely correct, and if I have done this I am guilty. On the other hand, no one should have any planks in his philosophical platform that are clearly demolished by the findings of the science of biology.

The most important message of this letter is that you should very carefully study the writings of those who you consider your adversaries....

Cordially yours,

Ernst Mayr

P.S. I am enclosing a short dictation [on "Science and Religion"], possibly to be used by me in a future book. [See Greene to Mayr, January 17, 1990 for comments thereon.]

December 18, 1989

Dear Ernst:

A brief letter to wish you and Mrs. Mayr a joyous Christmas season and a happy and productive new year....

By this time, I hope, you realize that my objections, such as they are, are not to evolution or to science properly conceived or to Darwinism as a scientific theory but rather to naturalism as a total world view. I must concede, however, that many of my good friends subscribe to some form or other of naturalism and lead exemplary lives, much more useful to mankind than mine. In his *Foundations of Belief* (1895) Lord Balfour* raised the question whether naturalism in its late nineteenth century form could, when shorn of its parasitic borrowings from classical and Judaeo-Christian sources, support a high civilization. Julian Huxley tried to show that it could, but, as you know, with arguments I find unconvincing. Time will tell! You may be interested in some of my ideas set forth in *History, Humanity and Evolution*, the festschrift Jim Moore has edited in my honor and now, at last, available from the Cambridge University Press. Jim will be here in March to help celebrate the event. We all need our "due meed of glory"!

With high and warm regard-

John Greene

---

* See the essay "Darwin, Huxley and Balfour and the Victorian Crisis of Faith" in the present volume. Balfour was not elevated to the peerage until 1820.

January 17, 1990

Dear Ernst:

I don't know where to start in commenting on your MS "Religion and Science" [mentioned in the postscript to Mayr's letter of December 18, 1989]. My general ideas on the historical relations of the two in Western culture are indicated in my book *Darwin and the Modern World View*. Here I can only make a few comments.

1. I am glad that you recognize the positive as well as the negative role of religious ideas and institutions with respect to the rise and development of modern science. As I have argued in my *Revue de Synthèse* essay, Judaeo-Christian creationism was an essential element in the rise of the science of mechanics and the mechanical world view; likewise it inspired a great deal of excellent work in natural history in the guise of what I have called "Christianized Aristotelianism." When combined with the British competitive ethos it enabled Darwin and Wallace to view evolution by natural selection as a beneficent result of "laws impressed on matter by the Creator."

2. I have reservations about your attempt (à la Andrew Dixon White) to reduce the conflict between science and religion to a conflict between science and theology or between science and Biblical dogmas. The Bible is essentially a narrative except for some of St. Paul's writings, which represent the beginnings of a theological interpretation of the Biblical narratives. Moreover theologians in the various Christian churches have differed substantially in their interpretations. St. Augustine seems to have been fond of allegorical interpretations. And the science of the day, in various historical epochs, has influenced theological interpretation of Scripture. Geocentrism in cosmology owed more to Aristotle and Ptolemy than to the Bible. As to the fixity of species, I know of no church that ever declared it an article of faith before evolutionary ideas began to circulate. So far as I know, Linnaeus was never attacked on *religious* grounds for suggesting that new species may originate by hybridization of existing species. So far as I can see, conflict tended to arise when certain scientific ideas became embedded in the churches' understanding of nature and thus became obstacles to the acceptance of newer scientific ideas.

At bottom, however, the conflict is essentially epistemological, at least on the intellectual level. If scientific ways of knowing reality are the only valid ways, we can know nothing about God or morality, since science as currently conceived deals only with relationships among phenomena considered abstractly without reference to values. But on this assumption neither can we know why science (or anything else) is important, why the passion for truth is noble and morally binding, etc. etc. In these questions we are thrown back on philosophical reflection, introspection, intuition, and (in Christian terms) some notion of revelation through historical events. As you say, everyone is religious in some very general sense in matters of what Paul Tillich called matters of "ultimate concern," but science gives no guidance here. Some scientists, such as Clerk Maxwell, Dobzhansky, R. A. Fisher, and others, find guidance in the Christian tradition, others in other traditions. All are entitled to say their say so long as they do not represent their way of making experience as a whole intelligible as the finding of science or a necessary deduction therefrom. By the same reasoning religious persons should not present their religious beliefs as "creation science." Scientism is equally objectionable at both ends of the spectrum.

3. I quite agree with you that, generally speaking, it is not science that leads men and women either toward or away from theism or other religious beliefs but rather reflection on human experience, especially one's own experience but also the history of mankind, the problem of evil, the feeling of moral obligation and moral guilt, etc. These are the true sources of what you call "religiosity," but religiosity can take many forms, as William James pointed out long ago.

4. I wish I shared your belief that scientists generally are not interested in attacking traditional religious beliefs or in propagating their own forms of religiosity. If this were true, I would not have bothered to write or publish *Science, Ideology, and World View*, nor would I have called the spate of writings by biologists,

paleontologists, etc. on human duty and destiny "the Bridgewater treatises of the twentieth century"....

Cordially,
John Greene

NOTE: The Mayr-Greene correspondence lapsed after 1991 but was resumed in the summer of 1996 on the subject of biological progress.

August 6, 1996

Dear John,

You are quite right, I haven't written you in a long time. But time races by at such a speed!....

Now to your letter. The trouble with the objection to the word *progress* is, that so many people are still teleologists. They think that there must be some force pushing toward progress. The beauty of Darwin's thought is that with genetic recombination and variation you produce new combinations in every generation and those who in one way or another are a little better than their competitors will, so to speak, automatically survive and reproduce. It is the same non-teleological process that has given us a motor car that is so much better than Ford's Model T car....

Best wishes as ever-
Ernst

August 28, 1996

Dear Ernst:

It was a great pleasure to hear from you and to know that you are in good health and spirits, so much so that you are planning trips to the Grand Canyon and to Paris!....

I am afraid that we shall never agree about the adequacy of the theory of natural selection as constituting a full and sufficient explanation of the existence and evolution of organisms on the planet Earth. Somewhere in my writings I have said that the theory of natural selection presupposes the existence of organisms as going concerns, and I find the same idea expounded much more fully in Errol Harris's *The Foundations of Metaphysics in Science* (chapter on "Evolution," pp. 226ff.) setting forth his holistic concept of nature. p. 231: "Coherent structure must be presupposed as a basis for evolution; and more than that, a coherent structure which reproduces itself and which automatically adapts itself, within a limited but relatively wide range, to environmental alteration. In other words, inherent adaptability is an indispensable prerequisite to evolution; so that, however much may be effected by random mutation and natural selection, they cannot be the only determining principles in the evolutionary process. Once the assumption of auturgy is made, however, any fortuitous change which is assimilable by the system may be a means to further integration and self-maintenance, for it can be incorporated into the system and used to adapt to new conditions....[p. 246] This self-adjustment within the system discloses the activity of a positive, integrating agency cooperating with natural selection to effect adaptation and generate 'an exceedingly high degree of improbability'. Selection inevitably preserves and intensifies the effects of this nisus to integration and sifts out those which tend to impede its operation....This functional property we can now recognize as auturgic wholeness."*

As you can see from this passage, Harris's point of view is a broader version of your "somewhat holistic approach" in your essay "The Unity of the Genotype" emphasizing "the internal cohesion of the genotype." Harris generalizes this approach to embrace nature as a whole, physical and biological and psychological. He concedes the difficulty of formulating the postulated "nisus to integration" scientifically, but argues that the scientific facts don't make sense without some such concept. I tend to agree with him. I knew Harris slightly when we were both teaching at the University of Kansas, but I never read anything of his until this year, when I saw his *Foundations* advertised in a flyer distributed by the Humanities Press. His familiarity with scientific literature—physics,

---

* Errol Harris, *The Foundations of Metaphysics in Science* (New Jersey and London: Humanities Press, 1993), 231-232, 246-247. Quoted with permission.

biochemistry, biology, psychology is impressive. I gather that he is in retirement in England, from whence he came originally.

One final word on "progress" in evolution. I simply do not understand your notion that the evolution of the motor car is "non-teleological and hence an appropriate analogy to the evolution of plants and animals." Henry Ford was as teleological as can be imagined, and so were all the other entrepreneurs who devised improvements aimed at dominating the market place. My Plymouth Breeze is a product of human ingenuity driven by desire for profit and love of tinkering, not by random variation and selection of the market place....

Cordially,
John Greene

October 31, 1996

Dear John,

I was delighted to see that you are willing to put your reservations about natural selection openly on paper. It is my experience that all those who question natural selection vastly underestimate the amount of genetic variation. No two individuals are ever the same and among the infinite number of combinations some have a chance to survive more easily than others. Natural selection goes right back to the origin of life and according to Manfred Eigen it plays an important role even in the pre-biotic era. What natural selection picks is not always the best solution. We would not have so much extinction if natural selection was more effective, and, in the spirit of modern science, I am perfectly happy with natural selection until somebody comes up with a better solution. There certainly have been many attempts in the last 137 years but none of them was in the slightest successful.

Now to your comments on progress and teleology. In the first paper (1974) in which I showed that the term teleological had been applied to four entirely different kinds of phenomena I said that I would not include in my analysis the human activities for which the words purpose and intention were traditionally employed. This was a mistake. Such purposive activities are not restricted to the human species but may occur in any organism capable of thinking. A pride of lionesses which splits into two in order to attack a victim from two opposite sides is certainly carrying out a purposive activity. Eventually every act of our daily life is in this category....

When Ford or any other car manufacturer incorporates an improvement in his car this is certainly a purposive activity. However, Ford in 1900 did not have as his aim (telos) the car of the year 2000 or 2050. Neither does natural selection think of an ultimate telos when favoring this survival of a particular individual. It is therefore totally misleading, for instance, to say that the eye has the purpose of seeing. No, the eye has no purpose, however, the eye, as a product of natural selection, is adapted for vision. Any sloppy way of using the word purpose is bound to create confusion....

I do not expect you to agree with me but at least I want to state clearly why I have opinions that are different from yours....

Yours ever,

Ernst Mayr

November 7, 1996

Dear Ernst:

It was good to receive your delayed letter and to know that you have survived your Grand Canyon flight and your trip to Paris. How you do get around!....

I am afraid I don't understand your argument about the supposed analogy between the "improvements" (Darwin's term) produced in organisms by natural selection and the improvements produced by automobile manufacturers in the motor car. My point was that the variations in organisms are presumed to be random with respect to the needs of the organism in its struggle to survive and reproduce whereas the improvements in the motor car are specifically intended and designed to increase the survivability and market share of a particular line of cars. In the first case the variants are happenstance; in the second they are designed to increase efficiency, attractiveness, etc. In the latter case they are teleological in having a purpose or end, if only the purpose of selling the maximum number of cars.

I would be interested in having your reactions to the line of argument proposed by Errol Harris in his *Foundations of Metaphysics in Science* and quoted in my letter to you of August 28. What do you think of his idea that the discoveries of modern science suggest a "nisus toward integration" in nature? Michael Ghiselin rejects any such notion as sounding "like a lot of mystics that I have read." But there are ideas which reason suggests to the reflective, well-informed person (e.g. Democritus's atomic hypothesis) and which are persuasive even though they cannot currently be substantiated scientifically. Harris argues that modern science reveals a nisus toward integration even in the atomic world. Another book that would interest you if you have not already seen it is Evelyn Fox Keller's *Refiguring Life*, which seems to lend some plausibility to Harris's line of argument. I was particularly struck by her quotation on pp. 22-23 from Richard Lewontin to the effect that:

> DNA is a dead molecule....[It] has no power to reproduce itself. Rather it is produced out of elementary materials by a complex machinery of proteins. While it is often said that DNA produces proteins, in fact proteins (enzymes) produce DNA....Not only is DNA incapable of making copies of itself,...but it is incapable of 'making' anything else. The linear sequence of nucleotides in DNA is used by the machinery of the cell to determine what sequence of amino acids is to be built into a protein, and to determine when and where the protein is to be made....In fact, an egg, before fertilization, contains a complete apparatus of production deposited there in the course of its cellular development. We inherit not only genes made of DNA but an intricate structure of cellular machinery made up of proteins.

Do you see any teleology here? Can we have a "machinery" for determining a sequence of amino acids and the location in which a protein is to be made without some element of final cause? The definition of a machine is "an artifact designed to accomplish some purpose."

Cordially,

John Greene

November 27, 1996

Dear John,

....Now as to my comparing progress in motor cars with "progress" in evolution I am afraid that you have missed a number of points. Even though genetic variation does not answer any needs, selection would not accomplish anything if there were not fitness differences among the millions of new genotypes continuously produced. The situation in reproduction of novelty in motor cars is not as drastically different as you think. A very high percentage of the variance produced by car manufacturers turned out to be useless or even bad. Just think of the failure of the infamous Edsel. But there are some that are successful and the market (equals selection) will pick them up.

I do not know whether you consider natural selection to be a teleological process. This is, however, what Francisco Ayala does. I do not agree. If you adopt that interpretation then anything any organism does is teleological. The actual process of natural selection is, as from Herbert Spencer and Alfred Russell Wallace on many later authors have pointed out, a process of elimination. The "selected" individuals are those that are left over after the less fit ones have been eliminated. Do you call that a teleological process?

Evolution as seen by the orthogenesists like Berg, Osborn, Teilhard de Chardin indeed is a teleological process. But Darwinian evolution definitely is not, nor is any single selective event. There is no world spirit or supreme being which sees to it that every step is "for the best," as it should be if it were teleological. I realize that you will not agree with me but this is the way it looks to me....

Cordially yours,

Ernst Mayr

January 1, 1997

Dear Ernst:

I guess we shall never agree about the supposed analogy between technological progress (as in the motor car) and "progress" in organic evolution. In one case the variations are *intentionally* aimed at meeting (or creating) the demands of the market place; in the other the variations are random with respect to the organism's needs as dictated by environmental circumstances. This seems to me a crucially important difference. I am interested that you seem to have abandoned completely the notion of positive "selection". Darwin would roll in his grave! There is only the elimination of "unfit" organisms, the fit being those that survive. And so we come back to the ambiguities in the concept of fitness. Shades of Empedocles!....

Cordially,

John Greene

P. S. Shall we redo Darwin's title to read "the Elimination of the Unfit Races" instead of "the Preservation of the Favored Races"?

January 25, 1997

Dear John,

....You raise a number of interesting points in your letter. What is so exciting about "non-random elimination"? Spencer saw it too and so did A. R. Wallace, when they proposed survival of the fittest. And since Darwin also adopted it, or at least tolerated it, he would certainly not "roll in his grave." Many animal breeders use the same procedure, but call it "culling." Eliminating those not worth breeding. The fittest are not to be defined by their survival, but they survive because they have properties that prevent their elimination.

And in the case of progress due to the Darwinian process, you apply unnecessarily severe criteria. There is nothing in the *principle* of selection that specifies that the variation must be random. Darwin also allowed for all sources of variation, including use and disuse and even occasionally direct induction by the environment. Not all gene mutations are random, there is a good deal of "biased variation," as for instance the segregation distorter gene. "Intentional variation," as you call it, leads of course much faster to "progress." What the car builders achieved in 100 years would have taken unbiased variation at least 5 million years.

Exactly the same argument has been urged against Darwinian evolutionary epistemology. There also 2 critics claimed that it was not Darwinian because the variation of conjectures and theories was man made, and not random. But again the answer was that the nature of the variation was irrelevant, but the basic process was Darwinian, consisting of variation and selection.

To judge from your letter, you will find much in my new book that you will disagree with. [i.e., Mayr's *This Is Biology*] That should make you happy!

Cordially,

Ernst Mayr

March 6, 1997

Dear Ernst:

Having just survived my 80th birthday...I sit down belatedly to answer your letter of January 25th....

I shall take under advisement your latest formulation of the principle of natural selection. Offhand I don't see that it removes the difficulties associated with that principle, but rather defines it in negative rather than positive terms. In the process the whole idea of "selection" is imperilled. Those organisms survive that are not eliminated. They are not eliminated because they have properties that "prevent their elimination." Darwin's conception, imbued with his evolutionary deism, is much more positive. The "favored races" are "preserved" and subjected to still new trials and ordeals in a never-ending process of improvement. I am also struck by your suggestion that the variations favorable to survival in particular circumstances need not be random with respect to the organisms' needs in the survival game. This is scarcely orthodox neo-Darwinian theory; it would seem to imperil the anti-Lamarckian arguments of the neo-Darwinians....Is your new book out yet?....I look forward with pleasure to reading it.

Cordially,

John Greene

NOTE: Soon after this, Professor Mayr mailed me a copy of his latest book, *This Is Biology*, a fitting testament to his continuing intellectual vigor and his abiding faith in neo-Darwinism as the surest guide in biology, philosophy, and the conduct of life. My critique of *This Is Biology* may be found in a forthcoming issue of *Biology and Philosophy*.

III

FINAL REFLECTIONS

12

THE DARWINIAN REVOLUTION
IN SCIENCE & WORLD VIEW

The Count de Buffon, writes Jacques Roger, was *le naturaliste le plus important entre Aristote et Darwin.* In so doing he designates three key figures in a major transformation in Western thought. To outline the main steps in this transformation with some added reflections on the Darwinian revolution in our own time is the purpose of this essay.

It was Aristotle who set forth a point of view with respect to living things which dominated Western thinking until the publication of Charles Darwin's famous treatise *On the Origin of Species.* Aristotle was the first to see interest and dignity in the many forms of life, from the lowest to the highest, to preach and practice extensive observation of living creatures, and to create a conceptual framework within which to interpret the facts of natural history.

Like Darwin, Aristotle interpreted nature by analogy to human activities. The works of animate nature, he declared, are like works of art or artifice. To understand them we must take account not only of the material and efficient causes that influence their constitution and behavior but also of the formal and final causes. The acorn always grows into an oak, never into an elm or ash or horse. Every living thing undergoes a development dominated and directed by its peculiar form. Moreover, all the parts of the organism work together to maintain it as a going concern and to adapt it to its mode of life in its environing circumstances. The existence and perpetual regeneration of natural kinds, each member of each kind realizing its own form of being, each with parts adapted to each other and to the organism's needs in its interactions with other organisms and the physical environment, this *oeconomia naturae* (so like the economy of a rationally ordered household) could not be explained by the operation of material causes alone, Aristotle argued. The natural world was a cosmos in which formal and final causes, interacting with material and efficient causes, assured that plants and animals in their unending life cycles imitated the uniform circular motion of the heavenly bodies and, in so doing, achieved that degree of realization of the beautiful and the good which was possible for them as sub-lunar beings. "I add Beauty," says Aristotle, "because in the works of Nature purpose and not accident is predominant; and the purpose or end for the sake of which those works have been constructed or formed has its place among what is beautiful."[1]

Armed with his basic analogy to works of art and artifice, with his metaphysics and his logic of class division and species definition, and with information gathered from his own researches and the reports of others, Aristotle proceeded to construct a science of natural history ranging over the fields we would now call comparative anatomy, taxonomy, embryology, ecology, and animal psychology. His point of view was non-evolutionary. The world, he thought, was eternal and had from eternity exhibited the graduated series of organisms—the scale of nature or great chain of being—that greeted the eye of the observer in every age. Accepting the variety of animal forms as given, Aristotle undertook to analyze them functionally and to differentiate the natural kinds by comparative study of their anatomical parts, modes of reproduction, lifestyles, and character traits, subdividing the blooded animals into viviparous and oviparous, the viviparous into quadrupeds and human beings, and so on until he arrived at the ultimate species, the members of which could not be further differentiated by characters essential to their very nature but only by accidental differences produced by material causes. The point of view throughout was teleological. The aim was to define the essential nature of each kind and to display its attributes, its structure, physiology, biochemistry, behavior, and the like—as adapted to and flowing necessarily from that essential nature. "As its very essence includes the power to fly," writes Aristotle, "a bird must have something it can stretch out, and wings provide this."[2] Likewise with respect to man's physical attributes: they serve the needs and purposes of a rational animal.

> Man is the only animal that stands upright, and that is because his nature and essence is divine. Now the business of that which is most divine is to think and to be intelligent; and this would not be easy if there were a great deal of the body at the top weighing it down, for weight hampers the motion of the intellect and of the general sense....And since man stands upright, he has no need of legs in front; instead of them Nature has given him arms and hands. Anaxagoras indeed asserts that it is because he has hands that man is the most intelligent of the animals; but surely the reasonable point of view is that it is because he is the most intelligent animal that he has got hands. Hands are an instrument; and Nature, like a sensible human being, always assigns an organ to the animal that can use it....[3]

Such was the science of natural history that emerged from Aristotle's wide-ranging philosophical inquiry into the hitherto unexplored world of living beings. It was a profoundly non-evolutionary science, but it introduced ideas and raised questions that were to play an important part in the rise of evolutionary theories many centuries later.

For 2,000 years after Aristotle the science of natural history made little headway. Theophrastus applied Aristotle's concepts to the study of plants with some success, but soon afterwards scientific natural history gave way to the herbal and to encyclopedic compilations like that of Pliny the Elder. Comparative anatomy lingered on as an adjunct of human anatomy in the medical schools, but with little reference to the problems of natural history. A new natural history based on Aristotle finally emerged in the sixteenth and seventeenth centuries, but it was preoccupied with naming, classifying, and describing the thousands of new plants and animals made known by expanded research and by European voyages of discovery and colonization in America and the Far East. Under the pressure of this growing mass of information the herbal and the encyclopedic catch-all yielded to systematic natural history, the principles of which were gradually worked out by naturalists like John Ray, Joseph Pitton de Tournefort, and Carl Linnaeus.

The new systematic natural history was in many respects a Christianized Aristotelianism. Aristotle himself had been more concerned with defining essences and explaining animal structure and function in terms of these than with classification. But, as James Larson demonstrates in his excellent study *Reason and Experience,*[4] Aristotle's distinction between natural and artificial methods of division, his procedure (analogous to logical division) for arriving at specific essences by dividing and subdividing according to essential characters, his identification of functional importance with essentiality, and his doctrine of the vital unity of plants and animals with respect to the basic functions of nutrition and reproduction—all these were of the utmost service to naturalists seeking to discern rational order among the myriad forms of life.

At the same time, Aristotle's static, teleological philosophy of nature, suitably Christianized, provided the conceptual framework within which systematic natural history was practiced. The various natural kinds, instead of being eternal, were now regarded as created by God in the beginning and, like the other basic structures of nature, "by Him conserved to this Day in the same State and Condition in which they were first made,"[5] as the English naturalist John Ray put it. And the immanent means-ends rationality of nature, Aristotle's *oeconomia naturae*, was now viewed as the wise contrivance of a transcendent Creator, with the result that the balance of nature and the adaptation of structure to function were no longer thought to be more or less perfect, as Aristotle had supposed, but absolutely perfect, since they were the handiwork of an all-wise and all-powerful Creator. The hierarchy of levels of being, rising from the inorganic to the sentient and rational as Aristotle had observed, was now seen as a created order in which the inorganic ministered to the needs of the organic and the organic to those of the sentient and rational, both on the planet Earth and in the innumerable worlds scattered throughout space.[6]

In such a created order there was nothing left for the natural historian to do but to name, classify, describe, and admire the wonderful works of creation and, if possible, to discover the natural method of classification reflecting the patterns the Creator had in mind when he created living beings. True, there were some apparent exceptions to the stability and perfection of the structures of nature: cabbages that failed to breed true, the new star that appeared in 1572, fossil remains of creatures for which no living counterparts were known, hybrid crosses between species that occasionally produced fertile offspring—but these anomalies could safely be ignored or explained away by one means or another. Structure and wise design were the basic attributes of nature. Change was superficial, adding variety and interest but never altering the created order of things.

This Christianized Aristotelianism reached its climax in the writings of the French zoologist Georges Cuvier, "the Aristotle of the nineteenth century," as he was known to his contemporaries. In Cuvier's work, natural history and comparative anatomy were reunited. John Ray, Linnaeus, and other naturalists had drawn on the work of Aristotle and other comparative anatomists in framing their main categories of animals, but they were not themselves anatomists. Cuvier, on the contrary, took up comparative anatomy, mastered it completely, and applied it systematically not only to the classification of living animals but also to the reconstruction and classification of extinct animals. Adopting Aristotle's principle that function determines form, he applied it to reconstructing extinct quadrupeds, explaining that "the seemly harmony between organs which interact is a necessary condition of existence of the creature to which they belong and…if one of these functions were modified in a manner incompatible with the modifications of others the creature could no longer continue to exist." Like Aristotle, Cuvier thought that the "seemly harmony" among the organs and between them and the requirements of the environment could not be accounted for without invoking an ordering principle, which, in Cuvier's natural history, was the wisdom of the Creator. The internal and external conditions of existence, he declared, were the final causes of the organism's structures.[7]

Cuvier's demonstration that considerable numbers of quadrupeds which had once roamed the Earth were no longer extant raised difficult questions about the static creationism presupposed by his science, however. If the surface of the earth had undergone extensive revolutions in its flora and fauna, as the latest discoveries seemed to indicate, how were these facts to be reconciled with the Christianized Aristotelianism that dominated scientific research in natural history? Cuvier himself suggested an answer in the "Preliminary Discourse" to his *Fossil Bones of Quadrupeds*, published in 1812. In this essay may be found the first hints of a theory of successive creations and extinctions of plants and animals accompanying sudden alterations in the positions of sea and land brought about by geological upheavals produced by unknown causes different in kind from any operating on the surface of the present Earth. By means of this theory the static view of nature and natural history and its accompanying static design argument were reconciled with the patent fact that the organic and inorganic structures on the earth's surface had undergone profound changes long antedating human history. Species could still be regarded as created and wisely adapted to their conditions of life. Natural history could still be conceived as the science of naming, classifying, and describing the productions of the Earth. Man was still the crown of creation, the last in a progressive series of the works of omnipotence. And the most recent of the great catastrophes in the globe's history could, if one chose, be identified with the Biblical flood.[8]

But the Christianized Aristotelianism of Linnaeus and Cuvier did not hold the field undisputed. There were two rival approaches to the study of natural history, one leading away from the path Darwin was to follow, the other leading toward it. The first of these, advocated by Étienne Geoffroy St.-Hilaire, Lorenz Oken, and others, involved a Platonic search for a science of pure form in which all living things were conceived as modeled on a few archetypes, form determining function instead of the reverse.[9] The other approach drew on the dynamic and causal view of nature set forth by the Count de Buffon in his *Natural History, General and Particular* (1749-1788). The roots of Buffon's revolutionary ideas, so clearly described in Jacques Roger's *Buffon*, are to be found, not in Aristotle's writings, but in the mechanistic deism of René Descartes' *Principles of Philosophy* (1644). It was Descartes who first proposed a systematic alternative to Aristotle's philosophy of nature, substituting for Aristotle's world of forms and qualities the idea of nature as a law-bound system of matter in motion created by God and governed in its operations by divinely ordained mathematical laws of motion discoverable by human reason. Unlike Sir Isaac Newton, who was a static creationist, Descartes suggested that the Creator, instead of forming the world as we now see it, may have chosen to create matter more or less evenly distributed throughout space, leaving it to form itself into stars, solar systems, and the like through the operation of the laws of nature. In his famous vortex theory, the first mechanical explanation of the origin of the solar system, Descartes introduced a new kind of scientific enterprise—that of deriving the present structures of nature from some previous, more homogeneous state of the system of matter in motion by the operation of natural laws and processes.

In astronomy this kind of scientific speculation led in the eighteenth century to Immanuel Kant's cosmic evolutionism and the Kant-Laplace nebular hypothesis concerning the origin of the solar system. In geology Descartes' method led to the idea, now called "geological uniformitarianism," that all geological phenomena must be explained as having been produced by the daily action of known processes of erosion, deposition, volcanic eruption, and the like instead of by world-wide floods or other giant catastrophes. This method of reasoning led, in turn, to a vastly expanded time scheme. It also upset the traditional assumption that the inorganic world exists to serve the needs of organic beings. It was this mode of geological reasoning to which Charles Darwin was converted when he read the first volume of Charles Lyell's *Principles of Geology* on the voyage of the *Beagle*.

In biology (or natural history, as it was then called) Descartes' project of deriving the present structures of nature from the operations of the law-bound system of matter in motion led through the Count de Buffon, Erasmus Darwin, and Jean Baptiste de Lamarck to the idea that the present species of plants and animals were derived from earlier forms of life through a process of descent with modification arising out of the interactions between organisms and their environing circumstances. Buffon's revolutionary impact on the science of natural history, turning it into a history of nature,

is described succinctly in Jacques Roger's masterful account of
Buffon's life and work:

> Cette remontée dans le passé de la Nature est la conséquence logique,
> quoique lointaine, de la définition même de l'espèce que Buffon avait
> esquissé des 1749. Mais, parti du simple renouvellement des formes,
> Buffon est passé à leur 'dégénération', à leur diversification et à leur
> multiplication....Par sa facon de concevoir l'histoire des animaux, par sa
> définition de l'espèce, par le nouveau mode de classification qu'elle
> presentait, cette histoire naturelle rompait profondement avec les habitudes
> intellectuelles de son temps. Sans doute, la réalisation n'était pas toujours à
> la hauteur des ambitions, et Buffon en était conscient. Mais il avait posé de
> nouvelles questions et imposé de nouvelles directions de recherche, que
> personne ne reprendra exactement dans les mèmes termes, mais que
> personne non plus ne pourra ignorer après lui. Aucun naturaliste sans
> doute, depuis Aristote, n'avait si profondement transformé sa science.
> [*Buffon*, pp. 440-441].

Buffon's thinking about the changes undergone by animals in
the long course of time was too much dominated by the idea of
decline from original vigor and perfection for him to conceive of
evolution in the modern sense as a transition from simple to complex
forms. That was left for his protégé Jean Baptiste de Lamarck. From
his geological studies, conducted on uniformitarian principles,
Lamarck concluded that the surface of the earth had undergone
constant slow change over hundreds of millions of years and that
consequently the species of plants and animals must have changed
too, or they would have become extinct. The so-called extinct
species described by Cuvier and others, Lamarck believed, were
simply the ancestors of the organisms now inhabiting the earth.
About the same time it occurred to Lamarck that the graduated series
of organic forms rising from the simplest organisms to the highest
plants and animals—Aristotle's scale of nature—might represent the
path that nature had followed in producing the present array of
organic forms. As to *how* these organic transformations had taken
place Lamarck had no convincing explanation. He spoke vaguely of
"the cause in nature which tends toward complexity." He appealed
to the principle of use and disuse and imagined that the "felt needs"

of an animal could cause body fluids to flow to the region of the body where a new organ was needed and thus produce the needed organ. In England, Charles Darwin's grandfather, Erasmus Darwin, propounded an evolutionary hypothesis of a similar kind, pointing to evidence from comparative anatomy, embryology, and vestigial organs in support of his speculation.

It is worth noting that both Erasmus Darwin and Lamarck arrived at their theories of organic evolution within a framework of evolutionary theism. Thus Erasmus Darwin, "meditating [as he tells us] on the great similarity of the structure of warm-blooded animals...and...the great changes they undergo both before and after their nativity," asked his readers to imagine that all these warm-blooded animals had developed from "one living filament, which THE GREAT FIRST CAUSE endued with animality, with the power of acquiring new parts attended with new propensities" over a period of "millions of ages." It was evident, Darwin added, that "all nature exists in a state of perpetual improvement by laws impressed on the atoms of matter by the great CAUSE OF CAUSES".[10] And Lamarck, in turn, assured his readers that the "Sublime Author of Nature" had so arranged the properties of living matter that the progress made toward higher forms of life in the interactions between organisms and their surroundings would never be lost. As we shall see, Charles Darwin fell heir to the viewpoint of evolutionary theism.

It was at this point in the history of science that Charles Darwin entered the scene. He was born in 1809, the year in which Lamarck published his *Philosophie Zoologigue*. Besides being born later, Darwin had several other advantages over Lamarck and his grandfather. Unlike them, he had an opportunity to study the geology, flora, and fauna of South America, parts of Australia, and various islands of the Atlantic and Pacific oceans at first hand on the voyage of the *Beagle*, an opportunity few naturalists could match. Second, he possessed not only the propensity and talent for speculation of Lamarck and his grandfather but marvelous powers of observation as well and a determination to test all his theories by extensive observation and experiment. British science at this time was heavily empirical and anti-theoretical, and Darwin knew that he must be prepared to support whatever theories he might propose with solid evidence. Thirdly, Darwin had from his father sufficient income to devote himself totally to a life of scientific research and writing, and his chronic illness protected him in this cloistered life even further.

We come now to Darwin's great contribution to biological science, namely, that whereas others had speculated that a process of organic evolution might have taken place, offering only scattered evidence in support of this idea and suggesting no believable mechanism of organic change, Darwin constructed a theory of species modification and evolution by random variation, struggle for existence and natural selection, explored its consequences, and spent twenty years experimenting and gathering evidence from comparative anatomy, morphology, geographic distribution, taxonomy, animal behavior, the fossil record, and other sources in support of his theory, revising it from time to time in the light of new discoveries, and testing it in every way he could think of. It is only within the past ten or fifteen years that scholars have come to appreciate fully what an ambitious, tough-minded, wide-ranging, and tenacious theorist this man Charles Darwin was.[11] One could point to similar examples of systematic, hard-headed scientific reasoning and testing in the physical sciences, but Darwin was the first such theorist in the field of natural history, with the possible exception of Aristotle.

Shortly after returning from the voyage of the *Beagle*, as he meditated on what he had seen and on the fact that the ornithologist John Gould classified the mockingbirds collected on several of the Galapagos Islands as different species (not mere varieties of a single species), Darwin adopted an evolutionary point of view and set out to construct a theory as to how organic change comes about. In the years 1837-1838 he tried various theories, one of them decidedly Lamarckian in tone. Finally, late in 1838, after reading Thomas Malthus's *Essay on the Principle of Population*, it dawned on Darwin that if plant and animal populations, like human populations, tended to multiply exponentially, there must ensue a struggle for existence *within* as well as *between* species and that those individual plants and animals that happened to possess characteristics well suited to environing circumstances would be more likely to survive and reproduce than those individuals with less well adapted traits. Thus, by a process of selective elimination and differential reproduction (or "natural selection," as Darwin called it by analogy to the selection practiced by plant and animal breeders), the character of a given population would gradually change as individuals with certain favored traits flourished and multiplied and their brothers and sisters with less favored traits became less and less numerous in the population.

Having hit upon this idea and on the analogy between natural selection and artificial selection, Darwin proceeded to construct his theory, work out its implications for all the fields of natural history, and then make experiments and gather facts to test whether the predicted consequences of his theory held true in nature. When he would have been ready to publish his ideas if left to himself no one knows. Fortunately for science, Alfred Russel Wallace, who had been seeking to discover the mechanism of evolution in the Malay Archipelago for several years, sent Darwin in June, 1858, an essay setting forth a theory of evolution remarkably like Darwin's. Darwin was now forced to rush into print with an "abstract" of the treatise he had been working on.

Darwin's *Origin of Species* was the last and heaviest of a series of blows that brought about the collapse of the biological point of view Aristotle had propounded more than two thousand years earlier. Darwin's book not only overthrew the idea of the fixity of species; it also challenged Aristotle's assumption that the adaptation of structure to function and of organism to environment presupposed some teleological principle, some means-ends rationality, some final cause or causes in nature. With the demise of Aristotle's maxim that "Nature does nothing in vain" went the static design argument of John Ray, Linnaeus, Cuvier, and Archdeacon Paley's *Natural Theology*. At the same time, Darwin's theory undermined Aristotle's idea that the essence of a species was the primary explanation of the attributes of its members, who, being alike in form and essence, differed only in non-essential traits produced by material causes. In Darwin's view there was no specific essence, whether of the human species or of any other. A species was simply a well marked variety, a population of similar yet varying individuals, an entity which, when subjected to random variation in the offspring and the selective action of environing circumstances, underwent changes in the hereditary disposition and the observed character and behavior of its surviving members. In short, struggle, chance, change, and individuality, each of which had been assigned a negligible role in the Christianized Aristotelianism of Ray, Linnaeus, and Cuvier, now became the architects of the world of living beings.

But Darwin's argument in the *Origin of Species* was not purely scientific. He attacked static creationism not only with scientific arguments but also by suggesting an evolutionary creationism in its place. In the closing paragraphs of his masterwork he argued that his view of organic life as having evolved through the action of "laws impressed on matter by the Creator" (compare Erasmus Darwin's expression, quoted above, p. 269) gave a nobler view of the Creator than did static creationism. Some writers have attempted to dismiss this language of Darwin as having been inserted by him to placate the public or his wife or both, but this interpretation will not bear close scrutiny. From the 1830s onward we find expressions of this kind in his private notebooks. In Notebook C he refers to the static creationist view as a "miserable, limited view," and in his "Notes on Man" he describes the natural laws governing organic change as "his most magnificent laws." Indeed, one cannot help thinking that Darwin's evolutionary theism was an important psychological and spiritual support for him during the long years of intense labor on a theory he knew must subject him to merciless criticism from static creationists once it was published. Would he have endured to the end if he had not believed that his theory provided a nobler idea of God than the "miserable, limited view" of static creationism?[12]

But we have not yet discussed the most revolutionary aspect of Darwin's theory, namely, its implication that humankind in all its aspects—physical, mental, moral, esthetic, religious—was a product of the same processes of random variation, struggle for existence, and natural selection (aided, Darwin thought, by sexual selection and the inherited effects of mental and moral exertion) that had produced all other living forms. It was this application of his general theory, set forth in *The Descent of Man*, that became, and continues to be, the storm center of the controversy surrounding Darwin's name. Most people care little how plants and pigeons and monkeys originated, but the question of human nature and its origins touches us at the center of our existence as rational, moral beings.

Darwin was not the first to suggest that the human species was a product of organic evolution. Lamarck had suggested this, and Darwin's own grandfather had implied it. But Darwin undertook to gather and weigh the empirical evidence pointing toward human kinship with the rest of the animal kingdom and to try to envisage as concretely as possible how human evolution had occurred. With respect to the physical similarities between human beings and the higher animals Darwin could draw on an extensive literature in comparative anatomy and embryology. But when it came to conceiving the evolution of human intellect, instincts, emotions, sexual differences, and religious, moral, and esthetic sentiments Darwin was pretty much on his own. It was a huge undertaking, begun in July 1838, in his private notebooks and continued intermittently but with unflagging purpose through the publication of *The Descent of Man* and *The Expression of Emotion in Man and Animals*. In his notebooks we see him ransacking the literature on man from treatises on morals and esthetics to travel books and works on human psychology, tapping his father's medical knowledge, studying his own behavior, his children's, and that of domestic animals and those in the London Zoo, observing, experimenting occasionally, and constantly developing and revising his theoretical framework.[13]

Darwin's method was twofold. On the one hand, he gathered evidence to show that human actions are not entirely the result of conscious thought. On the other, he looked for traces of intelligence, consciousness, esthetic preference, and the like throughout the animal kingdom, from worms and jellyfish to apes and human beings. He even discerned something like mental powers in plants in their sensitivity to stimulation, their transmission of information from one organ to another, and their variable movements in response to changing circumstances. In seeking to discover the biological bases of instinct, intelligence, imagination, memory, language, and esthetic and moral feeling he pointed the way toward comparative psychology, child psychology, cognitive psychology, psychoanalysis, ethology, sociobiology, and the biobehavioral sciences generally. Not since Aristotle had a single individual opened up such a wide field of investigation into the science of living things.

The theory of human evolution resulting from these years of research and speculation envisaged a complex interaction of the agencies of natural selection, sexual selection, and the inherited effects of habit, use, and mental and moral exercise. By sexual selection Darwin meant the genetic effects of competition among males for the possession of females, whether by physical prowess in combat or by superior attractiveness in courtship. To this agency he attributed not only the physical differences between men and women (other than the obvious differences in their reproductive organs) but many other human attributes as well. Courage, pugnacity, perseverance, strength and size of body, weapons of all kinds, bright colours and ornamental appendages, musical organs, both vocal and instrumental (hence possibly even language itself) had all, said Darwin, been indirectly gained by the one sex or the other through the exertion of choice, the influence of love and jealousy, and the appreciation of the beautiful in sound, color, and form.[14]

The chief agency in human evolution, however, had been natural selection in the competition of individuals, tribes, nations, and races, aided somewhat by the inherited effects of mental and moral effort. "I suppose that you do not doubt [Darwin wrote to Charles Lyell] that the intellectual powers are as important for the welfare of each being as corporeal structure; if so, I can see no difficulty in the most intellectual individuals of a species being continually selected and the intellect of the new species thus improved, aided probably by effects of inherited mental exercise. I look at this process as now going on with the races of man; the less intellectual races being exterminated".[15] The same competitive struggle, Darwin reasoned, would gradually improve human moral faculties. Those tribes in which the social instincts were most fully developed would "spread and be victorious over other tribes," and these, in turn would succumb to some other tribe "still more highly endowed." Thus the social and moral qualities would "tend slowly to advance and be diffused throughout the world," and virtuous habits, inculcated by education and religion over many generations, might well become "fixed by inheritance" and so bring about the eventual triumph of a high morality. The processes of evolution, Darwin concluded, had raised mankind to "the very summit of the organic scale," and there was hope that they would create for it a still higher destiny, so that Darwin and Lyell would eventually be looked back on as "mere Barbarians" by remote generations yet to come.[16]

* * * * * * * * * *

From what has been said it should be apparent that Darwin believed that he could sink human nature into nature-at-large without disturbing his own and his contemporaries' faith in progress, humanity, and the good, the true, and the beautiful. But this proved to be very difficult. Darwin himself never succeeded in resolving the conflict between his belief that competitive struggle between individuals, tribes, nations, and races had been, and continued to be, a primary engine of human progress and his equally strong conviction that man's "nobler instincts" leading him to care for the weak, the maimed, and the helpless must not be discounted or disregarded. Nor could he reconcile his instinctive admiration for nature's "endless forms most beautiful and most wonderful" and his "inward conviction" that they were not the result of "mere chance" with the mechanistic determinism of the physical science of his day and the "clumsy, wasteful, blundering, low, and horribly cruel" process of natural selection he himself had discovered. If man was purely and simply a product of nature, why should not nature's methods and norms govern human behavior? Darwin's champion, Thomas Henry Huxley, reflected long and hard on this question and finally concluded that social ethics, far from being patterned on the processes of nature, must actively combat those processes in the name of values of justice and mercy that had no basis in nature. But what room was there for values of this kind in the universe of

evolutionary naturalism, in a universe described by Huxley himself
as a "web and woof of matter and force, interweaving by slow
degrees, without a broken thread, that veil [of phenomena] which
lies between us and the Infinite.[17]

None at all, said Arthur James Balfour, Huxley's younger
contemporary rising fast in the Tory leadership.* All those Victorian
ideas and feelings about the dignity of man, the golden rule, the
passion for truth, and the love of beauty were derived, Balfour
noted, from conceptions of nature and human nature quite different
from those assumed by Darwin, Huxley, and Spencer. Their idea of
nature, inherited from Galileo, Descartes, and Newton, viewed
nature as a *sys*tem of matter in motion governed by inexorable laws.
Matter itself was mere brute stuff possessing only the mathematical
properties of size, shape, mass, and the like imposed on it by an
omnipotent Creator. There was nothing of life or mind or beauty or
purpose in it—all these were superadded to the material world by the
Creator. But with the progress of physical science and, even more,
with Darwin's theory of natural selection as the source of adaptation
and improvement in nature the Creator God disappeared, leaving
only the law-bound system of matter in motion grinding out its
products and threatening, as Huxley noted with some apprehension,
to make the realm of matter and law "co-extensive with knowledge,
with feeling, and with action." Where in this grim universe was
there room for freedom, spontaneity, beauty, purpose, morality
—where room for beings like Darwin and Huxley? Huxley might
rhapsodize about "Nature's grand progression from blind force
to.... conscious intellect and will," but was such a progress really
conceivable? Was not Huxley's vision of the liberally educated
man—"one who, no stunted ascetic, is full of life and fire, but
whose passions are trained to come to heel by a vigorous will, the
servant of a tender conscience; who has learned to love all beauty,
whether of Nature or of art, to hate all vileness, and to respect others
as himself"—drawn from quite different sources than the
evolutionary naturalism Huxley professed?[18]

---

*See above, pp. 56-61, for a full account of Balfour's views.

There was, said Balfour, a profound "inner discord" between the values and ideas Darwin and Huxley derived from their Western heritage and those implicit in the world picture presupposed by their evolutionary naturalism. This discord could not continue indefinitely, Balfour insisted. Either science-based conceptions of nature and human nature would be revised to make room for freedom, purpose, and intellectual, moral, and esthetic creativity or Western culture would descend to a level consistent with Huxley's picture of nature as a "realm of matter and law...co-extensive with knowledge, with feeling, and with action."

Such, was Balfour's prediction in 1895. To what extent has it come true? Alas, the inner discord he discerned between traditional Western values and the portrait of man and nature painted by writers claiming to speak for science is still with us. B. F. Skinner tells us that we have moved beyond human freedom and dignity to a world of conditioned responses. Edward 0. Wilson adds that man is an accident of mechanistic evolutionary processes that might well have gone in a very different direction and that the human mind is "an epiphenomenon of the neuronal machinery of the brain," which, in turn, exists "because it promotes the survival and multiplication of the genes which direct its assembly."[19] Altruism, we are told, is a biological device built into our genes in the struggle for existence. The discrepancy between these views and the conceptions of man and nature undergirding Western civilization is blatantly obvious. It has produced a schizophrenia in our culture that threatens to tear it apart. At one extreme, the advocates of evolutionary naturalism try to persuade us that the values we hold dear are ratified by evolutionary biology despite appearances to the contrary. At the other extreme, Christian fundamentalists reject evolutionism root and branch and with it the whole of modern science except its technological benefits.

Fortunately, however, there are some signs of movement toward conceptions of nature and human nature capable of alleviating the inner discord Balfour deplored. For one thing, the idea of nature Darwin and Huxley inherited from Galileo, Descartes, and Newton—nature as a lawbound system of brute stuff possessing only the mathematical properties imposed on it by an omnipotent

Creator—is now as dead as the dodo. This is partly because twentieth-century physics has revolutionized our conceptions of matter, space, time, and causation, relegating Descartes' mechanistic universe to the trash heap of once-glorious world pictures. But, even more, it is because Darwin and Spencer, by sinking man into nature, undermined Descartes' sharp separation of mind and matter. So long as human beings were thought to be outside of and above nature a mechanistic view of nature was possible, although it involved regarding animals as automata in the manner of Descartes. But when, following Darwin's work, mankind were conceived as part and parcel of nature, an insuperable contradiction arose. "A scientific realism, based on mechanism," wrote Alfred North Whitehead in 1925, "is conjoined with an unwavering belief in the world of men and of higher animals as being composed of self-determining organisms".[20] But how could this be? If human beings are a product of nature, must not nature share the psychic, goal-directed aspects of human nature? If not, how could natural processes have given rise to human beings?

Confronted with this dilemma, a considerable number of biologists (Julian Huxley, Bernard Rensch, L. C. Birch, and Sewall Wright among them) have adopted a philosophy of panpsychism, i.e. the belief that all the processes of nature have a psychic aspect. "Emergence of mind from no mind at all is sheer magic," writes Sewall Wright. "We conclude," he adds, "that the evolution of mind must have been coextensive with the evolution of the body. Moreover, mind must already have been there when life arose and indeed must be a universal aspect of existence...."[21] Only on this assumption, says Wright, can we reconcile our scientific knowledge, constructed by inference from our sense experience and based on deterministic or probabilistic notions of causation, with the private but absolutely primary knowledge each person has of his or her own stream of consciousness, a stream directed "toward the finding of an acceptable course through the difficulties of the external world by means of voluntary actions". A far cry this from Huxley's "realm of matter and law...co-extensive with knowledge, with feeling, and with action" and much more in tune with Darwin's view that the humblest animals, and even plants, show signs of psychic qualities.

But the revolution in our conceptions of nature precipitated by Darwin and his fellow evolutionists does not stop here. The idea of evolution has permeated the whole realm of thought, from physics and cosmology to anthropology, psychology, and metaphysics. Nature, Julian Huxley tells us, is a creative process, "unitary, continuous, irreversible; selftransforming; and generating variety and novelty during its transformations." "The universe," writes Theodosius Dobzhansky, "is the product of the evolutionary process....The inorganic and human evolutions are parts of a single process. Ultimately all evolution is one".[22] For these writers, nature has ceased to be a machine; it has become a creative process. The basic question from this point of view is not whether we are to believe in evolution but, instead, whether the idea of nature as a creative process makes sense without the accompanying idea of a creative ground of the process capable of envisaging the possibilities for good inherent in the process and of desiring their fulfillment. Oddly enough, the metaphorical vocabulary of modern evolutionary biology is full of words and phrases implying striving, aim, effort, realization of value, and the like. In his book *Evolution in Action* Julian Huxley personifies evolution and exhilarates his readers with an account of his hero's trials and errors, advances and retreats, escapes from blind alleys, and eventual achievements in realizing ever-higher possibilities. Theodosius Dobzhansky, George Gaylord Simpson, and other biologists use the same anthropomorphic metaphors, probably without thinking about it. But does the idea of creativity without any creative mind or purpose make sense? Do we speak of a sunset as a beautiful creation? We do not. When we hear of a creation, whether it be a symphony or a beaver dam or the nest of a bower bird, we instinctively ask: "Whose creation?"

In the first edition of his great work *On the Origin of Species* Darwin professed to find "grandeur in this view of life...having been originally breathed into a few forms or into one" and in the thought that "from so simple a beginning endless forms most beautiful and most wonderful have been, and are being evolved." In the second edition he inserted the words "by the Creator" after the word "breathed," and he retained that insertion through all subsequent editions, including the sixth and last. As has already been indicated, this change should not be interpreted as a concession to public opinion. It expressed Darwin's "inward conviction," as he later called it, that the evolution of nature's "endless forms most beautiful and most wonderful" could not have been the result of "mere chance." Twenty years later, when he came to write his autobiography, this inward conviction had been eroded by what Darwin described as "the horrid doubt...whether the convictions of man's mind, which has been developed from the mind of the lower animals, are of any value or at all trustworthy. Would any one trust the convictions of a monkey's mind, if there are any convictions in such a mind"?[23]

Darwin had reached the end of the trail in his spiritual evolution. Taking for granted Huxley's view of physical nature as a "web and woof of matter and force interweaving by slow degrees, without a broken thread, that veil which lies between us and the Infinite" and believing, like Huxley, that there was but one kind of knowledge and but one method of acquiring it, Darwin drew the inevitable agnostic conclusion. Human reason, evolved from the rudimentary intelligence of an ape-like ancestor, was capable of plumbing the secrets of the solar system and discovering the origin of species, but it was not to be trusted when it tried to penetrate to the ultimate source of being. But if, as modern evolutionary biologists tell us, nature is not a machine but a creative process, and if, as reason suggests, this creative process has a creative ground analogous, however roughly, to our own creative personhood, then why should we doubt our inward conviction that the endless forms most beautiful and most wonderful that so enchanted Aristotle and Darwin are an expression of a creativity incomparably higher and greater than any we can ever imagine? "It is not wisdom to be only wise," to "doubt the soul's invincible surmise".

George Santayana's poetic reference to the surmises of the human soul brings us to the last of the twentieth-century developments that bear on Darwin's project of viewing the human species as part of nature, namely, those developments in science and science-based technology that have given us the power to alter human nature radically and to render the Earth uninhabitable not only for ourselves but for thousands of other species as well. If human beings succeed in altering human nature by genetic manipulation, will this be a case of nature altering nature? And if the peoples of the world in their insane preoccupation with ethnic identity and national security precipitate a nuclear holocaust that makes our planet uninhabitable, will this be nature destroying nature? For Darwin and Spencer, human progress was the result of a gradual improvement in the intellectual and instinctual endowment of the surviving human race, brought about chiefly by natural selection and the inherited effects of mental and moral training. Progress was a necessary long-run result of the processes of nature-history. We now know better. The future of mankind lies not with the processes of nature but with human choices for good or ill. Science and technology only escalate the urgency of these choices without giving us the slightest help in making them.

Are human beings, as Darwin thought, totally a part of nature? If so, how can they comprehend and to an awesome extent control nature? If not, how are we to understand man's ambiguous existence as both a part of and not a part of nature? For my part, I rather like the attitude of Edward Tyson, the seventeenth-century comparative anatomist who made the first anatomical study of a chimpanzee in a book entitled *Orang-Outang: Or the Anatomy of a Pygmy*, published in 1699. After comparing the anatomy of this animal with that of human beings Tyson concluded:

> This Difference I cannot but remark, that the Ancients were fond of making Brutes to Men; on the contrary now, most unphilosophically, the Humour is, to make Men but mere Brutes and Matter. Whereas in truth Man is part a Brute, part an Angel; and is that Link in the Creation, that joins them both together.[24]

Whether we believe in angels or not, we shall find difficulty in conceiving humans as purely natural beings without running into hopeless paradoxes and contradictions. A being who can explore the galaxies to their farthest reaches, alter his own genetic constitution, and, by conscious choices, destroy the planetary environment that sustains him and all other living creatures is something more than a freak of nature, a "lucky accident" in Stephen Gould's terms.

In his autobiography Darwin tells us that he abandoned Christianity partly because he could not accept the "manifestly false history of the world" set forth in Genesis. Yet, ironically, the story of mankind's fall from grace recorded in the Bible, despite its historical inaccuracy, presents a far truer picture of the human condition than does Darwin's vision of gradual improvement in human nature and society brought about by natural selection and the inherited effects of mental and moral training. According to the Biblical account, it was not by partaking of scientific knowledge that our first parents lost their claim to paradise but rather by eating of the tree of the knowledge of good and evil, a tree unknown to science. It is that knowledge which constitutes our transcendence, our danger, our humanity. It was Darwin who showed us our kinship with nature, all living things being "netted together," as he expressed it, in a seamless web of being. It is we who must decide whether that kinship is to be cherished and improved or, instead, dishonored and obliterated by human pride and folly.

NOTES

1.   Aristotle, *Parts of Animals With an English Translation by A. L. Peck* (The Loeb Classical Library), London, William Heinemann Ltd, 1937, p. 101 (I.v. 645a, 24 ff.) See also Aristotle's *Metaphysics*, XII, x., 2-4, translated by Hugh Tredennick in the Loeb Classical Library (1936), pp. 167, 169: "We must also consider in which sense the nature of the universe contains the good or the supreme good; whether as something separate and independent, or as the orderly arrangement of its parts. Probably in both senses, as an army does....All things, both fishes and birds and plants, are ordered together in some way. Everything is ordered together to one end; but the arrangement is like that in a household,...in which everything contributes to the good of the whole." Aristotelian scholars do not agree as to the exact nature of Aristotle's teleology nor as to whether it extends to the universe as a whole (as the passage quoted above seems to indicate). The present interpretation draws on several of the essays in *Philosophical Issues in Aristotle's Biology*, Alan Gotthelf and James G. Lennox, eds., Cambridge, England, Cambridge University Press, 1987, and in *Aristotle on Nature and Living Things: Philosophical and Historical Studies Presented to David Balme on His Seventieth Birthday*, Alan Gotthelf, ed., Pittsburgh, Pa., Mathesis Publications, Inc. and Bristol, England, Bristol Classical Press, 1985, especially David Furley's "The Rainfall Example in *Physics ii 8*," pp. 177-182, and

Charles H. Kahn's "The Place of the Prime Mover in Aristotle's Teleology," pp. 183-206.

2.   Aristotle, *Parts of Animals*, IV. xii, p. 407 (693b, 13ff.)

3.   Aristotle, *Parts of Animals*, IV. x., pp. 371, 373 (686a, 25 ff.)

4.   Larson, James L. *Reason and Experience. The Representation of Natural Order in the Work of Carl von Linné*. Berkeley, Los Angeles, and London, University of California Press. On page 20 Larson writes: "The process of grouping plant forms on the basis of likenesses utilizes the same basic conceptual elements found in Aristotelian systems. These elements are three in number: types, differentiae, and an integrating structure. The basic units of order are fixed types or natural forms. These types, constituted from and defined by diverse but limited visual and tactile qualities, or differentiae, are integrated in a structure conceived as an ascending sequence of forms." Larson traces the development of this approach to the classification of plants from Caesalpino to Linnaeus, showing the difficulties encountered and the compromises arrived at in the attempt to follow Aristotle's dictum that divisions should be based on essential (i.e. major functional) parts, and showing also the problems posed (for Aristotle himself as well as for his followers) by the effort to reconcile the demands of Aristotelian logic with Aristotle's insistence that classification must express the relations of essences, in which case the naturalist must abandon the dream of a clear cut hierarchy of classes reflecting the order of nature in favor of a principle of continuity linking forms by multiple affinities. Larson regards this latter idea, derived ultimately from Aristotle's conception of the *scala naturae*, as more relevant to the quest for a natural method of classification than his method of logical division. (See Larson's Footnote 43, pp. 22-24.)

5.   Ray, John, *The Wisdom of God Manifested in the Works of the Creation*, 3rd ed., London, 1701, "Preface" (not paged).

6.   Greene, John C., *The Death of Adam: Evolution and Its Impact on Western Thought*, Ames, Iowa, Iowa State University Press, 1959, pp. 4-8.

7.   Cuvier, Georges, *Lectures on Comparative Anatomy*, William Ross, tr., 5 t., London, 1802-1805, t. 1, p. 45 ff. See also Greene, *op. cit.*, 169-173.

8.   Cuvier, Georges, "Discours Préliminaire," *Recherches sur les ossemens fossiles de quadrupèdes*, 4 t., Paris, Déterville, 1812. Cuvier did not explicitly propose a theory of successive creations, but his rejection of Lamarck's evolutionary hypothesis and the idea of spontaneous generation left him no other alternative unless he was prepared to believe that all extant and extinct species were present at the first creation, an idea which conflicts with his statement that the shelled animals, fishes, and oviparous quadrupeds appeared before the viviparous quadrupeds.

9.   Concerning the transcendental morphology of Geoffroy St.-Hilaire and others see Appel, Toby, *The Cuvier-Geoffroy Debate: French Biology in the Decades Before Darwin*, New York and Oxford, Oxford University Press, 1987, chaps. 4-6; also Russell, Edward S., *Form and Function: A Contribution to the History of Animal Morphology*, Chicago and London, University of Chicago Press, 1982, chaps. 4-7.

10.   Darwin, Erasmus, *Zoonomia; Or the Laws of Organic Life*, 4th Amer. ed., 2 v., Philadelphia, 1818, v. 1, 397.

11. Darwin's development as a theorist is described in Chapters 1-14 of Kohn, David, ed., *The Darwinian Heritage*, Princeton, N. J., Princeton University Press, 1985.

12. See Kohn, David, "Darwin's Ambiguity: The Secularization of Biological Meaning," *British Journal for the History of Science*, v. 22, 1989, pp. 215-239 for an excellent discussion of the extent to which Darwin's references to the Creator are to be taken at face value. "In short," Kohn concludes, "Darwin sought to make a rigorously non-Providentialist scientific utilitarianism safe for an enlightened form of Latitudinarian theism. Ultimately, these are contradictory positions. And the ultimate source of Darwin's ambiguity in the *Origin*, and in his later comments, is this clear contradiction."

13. See Gruber, Howard E., *Darwin on Man. A Psychological Study of Scientific Creativity.... Together with Darwin's Early and Unpublished Notebooks Transcribed and Annotated by Paul H. Barrett*, New York, E. P. Dutton and Co, 1974, Part I.

14. Darwin, Charles, *The Origin of Species and The Descent of Man*, New York, The Modern Library, 1937, p. 918.

15. Darwin, Charles, letter to Charles Lyell, Ilkley, Yorkshire, 11 October, 1859, quoted in Francis Darwin, ed., *The Life and Letters of Charles Darwin*, 3 v., London, John Murray, 1888, v. 2, p. 211.

16. Darwin, Charles, letter to Charles Lyell, Down, 27 April, 1860, quoted in Francis Darwin, ed., *More Letters of Charles Darwin....*, London, 2 v., London, John Murray, 1903, v. 2, p. 262. See also John C. Greene, "Darwin as a Social Evolutionist," in Greene, *Science, Ideology, and World View: Essays in the History of Evolutionary Ideas*, Berkeley, Los Angeles, London, 1981, chap. 5.

17. Huxley, Thomas Henry, "The Origin of Species," in *Darwiniana: Essays*, New York, D. Appleton, 1908, p. 58. First published in 1860.

18. Balfour, Arthur James, *Foundations of Belief*, London, Longmans Green, 1933, p. 13. Huxley, *Selections from the Essays of T. H. Huxley*, Alburey Castell, ed., New York, Appleton-Century-Crofts, 1948, p. 18, 21.

19. Wilson, Edward O., *On Human Nature*, Cambridge, Mass., Harvard University Press, 1978, p. 2.

20. Whitehead, Alfred N., *Science and the Modern World: Lowell Lectures*, 1925, New York, Macmillan, 1947, 110.

21. Wright, Sewall, "Panpsychism and Science," in J. B. Cobb, Jr. and D. R. Griffin, eds. *Mind in Nature: Essays on the Interface of Science and Philosophy*, Washington, D. C., pp. 82, 87.

22. Huxley, Julian, *Evolution in Action*, New York, The New American Library, 1953, p. 10. For Dobzhansky's views, see Theodosius Dobzhansky, *The Biology of Ultimate Concern*, New York, The New American Library, 1970.

23. Darwin, Charles, letter to William Graham, Down, July 3, 1881, quoted in Francis Darwin, ed., *Life and Letters*, v. 1, 285.

24. Tyson, Edward, *Orangutan Sive Homo Sylvestris: or, the Anatomy of a Pygmy compared with that of a Monkey, an Ape and a Man*, London, Th. Bennett, D. Brown, 1699, p. 55.

Acknowledgments

Permission has been granted by Kluwer Academic Publishers to republish, with minor changes, the following articles:

"The Interaction of Science and World View in Sir Julian Huxley's Evolutionary Biology," *Journal of the History of Biology*" 23 (Spring 1990), 39-55.

"On the Nature of the Evolutionary Process: The Correspondence Between Theodosius Dobzhansky and John C. Greene," *Biology and Philosophy* 11 (1996), 445-491 (abridged).

"Letter to the Editor," *Journal of the History of Biology* 22 (1989), 357-359.

"From Aristotle to Darwin: Reflections on Ernst Mayr's Interpretation in The Growth of Biological Thought, *Journal of the History of Biology* 27 (Summer 1992), 257-284.

"Science, Philosophy, and Metaphor in Ernst Mayr's Writings," *Journal of the History of Biology* 27 (1994), 311-347.

The Editors of the *Revue de Synthèse* have granted permission to republish the following articles from that journal:

"The History of Ideas Revisited," *Revue de Synthèse*, Quatrième série, no. 3 (juillet-septembre 1986), 201-228.

"The Death of Darwin?" by Ernst Mayr. Ibid., 229-236.

Éditions Klincksieck has granted permission to publish the original version in English of:

"La révolution Darwinienne dans la science et la vision du monde," in *Nature, Histoire, Société. Essais en hommage à Jacques Roger* (Paris: Editions Klincksieck, 1995), 79-97.

Professor Ernst Mayr has generously granted permission to publish his essay "The Death of Darwin?" and substantial parts of his correspondence with John Greene, 1980-1997.

The cover design was conceived and produced by Larry Wasiele of Storrs, Connecticut.

INDEX